THE LIFE OF PRICE DANIEL

TEXAS GIANT

THE LIFE OF PRICE DANIEL

TEXAS GIANT

DAN MURPH

Foreword by President George Bush

EAKIN PRESS  Austin, Texas

Dedicated to my parents,
who have always allowed
me to dream big.

FIRST EDITION
Copyright © 2002
By Dan Murph
Published in the United States of America
By Eakin Press
A Division of Sunbelt Media, Inc.
P.O. Drawer 90159 ⌨ Austin, Texas 78709-0159
email: eakinpub@sig.net
💻 website: www.eakinpress.com 💻
ALL RIGHTS RESERVED.
1   2   3   4   5   6   7   8   9
1-57168-571-5

For CIP information,
please access:
www.loc.gov

CONTENTS

FOREWORD

GEORGE BUSH
August 26, 1993

Dear Daniel,

As you prepare the biography on Price Daniel, I would like to add these simple words of respect and admiration.

Price Daniel served his state and nation with great distinction and also with total integrity. This last point is important, for there is so much cynicism around about public service and about politics.

Price and Jean Daniel became close friends of my parents when my dad and Price served together in the U.S. Senate. That friendship was built on mutual respect.

In my own political life a handful of people, who served before my time in public office, set standards that I tried to adhere to later on. Your grandfather was one such man.

Your biography must do him honor.

GEORGE BUSH

INTRODUCTION

On a chilly afternoon in the late 1950s, a dispatcher was sent aboard a southbound train with an urgent message for the governor of Texas. After making an exhaustive search of the train, the dispatcher returned with the telegram still in hand. "I can't find the governor," he said with a mystified look on his face. "All I saw was a little man shining his shoes." That lone, unassuming man was Price Daniel, a giant in twentieth-century Texas politics.

Having been elected to more major offices than any other public official in the history of the state, Daniel served as state representative, Speaker of the House, attorney general, United States senator, governor, and, in his later years, as a justice on the Texas Supreme Court. He was credited with winning the largest states' rights settlement in United States history, was responsible for bringing organized gambling in Texas to its knees, argued one of the landmark cases of the civil rights movement before the U.S. Supreme Court, nearly succeeded in his attempt to abolish the electoral college as the method of electing presidents, was on the inside loop of many critical decisions which made during the Vietnam War, led the largest narcotics investigation in the nation's history, and in the meantime oversaw the passage of more legislation than any other Texas governor.

Daniel often shied away from the national stage, preferring instead to concentrate his time and energies on Texas, which to him was somewhat of a nation in itself. Sounding the unbelievable battle cry, "I'd rather be governor of Texas than president of the United States," Daniel shocked the Washington elite by relinquishing his powerful seat in the United States Senate and returning home to run for governor. He said he missed the Texas air, wanted his kids to be reared in Texas schools, and could not bear to be away any longer. Texans took great pride in the loyalty of Daniel, who, as Reverend Billy Graham once said, "had all the ability to be president of the United States."

Perhaps Daniel could best be termed the grand finale of old-time Texas governors. Back when politics was fun and flamboyancy was a prerequisite to being elected, the maverick from Liberty, Texas, was at his prime. With an unlit cigar clamped loosely between his teeth and a small-rimmed Stetson perched atop his head, he took the state by storm with his unpredictable yet simple approach to the complex world of politics. "Anyone who thinks he can predict what Price is going to do is either naive or tragically complacent," one state legislator confessed. During his gubernatorial years, two of Daniel's closest aides joked that if he were walking through the woods and came across a wasps' nest, "He'd hit it with a stick just to see what'd happen."

Often when the Texas legislature finally reached agreement on a heavily contested issue, Daniel would have another ready to debate. Perhaps his political expediency was an attempt to take advantage of every single day in the office he had sought since earliest childhood, or was simply a result of his unyielding energy. Regardless, from the day the wavy-haired solon burst onto the state scene in the late thirties, Texas politics would never be the same.

Throughout his career, Daniel refused to lean on the crutch of labels to chart his course. Instead, he insisted upon making his own decision on each individual issue and, once his mind was set, all hell could not change him. On some matters such as states' rights, liberals considered him ultra-conservative. But at the same time, conservatives would insist that he was a liberal because of his relentless fight against a general sales tax. It is thus fair to conclude that Daniel had few loyal supporters, and few ardent enemies. His political friends and foes were won and lost by his latest actions. Those who venomously opposed him one election could likely be his biggest campaign contributors the next.

One observer, describing the governor as seemingly oblivious to the pained outcries or lavish praise from business, labor, or other groups, described Daniel throughout his career as having "gone his own way, charted his own course, and adhered to his own strictly-personal point of view." Even his closest friends knew it would be foolish to bank on his support. For in the end, Daniel was not afraid to buck the system when he felt the need. He always believed that if he was thinking straight, he could fly in the face of public opinion and convince people he was right. And, more often than not, enough like-minded people would eventually surface to reward him on election day. As one political foe remarked: "Half of his friends and most of his enemies may be defeated for reelection, but anybody who attempts to run on a hate-Price platform better have some other strong planks to lean on."

Daniel was handsome, stocky, ambitious, humorous, modest, and almost embarrassingly unsophisticated in his taste for material possessions. To him, life was an exciting adventure and not a single minute of one's God-given time should be wasted. From attempting to make a wild river navigable to searching for the whereabouts of a Napoleonic fort supposedly buried in the thick woods of southeast Texas, his time was spent in a vast array of projects. Up until his death in 1988, Daniel would devote his life to God, his family, and the state of Texas. Throughout his personal and political life, no challenge was too big and no cause too small.

As author, it is my duty to inform the reader that the subject of this biography was my grandfather. I have made every attempt to document each individual source in the comprehensive manner of the formal historian, bringing in opinions from both sides of the issues in an effort to produce a fair, definitive biography. I have injected my own opinions and conclusions, but these are not to be confused with prejudices. Given his history of editing everything he could get his hands on, Daniel would unlikely have approved of all that is included here. Certainly he would have suggested revisions or differed in opinion with some of my conclusions. In the end, however, I hope that this work will adequately fill out the mosaic of a fascinating life that left a large imprint on the annals of twentieth-century Texas.

CHAPTER 1

The Early Years

Marion Price Daniel, the father of the subject of this book, would never forget the day he ran away from home as a youth. Still in his early teens, the lad packed a small bag full of his belongings, draped it over his shoulder, and headed out the back door. In such a hurry to escape the demands of a strict home, he carelessly stumbled over a clothesline and was tossed to the ground. His mother laughed from the doorway as he quickly retrieved his possessions and disappeared into the unknown.[1]

Called M.P., he was one of ten children and had learned at an early age to fend for himself. After temporarily moving in with a family a few miles up the road in the town of Willis, Texas, he found a variety of jobs to make ends meet. From his father, a traveling preacher who was said to have baptized more than 1,200 people, he had acquired strict and disciplined work habits which impressed his employers. His father also bestowed upon him religious teachings and the importance of the church. Blended together, his strong faith and desire to complete anything he started made him an irresistible candidate for almost any job he desired.[2]

M.P. dreamt big dreams and instinctively seized every opportunity which came his way. At the age of twenty-five, he and a friend,

P.H. Le Suer, formed a newspaper partnership, owning and editing the *Willis Progress*. Just three years later, in March of 1909, the two men reported that they had received a "better proposition" in another small town a few miles to the south in Liberty County. The following month, M.P. and Le Suer were owners and editors of the *Daytonite*.[3]

Not an exceptionally tall man, M.P. possessed a slim, fit physique and a fondness for outdoor activity. His dress was neat and orderly, as were his methods of organization used both at home and the office. By his bedside he kept a detailed diary in which he chronicled his daily activities, similar to the well-organized business records which could be found neatly stored in a desk drawer at his office. A prolific letter writer, he kept organized files of his daily correspondence.[4] So particular was M.P. about organization that he had the following request printed across the bottom of his stationery: "My filing system is the most complete I have ever seen and you will assist me very materially in keeping it, so if you will, use paper sized 8½ x 11 inches in replying."[5] M.P. was determined to make a success of himself and to leave clear documentation of his endeavors along the way.

While residing in Dayton, M.P. developed a fine liking for a young schoolteacher in Stilson named Nannie Blanch Partlow. She came from a prominent family in Liberty County and had been raised with many of the same religious beliefs and hard-work ethics as M.P. Their relationship blossomed and soon led to the altar of Liberty's First Methodist Church. On December 23, 1909, they became man and wife.[6] An article appearing in the following day's newspaper described the scene: "Probably a more beautiful wedding has never been solemnized in Liberty—every detail being extremely elegant and marked with an emphasis that enhanced the sacredness of the occasion, the termination of an exceptionally happy girlhood and the beginning of a new life."[7]

M.P. and Nannie moved into a white-frame house on the south edge of Dayton. While Daniel worked from early in the morning until late in the evening, Nannie labored with equal vigor at home, cleaning and preparing the residence for the family she could not wait to bear. Before long, her dreams of having a child became a reality.[8]

Judd Mortimer Lewis, *Houston Daily Post* columnist and good friend of Daniel's, was informed by a letter from the proud parents that they had "an eleven-pound boy... three days old this morning at 5 o'clock and his mother calls him M.P., Jr. Having learned the type positions in the cases yesterday he will henceforth control the management of the *Daytonite*."[9] Judd joked with the Daniels that for the life of him he could not figure out the meaning of the initials "M.P." He wondered if it was short for "Merciful Providence"... "Mother's Pet"... "Muddy Pants"... "Metrically Perfect"... or "Mother's Punishment." In following correspondence he reckoned: "If we were in England we should want it 'Member of Parliament,' but as we are in 'Grand old Texas,' we will try not to let him be a 'Mere Printer.'"[10]

Marion Price Daniel, Jr. was born on October 10, 1910, and jubilantly ushered into the Dayton homefront Nannie had so diligently prepared. Before long, it was a regular occurrence for family members to travel from Liberty to set eyes on their newest descendant, whom they dubbed M.P., Jr. Miriam Partlow, Nannie's seventeen-year-old sister, was the most frequent visitor to the Daniel home and loved nothing more than making the six-mile journey to Dayton to hold her first nephew. Due to M.P.'s heavy work schedule, which kept him at the newspaper office a good portion of the day, he hired a nurse to help Nannie care for the child.[11]

Soon M.P. became interested in another journalistic venture, one which would require yet another move. After careful consideration, he packed up his possessions in the spring of 1912 and moved his family to Teague, Texas, where he formed a partnership with a gentleman named J.P. Yantis.[12] Together, the two men published and edited the *Teague Daily Herald* and proudly proclaimed the following statement in their first paper, dated April 1: "We are, as we ever have been, Jeffersonian Democrats.... Our families are here, we have bought homes here, and we have come to stay to identify ourselves with the best interests of the county for our common good."[13]

Despite such an optimistic beginning, M.P.'s new venture proved to be more of a personal burden than anything else. In a June 3 letter to Nannie, who was visiting friends in Dayton, he revealed: "I cannot possibly stand the strain I am under much longer.... I believe that I would go crazy if I had to put up with this much longer."[14] Within one month after Nannie received the letter, he and Yantis terminated their involvement with the newspaper. In a farewell editorial appearing July 1, 1912, M.P. announced that his interest in the newspaper had been sold: "We own nothing except our wife and baby, which we would not sell if offered a price which we could take." [15]

Upon returning the family to Liberty County, he formed the M.P. Daniel Real Estate Company and within a short while became postmaster at Dayton. However, his lifelong love of the printing press would soon carry his family to Coldspring, Texas, where he founded the *San Jacinto Times*. But once again, fatigue and disillusionment occurred within six months and the family returned to Liberty County. Before long, the couple would have two more mouths to feed. In 1913, M.P. and Nannie became the parents of a baby girl, Ellen Virginia, and three years later another son, William Partlow Daniel. [16]

Despite the inconsistency of the family's residence, the ensuing strain on finances, and the fatigue evident on the face of M.P., Nannie succeeded in providing a consistent and nurturing home for her oldest son. She taught him to read even before he entered school, causing his first-grade teacher to advance him immediately to the second grade. [17] From his father, Price Daniel learned the traits of discipline, hard work, and determination, which he would carry with him in his future endeavors. By the time he arose in the morning for breakfast, his father was returning from three hours of early morning work at the office. And when he began gathering his books for school, his father would beat him out the door again en route back to the office. [18]

Daniel would later trace his interest in politics and government back to his earliest days and the stimulating learning environment his parents had provided. Texas history books were placed in his hands as soon as he was able to read, and tales were commonly told of his ancestors and their role in the state's struggle for independence. He took great pride in knowing that his great-great-grandfather, Gen. Francis A.B. Wheeler, had fought alongside Andrew Jackson and William Henry Harrison before joining Stephen F. Austin's expedition to Texas. [19] But perhaps his greatest stimulus for a career in government service was his father. Although never having sought an office himself, M.P. actively campaigned for numerous candidates in a variety of elections and was always willing to share his exciting experiences with his son. He had helped organize the Democratic Party's first Executive Committee in Liberty County and was a delegate to most of the county and state conventions of his party. When later asked about the origin of his vast knowledge of Texas history, Price Daniel replied: "I suppose that if a person can be *born* with that interest, that is what happened to me."[20]

Also bestowed upon Daniel at an early age was the importance of family. Growing up on the corner of Grand Avenue and San Jacinto Street, he lived within a rock's throw of the entire Partlow family. His grandmother lived across the street with his uncle Dozier and aunts Miriam and Bee. His uncle Ray, along with wife Elnett, lived next door to them, and two houses down resided his uncle Gerald and wife Voe.[21] Some of Daniel's fondest childhood memories were of regular Sunday afternoon family gatherings at Gran's house. There he was free to talk, sing, and play for hours in the company of his own kin. This reliance on and devotion to the family unit that he learned to appreciate at such an early age remained with him through the years to come.[22]

Young Daniel also received his fair share of biblical teachings, both from the Partlow clan and his parents. Church was a mandatory activity on Sundays in the old Partlow house, and a family Bible was kept in a prominent place as a regular point of reference. Morality and decency were stressed above all else, as was the belief in the necessity of conviction and purpose in life. M.P. taught a Sunday school class of high school boys, and young Daniel would watch his father throughout the week study class materials and assemble maps in detailed preparation for his presentations. His mother was equally influential in his religious upbringing. Believing that one's soul would ultimately be either saved or lost, nothing in between, Nannie went out of her way to make her faith evident in her every action. She provided food for the poor who knocked on her door, and did not hesitate to preach to them the need to sanctify their souls. And to her oldest son, she stressed that he waste no time in sinful activities and become actively involved in the Christian movement. When Daniel eventually left home and embarked on a political career, nothing influenced him greater than the religious upbringing he had received on Grand Avenue.[23]

Like many other boys his age, Daniel exhibited a vivid imagination and sense of adventure. Since his earliest days visiting the old Partlow house, he had loved sitting in the living room and listening to his kinfolks tell wild tales about the rowdy days of frontier Texas.

Books, too, spawned his fondness for action and adventure, most notably Elbert Hubbard's *Little Journeys to the Homes of the Great.*

More often than not, his wild imagination put him in places and situations that led to trouble. On one occasion Daniel, at age five, and his sister Ellen, three, returned home after being out alone for several hours. When their father demanded to know their day's whereabouts, Daniel unhesitantly told him that Charlie Steusoff, the local druggist, had been kind enough to show them some interesting sights around town and give them two ice cream cones. As little Ellen hesitantly nodded in agreement, Daniel described in great detail their day's exploits. M.P. was so grateful for Mr. Steusoff's kindness that he paid him a personal visit to express his thanks for the generosity shown to his children, only to return home embarrassed. His son had made up the entire story.[24]

At an early age Price Daniel developed a fondness for talking, asking questions, and engaging in deep conversations. Once on a trip back from Dayton with his uncle Ray, he talked and talked until finally his uncle struck up a deal: "If you can keep your mouth shut until we get to Liberty, I'll give you a quarter." Daniel agreed to the terms, then ceased all conversation. As the two approached the outskirts of Liberty, Ray, fearing he would lose the bet, decided to try to provoke his nephew into saying something. Ray noticed a group of children playing in a schoolyard. "Why, look, Price," he said, pointing toward the children, "there must be at least, uh, eleven kids out there!" Daniel immediately blurted out, "Twelve!" Even the lure of money was shadowed by his desire to communicate.[25]

Much as his family influenced his religious beliefs and sense of belonging, the Trinity River brought Daniel a passion for history and learning which he would forever nurture. The river, on whose banks the town of Liberty had been founded, brought to his attention a rich past of Spanish and French explorers and military adventurers. Describing Daniel's early experiences with the river, one researcher noted: "As a boy he heard men pinpoint past events not by calendar years but by the river's major overflows. He watched farmers grow crops in its fertile soil deposits and helped ranchers tend cattle in its wet bottom-lands. He picnicked on its banks, fished its waters, and heard tales about boats sinking beneath its swirling currents."[26] In fact, Daniel's love of the Trinity River would stay with him until his death.

As a child, he had heard tales of how the Orcoquiza and

Attacapa Indians had camped on the river's banks and of sixteenth-century Spanish explorers who had mapped the Trinity's course. He was especially fascinated by the river's most infamous settlement, started by a group of French refugees who many historians believe were either planning to free Napoleon Bonaparte from exile at St. Helena or waiting for his freedom to escort him to Mexico City. Gen. Charles Lallemand had led several high-ranking French officers to America in 1818 to a riverbank site believed to be near present-day Liberty. They named their colony Champ d'Asile (Isle of Refuge). Apparently they schemed to sever Mexico from Spain when the emperor escaped and to use the fort as a base for the new empire. Unknown to Lallemand, the Spanish government soon dispatched a small force of 240 men from San Antonio to destroy the colony. By the time the force arrived, however, Lallemand had already moved the colony to Galveston Island.[27] Young Daniel began to study about the French and Spaniards and their relationship to the banks of the Trinity, as well as the leadership traits and characteristics of Napoleon. Over the years, he would acquire a personal library filled with extensive materials relating to Champ d'Asile and would never lose his fascination with Napoleon.[28]

As he continued to grow into an industrious young man, Daniel's relationship with his father also deepened. In the summer of 1922, the two rented a small waterfront house in Palacios, Texas. One day, swimming in the Gulf of Mexico, Daniel was pulled beneath the water by a strong undertow. Struggling to find his way to the surface, he felt his father's strong hands come beneath him, grab him on both sides, and push him toward daylight. For the rest of his life, he could not tell this story without becoming emotional. It was also during this excursion that he fired a shotgun for the first time. The following year, they traveled together to Vicksburg, Mississippi. When nighttime came, the father and son spread a quilt and slept under the moonlight. These trips not only introduced Daniel to the enormity of the world around him, but also helped build strong ties between father and son.[29]

M.P. expected a lot from his oldest son. Therefore, it was no accident that Daniel assumed many responsibilities at an early age. His first job as a lad was delivering newspapers for a Beaumont daily. He received his paper supply early each morning from the back of a railroad car, then rode his route before heading to school.

Soon he found another job delivering laundry door to door. It was on these rounds that he made a life-altering discovery. He noticed that there were many more white shirt collars in the laundry bags he delivered to Liberty's lawyers than to his other customers, and consequently he reasoned that they were making more money than the other townspeople. For the first time, Daniel viewed law as a possible career opportunity.[30]

At the advent of World War I, M.P. again began growing restless and desired a change from the land business. He wanted to enlist and fulfill his patriotic duty overseas, but scoffed at the thought of leaving Nannie behind alone with three growing children and the emotional strain that would result. For some time he had felt compelled to enter the ministry, so much so that in the summer of 1917 he traveled cross-state to become assistant to the chaplain at Camp Bowie, a large military training base located near Fort Worth. However, still uncertain about plans, he soon returned to Liberty, where, despite one semester when he left to attend Fort Worth's Southwestern Baptist Theological Seminary, he staked out his future in real estate. But by 1923, his desire to go into ministry intensified to such a degree that it led him to relocate his family to Fort Worth and become a full-time theological student.[31]

Fort Worth held many new and exciting experiences for twelve-year-old Price Daniel. Having well over 100,000 inhabitants, it was a far cry from the rustic, rural backdrop of Liberty to which he had become so accustomed. His usual daily ritual of spending hours fishing and skipping rocks off of the quiet banks of the Trinity River was now replaced by block after block of paved streets stocked with Model T Fords and tall buildings. But Daniel adjusted well to his new environment, and as a sign of his newfound urbanization was eager to catch the city streetcar each morning for a lift to school. Equally exciting was his spacious new residence. At 2005 Sixth Avenue, the attractive, white-frame house was located next to a small corner drugstore and within a short walk of the streetcar line.[32]

Daniel's active involvement in Fort Worth schools foreshadowed his future days as both college student and public servant. It was there that he would first begin assuming numerous jobs and assignments and follow them to fruition with the same confidence and determination his father so commonly displayed. After completing the 1923-24 school year at Daggett Elementary, he advanced to Jennings Junior High and a short time later was elected by his classmates to represent them as city manager during Boys' Week, an annual observance sponsored by Fort Worth civic leaders and designed to give certain students the opportunity to spend the week as honorary city officials. This was an experience Daniel would never forget, for not only did the sixteen-year-old get to ride in a downtown parade, but he also got his first real look at government in action, meeting officials and visiting city offices throughout the week.[33] The Liberty newspaper reported every detail, almost as if the Daniels had never moved away: "Daniel, representing Jennings Junior High, ran on a platform of a greater Fort Worth and promised to give his undivided attention on his day in office to that purpose. He was selected over Earl Dorris and Diamond Hill in the final run-off. Seven contested for the office..."[34]

While attending Jennings, Daniel became actively involved in the school's speech and debate program and, upon enrolling at Central High School in 1926, continued to nurture his desire for arguing in favor of just causes and speaking in public. Under the watchful eye of Marjorie Dickey, his peppy debate coach to whom he would be forever grateful for sharpening his logic and self-confidence, he continued to excel. She soon paired him with classmate John A. Lovell, and as a team the two young men excelled.[35] The semester's debate topic was: "Resolved that there should be a department of education with a secretary in the President's Cabinet." Daniel and Lovell were responsible for arguing as a team both the affirmative and negative positions. "Having administered defeats to Sunset and Forrest Avenue High Schools of Dallas in debates Monday," one newspaper reported, "the Central High School tonight will meet representatives of the Masonic School in the Central Auditorium at 7:30."[36] The Daniel-Lovell duo, again victorious, would eventually capture the city championship and advance to the state finals in Austin. Despite a valiant effort, the boys would concede first place to a team from San Antonio. On a small, crinkled sheet of paper, the dejected Daniel penciled a quick note of explanation to his folks: "Well, we lost but went down fighting. Am going to have a good time in spite of defeat. Your boy, M.P."[37]

The state finals had given Daniel his first taste of the city that, unbeknownst to him at the time, would serve as the backdrop for the majority of his future political endeavors. It was during this trip that he first set eyes on the Texas State Capitol, walked along Congress Avenue, and stared through the black-iron fence at the Texas Governor's Mansion.[38]

Upon prodding from his father, Daniel also became involved in the Reserve Officers' Training Corps (ROTC) while a student in Fort Worth. M.P. had told his son of the realistic possibility that the United States could be drawn into another war and, if nothing else, the program would reinforce the value of discipline. On the first day, the commanding officer asked a roomful of young men if anyone had the ability to type efficiently. Daniel might later have regretted being the first to shoot his right arm up in the air and volunteer, for thereafter he was called upon not only to do regular drill work but much office record-keeping as well. He was fond of the ROTC program and obviously benefited from the sense of pride and importance it bestowed upon its members by providing numerous opportunities for achievement. By the time of his graduation from Central High, he had advanced to the rank of captain.[39]

Despite Daniel's passion for debate and the ROTC, his greatest extracurricular interest at Central was journalism. Following in the tradition of his father, he excelled at the craft of writing and used it as an outlet for his productive energies and ideas. At the age of fifteen, he was named editor-in-chief of the *Fort Worth High School Student,* which proudly hailed itself as "the largest circulated school weekly in the United States." The publication represented eight city schools, and because none of the participating institutions provided any monetary support, Daniel was responsible for making it float. Along with his business manager, Charles Sharp, he worked long and hectic hours trying to find enough material to fill every page.[40] In one of his weekly editorials, he prophesied: "A graduate of high school that does not finish his education in any particular line, but wishes to be a 'jack of all trades,' will never meet success in life."[41] In addition to his devotion to this publication, Daniel became a reporter for the *Fort Worth Star-Telegram* and covered the city high school beat.[42]

Despite such a heavy load outside the classroom, he still managed to make superb grades. One newspaper reported: "In a Fort Worth school of 1,700 pupils, M.P. Daniel, Jr. won the distinction of being the only boy who passed the required examination and made the average grade of 98 percent. Only 11 girls did it. M.P. is a

Liberty boy. He is doing four years of high school work in three years."[43] Indeed, Daniel had successfully completed so much extra course work at Jennings that he was required to stay at Central for only one year. On June 2, 1927, he graduated magna cum laude and received an academic honor pin.[44]

That same summer, M.P. decided to move his family back to Liberty in hopes of cashing in on the great East Texas oil boom of the 1920s. Young Daniel would never forget his years in Fort Worth and the invaluable training and experience he had acquired in public speaking, debate, and journalism. The city had opened his eyes to a larger world and spawned a hunger inside the boy which would, from that time forward, create in him a desire to undertake one more activity, make one more accomplishment, and be willing to defend a justifiable cause.[45]

Daniel had also made an important religious decision while attending school in Fort Worth. Although having grown up in the Methodist church, where his mother's family had such deep roots, at the age of sixteen he walked down the aisle of College Avenue Baptist Church and committed his life to Christ. While participating in many denominational activities, he had made a decision to attend Baylor University in Waco, a strong Baptist-affiliated institution.[46] There is little doubt that M.P., whose family had connections at Baylor, pushed his son to attend the university. After all, one of Daniel's uncles was a famous Baptist missionary in China and his grandfather was a well-known Baptist minister. This Baptist-Methodist division was a source of conflict between his parents, but Daniel, ever mindful of making both happy, would remain an active member of both churches throughout his life.[47]

In August of 1927, Daniel wrote a letter to Baylor's student newspaper, the *Daily Lariat,* in query of a possible staff position upon his arrival in the fall. A somewhat optimistic reply from the newspaper's managing editor, Dave Cheavens, who would later become a political correspondent for the Associated Press, suggested that Daniel could receive a reporting job with "occasional movie passes" as his only payment. "However," the letter continued, "this year's reporters are next year's editors," and newspaper work was desirable because for a "slime (freshman) it offers a little, little more prestige than he might otherwise have."[48]

Later that month, Daniel wrote the following letter to the congregation of College Avenue Baptist Church: "Dear Brothers and Sisters, as I will be at Baylor University for the next several years, I wish to transfer my membership from your church to the First Baptist Church of Waco, Texas.... Am enclosing herewith a little check payable to the church. I do wish I could make it more, but am actually having to borrow this. In severing my relations with your church please be assured that I fully realize you have done far more for me than I did for you. I fully appreciate it all, and pray God's continued blessing upon you." [49]

In September, the time had come for Price Daniel to say good-bye to his childhood. Wearing a dark dress suit and lugging a new trunk his father had purchased as a parting gift, he was driven to the Liberty railroad depot. [50] M.P. watched the train slowly carry his son off into a new and dangerous world and hoped that he and Nannie had best prepared him for what it had in store.

CHAPTER 2

Baylor University

Located some twelve blocks south of Waco, Baylor University was the oldest institution of higher education in Texas. With nearly 2,000 students, it was rich in history and tradition, much to the liking of Price Daniel. But even more appealing was the university's strong affiliation with the Baptist church. Rules were strictly enforced, and decent conduct was mandatory for students to stay in good standing with university officials.[1] Daniel showed little concern for decorum the day he arrived on campus in September 1927. The lanky, wavy-haired young man from Liberty emerged from the back seat of a taxi, placed his bags on the nearest sidewalk, and immediately declared to a small group of onlookers: "I'm M.P. Daniel, and I'm a candidate for president of the freshman class!"[2]

During his first couple of years at Baylor, Daniel revealed a much more bumptious personality than the person who would ultimately receive some of the university's highest honors. He enjoyed tooting his own horn, and did not hesitate broadcasting to fellow students his desire to become governor of Texas. "We used to call him 'bigger and better Daniel,'" reminisced one classmate. Another peer fondly recalled this period in Daniel's life, remembering that he "loved the limelight and excitement." At the time, such pomposity was rare at a strict Baptist university such as Baylor, and even prompted a lecture from M.P. in which he pleaded with his son to be more humble. That preceded an incident where Daniel was pinned by a group of freshmen determined to deflate his ego. The boys ran clippers over the back of his head, leaving him no choice but to shear his remaining locks.[3]

Daniel also exhibited strong self-assurance with the ladies, once advising an attractive classmate that he would take her all the way to the Governor's Mansion, whereas her relationship with a certain football player had a darker and gloomier future.[4] In a brief essay written his freshman year entitled "My Ideal Woman in the University," he explained that his model companion must: "frequent the library for purposes other than checking out books or preparing a daily lesson... not always be worrying about her studies and examinations... be a good, hard worker, but refrain from boasting about it... be able to meet with ease every new occasion with which she comes in contact... and know how to act well everywhere." In conclusion he wrote: "I may add that I am glad that I haven't decided to wait until I find her before I associate with members of the fairer sex. If I did, things might get pretty lonesome before four years of this grind for higher education is complete."[5]

On one date, Daniel was the victim of a prank organized by some of his classmates. He had been told that the father of a young lady he liked was a bit overprotective. Arrangements were made for Daniel and the girl to meet one evening at a small bridge on the edge of campus. Not long after he arrived at the location and engaged in conversation with his date, a fellow student emerged from behind a tree wearing a dark trench coat, pointing what appeared to be a gun in Daniel's direction. Daniel, sure that the girl's angry father had followed her to the secret meeting place, took off in a dead sprint for cover as the prankster fired blank after blank from his gun. He ran zigzag patterns until finally disappearing from sight, sure that he had managed to dodge every bullet.[6]

Daniel's first taste of elected office came as chairman of the Freshman Banquet Committee. Although the university prohibited such functions, he discharged his duties as if the fate of the university rested on his shoulders. Writing to Dean W.S. Allen, eloquently requesting that the freshman class be allowed to have a banquet, and not wanting to engage in "a revolting attitude of a plea for our rights," he assured the dean that the class would sign a petition solely for "the spirit of the thing." He implied, however, that the class would prefer to communicate in a more mature manner. "We would have it understood that we readily see your justification in having passed a faculty ruling some five years ago prohibiting our class from banqueting," Daniel wrote. "But our point today is that we feel capable of conducting ourselves at an entertainment event in a manner that would be pleasing to the other students and faculty of the University..."[7] Days later, Dean Allen responded: "I am writing to notify you officially that the faculty Monday afternoon, February 13, declined to grant the Petition of the Freshman class.... As I stated to you in conference, the faculty feels that the present ruling should not be changed. The faculty honors the fine spirit of the freshman and also the fine way in which the petition was made."[8]

Daniel continued to pursue his journalistic ambitions by landing a job with Baylor's campus newspaper, the *Daily Lariat.* "He had a yen to be a writer," recalled Fred Hartman, the paper's news editor who would become Daniel's lifelong friend. "He was an alert reporter and, therefore, got the best assignments even though only a freshman." As promised, Daniel received an occasional movie pass as payment for his services with the newspaper.[9]

When the Democratic Party finalized plans to hold its 1928 national convention in Houston, Daniel worked to secure press credentials for himself and Hartman to cover the historic event. With a little help from his father, the budding journalist soon received assignments to cover the convention for not only the *Daily Lariat* but the *Liberty Vindicator* and *Progressive Outlook* as well. On June 22 a front-page article in the *Houston Post* hailed Daniel as "probably the youngest writer to receive assignment to the press box of the Democratic National Convention."[10] And in the *Houston Press,* a similar article read: "Texas boasts of producing the 'baby' of all news writers assigned to cover the National Democratic Convention. He is M.P. Daniel, Jr., sophomore at Baylor University, who is assigned a seat in the official press box to represent four Texas newspapers."[11] However, readers of both publications might have been surprised to learn that both articles were written and submitted to the newspapers by none other than Daniel himself.[12]

It was during this convention that Daniel, sitting in the press box beside his father and Hartman, got his first glimpse of some of the big names of Democratic politics. Observing the thousands of delegates who poured into the massive structure built solely for the occasion, he reported that "a person can barely budge his way." Flamboyant New York mayor Jimmy Walker "was given especial greeting from the womenfolk of democracy," he wrote. "In the Rice Hotel lobby he was surrounded by them and could not escape them until aided by several husky men from the Al Smith headquarters." And because of Al Smith's increasing popularity, Daniel speculated that "Sidewalks of New York" had become the most popular song in that part of the state. "It is heard from every band, radio, and phonograph. The lobby of the Rice Hotel each day rings with melodies from an old accordion, the owner of which has composed many songs honoring Al Smith and the city of New York." [13]

Daniel had some unforgettable experiences during the four-day convention. He and Hartman sat directly behind Will Rogers each day and commonly found themselves engaged in brief conversations with the famous humorist. But the high point was when Franklin Roosevelt, pulling himself forward on leg braces, made his way to the speaker's podium and jubilantly nominated for the presidency "one who has the will to win who not only deserves success but commands it. Victory is his habit—the happy warrior, Alfred E. Smith." Daniel was living his dream, experiencing firsthand the affinity between his two favorite professions—journalism and politics. [14]

Despite all of this, his most lasting experience during that week in Houston had nothing to do with the convention itself. One afternoon, on the way back to the hotel, he and his father began discussing politics. M.P. suggested that, should there be a vacancy in the state legislature, upon his eventual return to Liberty, his son may want to consider running. Daniel was thrilled at the prospect of seeking office, but even more so that his father would consider him worthy of such responsibility. The idea would remain in his mind for several years to come. [15]

Daniel and Hartman returned to Baylor from the convention enthusiastic and determined to help get Al Smith elected. They quickly threw together an Al Smith for President Club, and openly endorsed the New York governor in the *Daily Lariat*. But support for the urban, anti-prohibition Catholic was diminutive on the ultra-conservative Baylor campus. Recalled Hartman: "It went over like a lead pipe thrown in the middle of a lake." In fact, soon after formation of the club, someone broke into the newspaper office and stole the duo's supply of campaign paraphernalia. The incident only prompted them to write more pro-Al Smith editorials, until university officials grew uneasy and pressured the two budding journalists to recant. Finally, after much persuasion, Daniel and Hartman obliged.[16]

Much of the carefree spirit Daniel exhibited throughout his college days can best be detected in his correspondence with Hartman during breaks between quarters. In these letters the two young men confessed dreams, aspirations, and fears to each other in a style that Hartman would later describe "as dignified as the President would have with a Supreme Court justice."[17] In a January 23, 1929, letter to Hartman, Daniel expressed his admiration for a certain girl back at school: "There is no doubt that I love her now, but you know that I am not going to care for any girl more than she cares for me. So you can judge the amount of my love by the volume of hers, and vice-versa. There are still some things I do not like about her, and since she knows about it, I do not intend to care more for her until she cares enough to change in a way or two."[18]

Concerning Baylor, he wrote: "I am not going to go there another year if I don't have something very enticing in the way of a position to hold me. If this is not available, I would like to get my master's degree in the East. Then another year of my life, I would spend out of the United States. And if I wasn't too much in love, I would like to get some more degrees and what goes with them. There is no doubt that getting married holds a guy back in some ways. But it should push him forward in others. If it does not do more good than it does bad, then I am positively against it until I am thirty years old." In closing, he remarked: "Well, my chest feels clear again. By the way, I have just gained twenty pounds since coming home. So you see, I have a larger chest to clear."[19]

In somewhat of a foreshadowing manner, Hartman would address Daniel as "Dear Governor..." atop his return letters. "I doubt that I would make a very good politician," he scribed on January 29, 1930, "but I believe that I would make a good campaign manager! I wouldn't mind your being governor if you would appoint me to the highway commission..."[20] And when Daniel once confessed that he liked the same girl Hartman had been chasing back at school, Hartman wrote: "Now that you have fallen for Louise, differently from the rest, tell me this. It had not been for long had it? It makes me feel embarrassed to believe that you cared any more for her than I did but withstood out of friendship for me." [21]

Hartman, who described Daniel in his college years as having "ambition all over the place," was responsible for making an important decision in his friend's life. While passing time at the campus newspaper office, discussing Daniel's possible future in politics and the fact that he still referred to himself as M.P., Jr., Hartman remarked: "I hate to tell you this, but you're never going to get there. Was it T.C. Jefferson, somebody Houston, or W. Something Wilson? No! You're going to have to do something about your name or you're never going to be elected anything." He asked Daniel the meaning of "M.P.," and upon learning that the initials stood for "Marion Price," made a simple suggestion. "We both agreed that Marion wouldn't get it," Hartman recalled, "so then I said, 'Why don't you make it 'Price'? That's a good name—Price Daniel. I predict you'll go far with that.'" Hartman later called it "just a couple of kids in a wild college conversation." But from that moment forward, Daniel would seldom again refer to himself as "M.P." [22]

Knowing that his father was big on tradition, Daniel was reluctant to tell him that he no longer preferred to be called by his initials. Making this even more difficult was the fact that he was abandoning his father's own name. After careful consideration, he broke the news in a letter explaining the political implications. His father responded: "By all manner of means use the name you prefer best just as long as you do not prefer something besides the last name— which I am sure you never will. I agree that there is a psychology about all such things.... In making the change, just make it—and say nothing about it. Just sign your name, always, 'Price Daniel.' We will call you that and make everyone else call you that, so that it will be as 'household' as M.P., Jr. now is so." [23]

One of Daniel's more notable editorials in the *Daily Lariat* during this period applauded the election of Tom Connally from Texas to the United States Senate. "Write down one more colorful member in the upper house when Tom Connally, of Texas, moves over from the other side of the Capitol dome after the fourth of March," he wrote. "He is an orator; his speeches are full of wit and sarcasm, and he is gifted with an imposing appearance." [24] The article wound up on the desk of Connally, who wrote Daniel: "Your article appearing in the *Daily Lariat* regarding myself and my induction into the United States Senate has been called to my attention. I have read the article with a great deal of interest and am deeply appreciative of your kind reference as to my public service." [25] The letter held a touch of irony, for little did Connally know that the young Baylor student would one day oust him from the Senate.

Daniel's involvement with the college daily continued to intensify. He had served as a reporter, feature writer, copy editor, and news editor in his first two years at Baylor, but on the night of May 22, 1929, achieved his ultimate journalistic ambition. The Baylor Board of Publications selected him over six other applicants to fill a vacated position. In large print, the following morning's newspaper headline read: "PRICE DANIEL NAMED EDITOR OF 1929-30 LARIAT." [26] Daniel was ecstatic because, for the first time, he was in charge of a big and important operation. Its success or failure rested on his shoulders, and a large staff now turned to him for delegation of authority. In a congratulatory letter, an upperclassman expressed his joy: "I knew from the first you were the real thing. There's nothing phony or shallow about you.... You've won the greatest victory of your life.... I'll have to forget you were my slime.... Heartiest best wishes for a successful administration." [27]

One might look to Daniel's appointment as editor of the *Daily Lariat* as the turning point in his college experience. Up to this time, he had exhibited a flamboyant quality, seldom missing an opportunity to tout himself or broadcast openly his ambitions. But with this appointment came a large responsibility and a need to reflect some maturity in his daily columns. In his opening remarks, he wrote that students were welcome to visit the publications office, but warned: "We have no room for bull sessions, and you are not welcome if you come for that purpose." [28] He began winning the respect and allegiance of both students and faculty. Daniel had been popular before, but was now viewed as a hard worker who not only dreamt big dreams but possessed traits of leadership, commitment, and determination that could make them become reality.

Price Daniel's college career to this point could have been judged as a great success. In just two years at Baylor, he had already tackled his twin ambitions of becoming president of his class and editor of the college daily. And then that next fall, because students were allowed to begin law school in their third college year, he quickly undertook this challenge as well. His ability to pursue such a variety of activities and execute each as if it were his only priority prompted one journalism classmate to write: "In three years he will have an A.B. degree, where it takes most students four and sometimes five. Then in two more he plans to have a law degree and a possible m.a. degree; three degrees all in the time that it takes most students to get one.... Measure your achievements by what he has done and see if your ambitious nature has led you to accomplish as much as he has." [29] One professor who had since moved on to become president of another university in Arkansas wrote to his former student: "Ever since you arrived and even before you came to Baylor, I found a deep interest in you. You wrote well; you expressed always the highest ideals in thought as well as in act and conduct, maintained the esteem of all who knew you. I shall watch for your continued success as editor of the *Daily Lariat* next year and then on as a journalist through all the years to come." [30]

But Daniel's honeymoon with Baylor would soon come to an abrupt end. In December 1929, just before final examinations, he and five other students were caught being excessively rowdy on campus after having consumed alcohol in a university dormitory room. Dean Allen quickly commented: "They knew the rules of the university and the land. I can say only that their offense came during the time they were students at the University." [31] Consequently, the December 4 issue of the *Waco Times-Herald* reported that a small group of Baylor students, "among them a staff official of the *Lariat*," had been suspended from school.[32] Daniel was devastated, and regretted nothing more than telling his proud parents that their oldest son had foolishly jeopardized all he had worked so hard to achieve at the university. But before leaving Baylor, reverting to his pompous nature, he went to the dean's office and assured him that he would return, "bigger and better" than ever.[33]

Within a week the Baylor Board of Publications chose a new *Daily Lariat* editor, and Daniel was aboard a train heading home. Embarrassed and humiliated, he was met by his father at the Houston depot, and from there driven to Liberty. On the way, much to his surprise, M.P. confessed that he, too, had made some poor decisions in his earlier days, but this would not diminish young Daniel's disappointment with himself. Each day at home during his three-month leave would serve as a reminder of this episode and the ignorance he felt he had displayed.[34]

To help pass the time, Daniel worked hard throughout the winter milking cows and performing chores for his father. As tough as the suspension was, it proved to be even more difficult for his close friend Hartman, who also had been involved in the incident. Hartman had already graduated from Baylor and in the fall of 1929 was manager of student publications on campus. The two continued to write each other throughout their forced leave of absence, each assuring the other that he was not alone in having to endure the grueling penalty of putting their lives on hold. In a January letter to Daniel, Hartman wrote: "Of all of the fools I've ever met, I'm the biggest.... I made more mistakes per minute than you did per hour.... The year 1929 will remain a blotch on my life." Further on in the letter, Daniel was flattered to read Hartman's description of the *Daily Lariat* without his leadership, calling it "the most pitiful attempt at journalism I have ever seen.... What I am trying to tell you is that they miss your supervision, and from the look of the fillers even I am slightly missed." [35]

Daniel held no lasting resentment toward Dean Allen or the university for his expulsion. He knew he had violated the rules, and willfully suffered the consequences. But the incident did little to derail the young men's ambitions, for as permanent as the disgrace seemed at the time, the boys involved would eventually go on to succeed dramatically in their chosen professions. Suspended that cold night in December were the soon-to-be publisher of one of the largest newspaper chains in Texas (Hartman), an air force general, a United States senator and three-term governor, and an Episcopal bishop. [36] In 1987 Hartman sent Daniel a clipping which appeared in a San Antonio newspaper and poked fun at the irony of the suspension. At the close of an attached letter, he wrote: "My only comment about the clipping is that many serious events can be humorous 57 years later." [37]

Upon the long-awaited arrival of spring in 1930, Daniel once again enrolled at Baylor. As if never missing a single day of classes, he jumped head-first back into a schedule filled with long hours and demanding responsibilities. Within a short time, a newspaper sub-head declared: "PRICE DANIEL IS CHOICE OF JUNIOR CLASS FOR YEARBOOK HEAD." [38] He campaigned for and won the editorship of the publication, the *Round-Up*, and began to focus the majority of his time and efforts on this new job. The position enhanced his popularity on campus and frequently required him to go above and beyond the call of the average editor. The *Round-Up* reported that on one occasion, after judging a beauty contest on campus, "it had first seemed necessary to give Editor Price Daniel a police escort as he proceeded about his duties on the campus. Various defeated factions threatened bodily harm to the midget editor, but time healed the wounded vanities." [39]

As a growing leader on campus, he received ample experience speaking in public. Wrote one classmate: "His ability as a speaker has made him very much in demand, not only at pep rallies, but gave to him as a slime the high honor of carrying a heavy siren to all the football games—something for which we all remember Marion Price." [40] During chapel hour on Armistice Day, 1930, Daniel addressed his fellow classmates: "Since the college students were the first to respond to the call of the great War, let them be the first to respond in the promotion of the peace of the world." He also praised President Wilson and his untiring efforts to solve problems in a peaceful manner. "Those men were fighting for eternal peace— let us as the men of tomorrow give ourselves to the cause and abolish war." [41] Another address given the following year at the Baylor law banquet prompted a glowing response from Baylor President Pat Neff. "Your address, 'The Courtship of the Law,' was in a high degree enjoyed by all," wrote the former Texas governor in a May 6 letter to Daniel. "I shall watch you climb the ladder of success with ever increasing interest." [42]

Under Daniel's leadership, the 1931 Baylor *Round-Up* was accorded All-American honors by the Scholastic Press Association, the highest rating given by the organization. An article printed in the Liberty newspaper, praising its hometown prodigy for his latest accomplishment, reported: "The annual is well printed, handsomely bound and well edited, and is one of the most attractive publications of its kind we have ever seen." [43] In some ways, the small article was almost as important to Daniel as was his yearbook accomplishments. He had proven both to himself and his friends back home that he had overcome the suspension and fulfilled his promise to Dean Allen by returning to Baylor "bigger and better than ever."

One of his more infamous exploits at Baylor was the formation of a jazz band called the Varsitonians. Self-billed as providing "the South's finest college music," the group traveled to engagements in faraway cities such as Dallas and Houston in an old truck with bright letters on each side proclaiming: "Price Daniel Presents Doc Mize and his Varsitonians." The irony of his involvement with the band was that he could not read a single note of music. Assuming the role of organizer and promoter, he sought publicity, scheduled engagements, and handled the money. He conceded in a letter home to his mother that his primary duty was to "announce the solos and the names of the tunes," and that "all I do is keep time and smile at the people." [44] In another letter, he wrote: "Tuesday night we played at Austin with nearly 2,000 on the floor. Made ten dollars apiece. Last night played at Temple, but didn't have a very good crowd. Friday night at the hotel should be good, and then Saturday night in Dallas we will make a few more. That will help out financially, but it doesn't help out when it comes to getting rest and doing good studying." [45] Most noteworthy about the band's engagement in Austin was that it was booked by none other than the University of Texas student body president, Allan Shivers, another future governor. [46]

M.P. and Nannie had serious reservations about Price's involvement with the Varsitonians, fearing for his safety on the road every weekend as well as the strain it was placing on his classwork. In order to convince his parents that the effort was worthwhile, he scheduled an engagement in Liberty. Covering the performance, a local newspaper reported: "Price Daniel and his Waco Varsitonians played for a holiday dance at the fair grounds pavilion last Wednesday night, and reports are that the evening's music was considered exceptionally pleasing. Mr. Daniel, who is a senior in the Baylor Law School, was given a splendid ovation by his many Liberty friends." [47] Despite being impressed by their son's performance, M.P. and Nannie were still concerned that the band was consuming too much of his time. They were not alone. Allen G. Flowers, dean of the Baylor law school, also objected to one of his students piddling around with such a whimsical activity. [48] Even a fellow classmate warned him: "Dear Senator, be careful old man that you don't spread yourself too thin! Many a capable man has spread himself into mediocrity that way. It's not quantity, but quality, of work that counts." [49] For a while, the more those close to him disapproved, the more involved he became with the band. In another letter home, he boasted: "I have played before three dances, one banquet, twice on the radio, once at the theater, and once in

Waco Hall on the stage. We are dealing with the theater here now to play a four-day run at the best theater in town." [50]

Before long, as his parents had predicted, the rehearsals and weekend engagements on the road, combined with the increasing demands of law school and other commitments on campus, began taking their toll. In a letter to his mother Daniel admitted that he had been under "such a strain and rush... I just keep on the steady go from seven in the morning until eleven and twelve at night." [51] It soon became clear that something had to give in his grueling schedule. Finally, on January 6, 1932, in another letter to his mother, he wrote: "Well, the orchestra won't bother [me] anymore now. I am an ex-director. Retired Monday of this week." [52]

One only has to skim through the pages of the 1930–31 yearbook to see how involved Daniel had become in numerous activities on campus. He appeared in a picture with the Nose Brotherhood, captioned the "Most Reputable but Ignorant Legal Representative and Attorney General Whistle Nose Daniel." In another, sporting a small, black bow-tie, he was listed as a field manager of the Lawyer–Premed Football Game. The yearbook also chronicled his relationships with female students on campus, suggesting: "A welcome addition to the college curricula would be a course in Women. We might suggest for instructors in Women 101, 102, 103, 104, such scholars as Price Daniel, Jack Runnels and Sam Allesandro." In addition, the face of the small-framed, wavy-haired student is seen peering over the shoulders of fellow members of the Chamber of Commerce, the debate team, Sigma Delta Chi, Pi Kappa Delta, Kappa Epsilon Alpha, Forum, and the Varsitonians. [53]

Daniel continued to see many girls throughout his college experience, but had trouble finding compatible mates on campus who met his rigid requirements. Of course they had to be pretty, but he was looking ahead and seeking a special someone who also possessed grace, intelligence, and a keen knowledge of history and current events. In a letter home discussing his relationship with a young lady named Sarah, he wrote: "Don't think I am serious about liking her. I just go with her because I like her better than any of the other girls, but we certainly have no serious intentions." [54] He also received an earful of dating advice from male friends on campus, each of whom thought he knew a perfect mate for the future politician. "Keep on balking at falling in love with a girl," wrote one classmate. "Unless you change your ambitions somewhat, love won't be so kind to you. Your former stand was theoretically ideal, but hard to maintain.... I have the confidence in you to think that you won't do anything rash. Lou would make a good wife and would be a suitable mate for the governor of Texas." [55] But regardless of the intensity of his search, Daniel would not find his soul mate on the campus of Baylor University.

Despite his assiduous involvement in collegiate activities, he always tried to keep in touch with family. Whether by letter or occasional weekend visits to the old Partlow house, he never drifted too far from the ancestral bond which characterized much of his childhood. And when his conscience told him every now and then that his letters home were becoming too infrequent, an apology would commonly arrive in an envelope on San Jacinto Street in Liberty. "Please believe me when I tell you that from now on I am going to write to you often and regularly," he professed to his mother. "My neglect does not show in any way the lack of love that sometimes is shown by children not writing their parents. I think of you all of the time and just hope that you will take care of yourself for now until summer when I can be with you for the rest of our lives.... It is my foremost desire for my life that I shall have many years with you and Grandmother during which I can in some ways repay you for what you have done in this world for us, and to show you my love." [56]

A couple of weeks later, Daniel wrote a similar letter to his father. M.P. fired back a scolding reply: "Yours of Feb 3rd—postmarked Feb 6th—came in this morning's mail, after I had given up all hopes of ever hearing from you again. If you could only know the strain and worry of a man's heart and the depth of love which permeates the very few, apparently, especially when one feels that there is but one person in the world on whom he could have depended, and then have that one neglect you as I have been neglected, you might realize my position and be able to sincerely ask God's forgiveness for your SEEMING ingratitude.... From here on out, I shall just grin and endure and expect nothing, even from you." [57] This angry outburst must have stung deeply.

Several professors at Baylor had done wonders in nurturing Daniel's interest in law and public service. But none so influenced the budding statesman as Charles D. Johnson, head of the journalism department. In him, Daniel found both a friend and scholar, someone who encouraged him to be all that he possibly could be. Looking back on those years, he would fondly recall: "Dr. Johnson used to teach journalism about half of the hour and then talk about life in general the other half. His philosophy was wonderful and inspired all of his students." [58] In fact, it was Dr. Johnson who caused Daniel to ponder his own future, to set goals and priorities for the years to come.

One day in particular, Dr. Johnson told his class of a man who had written a letter to himself, ten or twenty years hence. Stressing the importance of setting goals for the future, Johnson suggested to his students that they do the same. In Daniel's letter, addressed to himself and not to be opened for twenty years, he listed goals he hoped to reach for each of the years or intervals in the future. Some of his plans centered around service to the Lord, what he wished to do for his family and for the betterment of mankind. As for his political future, he planned on going to the legislature, then being county attorney, district attorney, running for attorney general, and then for governor. A classmate by the name of Frank Wilson, the only person Price let read the self-addressed letter, kindly suggested that his aims were probably set too high and too fast. Years later, as governor of Texas, Daniel would appoint then Judge Frank Wilson to the Court of Appeals in Waco. [59]

Daniel had served Baylor well. Having held "the highest positions that the university could offer," as one newspaper reported, the Liberty boy was twice class president, editor of both the yearbook and college daily, secretary of the Chamber of Commerce, member of the Scholastic Societies of the South, and leader of the university in debating and oratorical honors. [60] Perhaps more importantly, he had successfully reintroduced himself to a university which had expelled him a short time ago for "unacceptable behavior." As president of Baylor, Dr. Herbert H. Reynolds would later write: "Price, a lifelong Baptist, never failed during his forty years of public service to acknowledge the role of his faith and to make it a part of his life. His life was truly an exemplar of what Baylor strives for in her graduates." [61]

In return for his years of service and devotion, Baylor more than repaid Daniel by providing significant influence on his future political career. It was on the Waco campus that he refined his oratorical skills by participating in intercollegiate debate activities. It was at Baylor that Daniel not only made his first speech before a large group of people, but also was first afforded the opportunity to run for elective office. As the president of many campus organizations, he developed leadership skills. And, having been suspended from school, Daniel learned the importance of walking a straight moral line in order to succeed in public life. Perhaps more importantly from that experience, however, he learned that he had the ability to rebound from defeat or failure. Indeed, Baylor served as a catalyst for his political aspirations.

The university also provided a sound framework for Daniel's future political organizations. Having been involved in so many clubs and campus organizations, he accumulated many close and lasting friendships at Baylor. And because he made no secret of his future political aspirations, his friends pledged their support in advance and encouraged him to let them know when they could be of assistance. When these classmates graduated and dispersed back home to their respective rural towns, farms, cities, and suburbs across the state, Daniel inherited a strong network of support across Texas. They were at his fingertips to call upon when the time was right. On down the road, when he was seeking statewide office, it was this group who knocked on doors for him, spread his campaign message to friends and co-workers and, in the end, helped send their old Baylor classmate to the Governor's Mansion.

During his final days at Baylor, Daniel received one last letter from his father. Neatly typed, the letter read: "Be careful not to overlook anybody or anything. Give everybody and everything proper attention and then come on home. Yours, Dad." Then, scribbled at the bottom in pen were these words: "Somebody loves you wherever you go—I want you to know." [62] Daniel was aware, however, that the relationship between his mother and father had slowly deteriorated during his absence. His brother had warned him in a letter before his return to Liberty: "I feel that you and I are going to, in the very near future, support and wholly take care of mother. In other words, I mean that our parents will never be together again. Dad never speaks to mother unless he can help it. I can't see that it can go on this way forever. He still gives her money (little) but, you know, it's not the money but the social conditions. Whatever happens, we must take care of her and see that she is happy." [63]

CHAPTER 3

Country Lawyer

During Price Daniel's absence from Liberty, the rustic town had undergone a high degree of maturation. Upon his return in the summer of 1932, he was surprised by the steady stream of automobiles around the old downtown courthouse. The population had swelled beyond 2,000 residents, and many new homes had been constructed on what had been desolate fields. But even more impressive was the degree to which Liberty seemed to be surviving the national depression. At a time when Americans were electing Franklin D. Roosevelt to provide hope and economic relief, Liberty was home to more than eighty successfully operating businesses.[1] Twenty-one-year-old Daniel was glad to be back, and armed with high hopes and a law degree, was convinced that there was no better place to get started.

His parents now divorced and his brother off to college at Baylor, Daniel moved in with his mother and sister. He then located a small, second-story office in the same building occupied by his father to set up his own law practice. With not much more than a desk, chair, bookcase, and a 1911 Texas statute book, the office was just efficient enough for a young lawyer to open shop. As a finishing touch, he proudly displayed a white, wooden shingle outside his office door which proclaimed in big black letters, simply, "PRICE DANIEL, LAWYER." And despite the numerous accomplishments yet to come, he would never outgrow the modest, weather-worn shingle. From that moment on, it would proudly hang outside every legal office he occupied throughout his entire professional career.[2]

Daniel quickly adjusted to his role as an attorney. As one observer noted, "He keeps his arguments to the point at issue and moves about briskly, with the air of a man who knows what he is doing every minute. Though he avoids showmanship, there is enough of the actor in him, when he has the floor, to create a commanding, almost a crusading, impression."[3]

In June 1932 Daniel wrote a letter to Dean Flowers at Baylor recounting his early success: "One of the first things I want to tell you is that I won my first District Court case. It was a bootlegging case, but he was innocent of the charge. Paul Grogan was with me in the case and we were successful in satisfying the jury of our client's innocence. I have been in my office now for a week, and am doing right well."[4]

Daniel soon found himself immersed in one of the most infamous criminal cases in the history of Liberty County. The crime occurred in the early morning hours of November 14, 1932, when a night watchman for the Texas Gulf Sulfur Company was killed on duty. Doc Woods Browney was sitting in his car alone, guarding plant facilities near Moss Bluff, when someone slipped up beside the car, poked the barrel of a shotgun through the back driver's side window, and exploded two charges into his head at point-blank range. Immediately, three suspects were arrested: Bee Barrow, a local mechanic and wood chopper; Pearlie Browney, the victim's wife; and Mrs. R.O. Sherman, Pearlie Browney's mother.[5]

The three suspects sought legal assistance but had trouble finding a lawyer who would put his reputation on the line in such a case. Most legal counselors felt sure that at least one of the three suspects would receive the death penalty, and that such a sentence would inevitably tarnish his or her career in Liberty. The trio first visited a friend of the Sherman family, a local lawyer by the name of Thomas J. Hightower. Known throughout Liberty as a competent and skillful defense attorney, Hightower was also reluctant to take such a risk. However, he suggested to the desperate suspects that a new attorney by the name of Price Daniel had recently set up a practice in town and, because most new lawyers are in desperate need of clients, he might be interested in the work. After extensive persuasion, Daniel agreed to represent the three defendants charged with the murder of Doc Woods Browney, and, utilizing some swift conversion tactics of his own, convinced Hightower to share the case.[6]

The trial began in March 1933, at which time Bee Barrow testified that he slew Browney the night of November 14 upon the prodding of the other two suspects. According to Barrow, Mrs. Browney and her mother had plotted the slaying so that the bride of six weeks could collect $6,500 in insurance money on her husband's life. "She drove me to it—that woman made me kill him," Barrow had reportedly cried upon his arrest. "God, how I wish it hadn't of happened!"[7] He had been jailed immediately following the discovery of the body, whereas Browney and Sherman remained out on bond until the trial.

By agreement, Barrow's full disclosure of evidence earned him nothing harsher than life imprisonment. However, the district attorney demanded the death penalty for Browney's widow, and as a result the trial soon created a colossal following in Liberty County. The excitement prompted one newswoman to write: "This case has undoubtedly attracted more interest than any in this county in several decades."[8] As witness after witness was called to the stand, the courtroom remained packed to capacity, with many people forced to sit on the floor or stand along the walls. Even members of the Daniel family were required to arrive early to get seats. They placed sack lunches under their bench in anticipation of staying the entire day.[9]

Daniel and Hightower had their work cut out for them, and were forced to rely primarily on the testimony of their client. Mrs. Browney testified that, on the night of her husband's death, Barrow came to her house and told her he was going down to kill her husband. The two had lived together prior to her marriage to Browney, and according to the defendant, Barrow had grown insanely jealous.

"He left," she declared. "I didn't mention it to anyone because I didn't think he would do it. Later he came back and said, 'Well, I killed him, and if you tell anyone about it I'll kill you.' I went to sleep because I did not believe Barrow. The next morning, when Mr. Browney failed to return home, my mother and I started toward the sulfur lease and a man drove up and told me my husband had been murdered. It flashed through my mind that Barrow might have done it. I was grieved on the way there." That last remark by Browney was in response to testimony from a state witness who claimed to see the widow reading a newspaper at the head of her husband's casket when the officers arrived to arrest her. [10]

Hightower asked Mrs. Sherman, Browney's mother, if she had ever asked Barrow to kill anyone. The older woman shouted and raised her hands: "Lord, no! I never asked him to kill anybody. Great God, no!" [11] The testimony was highly dramatic, but Daniel was convinced it was not nearly enough to spare his clients. To sway the jury, he needed more evidence, such as testimony from an outside party impartial to the final ruling.

His prayers were soon answered in a man by the name of John Wesley Henson, a former cell mate of Barrow who suddenly came forward with shocking testimony. Henson claimed that Barrow, while listening to another prisoner read scripture from the Bible, confessed he had implicated Mrs. Browney in the murder because he did not want any other man to have her while he was in jail. With Henson's testimony to back them up, the two young attorneys claimed that their client, Pearlie Browney, was framed by Barrow in the murder of her husband. [12]

After days of electrifying testimony from a host of colorful witnesses, the verdict arrived. Pearlie Browney received a thirty-five-year prison sentence. The case was eventually appealed, reversed, tried again, and finally concluded by a Liberty jury in July of 1935, which shortened her sentence to only ten years in prison. Upon Daniel and Hightower's insistence on continuing the appeal process, Browney shouted: "I'll be damned if we're going to appeal this case. I'm going to take it!" [13] The following morning, Pearlie Browney was driven to the Huntsville State Prison, where she remained until her parole six years later.

Daniel gained invaluable public exposure from the Pearlie Browney case. As reporters arrived from such cities as Houston and Beaumont to cover the trial, many people were introduced to the young and talented Liberty lawyer through a throng of newspaper accounts. The trial also helped him land a capable law partner in Thomas Hightower. A rather slender man with a country drawl, Hightower was ten years Daniel's senior and an immense addition to his practice. The two consolidated supplies and equipment, and soon began sharing work and profits resulting from a vast array of both land and criminal cases.[14]

Daniel seemed to think of his legal career as an adjunct to his political aspirations. He had hardly settled in Liberty before becoming interested in entering his first race. In November 1933, when state Rep. John G. Ross resigned to seek another office, Daniel felt sure that his chance had finally arrived. By the time Governor Miriam Ferguson called a special election for December 16 to fill the vacancy, he was prepared to put his career and reputation on the line in quest of the vacated post.

Daniel's formal announcement of his candidacy appeared in a few local newspapers on the morning of November 24, 1933: "I wish to assure you that no person has solicited me to run for the office. It is my own desire to serve this district as representative in the Texas legislature, and my campaign is not financed, backed or aided by any person or organization. I will depend solely upon my friends, and those of you who become satisfied with my qualifications between now and December 16, to elect me to this office. By conducting such a campaign, if elected I will owe no campaign debts and will have no political obligations to pay while I am a member of the Legislature, and I will be in a position to serve you in a fair and impartial way, showing special favor toward none, but consideration for all. The position I seek at your hands is one of high honor and great responsibility; it is one in which a man can be of real service if he is sincere and serious in his efforts. I thank you for your consideration, and if elected, I will work untiringly to serve our State and the best interests of every person in the two counties of the 14th District." [15]

Having so frequently voiced his political ambitions to whomever would lend an ear at Baylor, Daniel, for a political newcomer, took unusually well to campaigning. He was always on the go, visiting communities such as Batson, Rye, Romayor, Moss Hill, Hull, Daisetta, Raywood, and Honey Island with literature in hand. He dashed into barber shops, grocery stores, fire stations, garages, restaurants, and stood on street corners in an effort to shake hands with as many people as he could possibly reach.[16]

Daniel received glowing endorsements from the Liberty press, which was obviously hungry to write about a young and energetic hometown boy who aspired to such ranks. One newspaper described him as a "clean, courageous, energetic, and ambitious young man, highly intelligent, courteous," and a host of other colorful adjectives fit to describe a prince. "The *Courier* predicts that his name will be heard around Texas in the political affairs of this State. . . . Men like young Daniel are needed in politics." [17] Another article stated that "if all men in public service were of the type of this young gentleman, there would be no 'forgotten man,' because the interests of the great plain people would be safeguarded and protected." [18] In addition, the young candidate received a glowing endorsement from ten members of the Liberty County Bar and, in the opinion of many pundits, appeared to have victory assured.

Little did Daniel know at the time, however, that another recent college graduate in nearby Hardin County was also planning to make an early entrance into state politics. Alf Weldon Roark, twenty-two years old and fresh out of Texas Christian University in Fort Worth, was the son of a well-known Saratoga physician and had recently landed a teaching position in the town of Cleveland. He was clean-cut, articulate, and highly respected by those with whom he had crossed paths. An energetic campaigner with a wealth of contacts, he was able to collect sizable support in Hardin County within a short period of time and thus assure a close election. [19]

Daniel received invaluable help from the Partlow family. They introduced him to friends, helped him organize speaking engagements, and even hosted small neighborhood get-togethers. But none labored so vigorously as Daniel's father, M.P., whose ties with a vast array of folks in southeast Texas proved an immense help to his son's campaign. To his friends, the elder Daniel wrote scores of handwritten, personal letters of endorsement which often maintained a surprising level of objectivity, especially considering that the letters were in reference to his own boy. In a letter to a friend in Romayor, he wrote that opponent Alf Roark was a fine young man, and "as far as character is concerned, it is my honest belief that Price and Alf are equals." But the difference, he maintained, was the level of experience between the two. He suggested that because of his travels and legal education, young Daniel was obviously superior. [20] But M.P. did not want to have a visible role in the campaign, preferring instead to work behind the scenes and let his son have the satisfaction of calling his own shots.

To a friend in Silsbee, M.P. wrote he was "confident that, knowing who the father of the boy is, you will throw your shoulder to the wheel and do everything you can for the election of Price." [21] To a judge in Orange, he confessed: "I am bold to say that he is better qualified to fill the position he seeks than any young man in our district."[22] And to a closer friend, he gave secret orders to travel to Silsbee to help stir up support. "Make a house-to-house canvass among the Baptist people—and talk to any others which they think proper to talk to," he wrote. "Do not make it a Baptist affair—but certainly the Baptist people should support Price.... Read this letter carefully, then destroy it and go to Silsbee.... Never mind answering this letter but send me a telegram simply saying, 'I will be there Sunday,' or whatever day you can get there. Do not say in the telegram where you are going. Simply say you will be there such and such a day. Send the telegram collect."[23] The next day, M.P. received a Western Union message from Newton which stated in its entirety: "I will be there Sunday evening."[24]

M.P. understood that Alf Roark's father was a good friend and distant relative of, and had even worked in political campaigns for, Congressman Martin Dies, someone whose support would likely be enough to sway the race in Roark's direction. M.P. knew that it was thus highly unlikely for the congressman to endorse young Daniel over Roark, so the best alternative would be to keep Dies out of the race altogether. After cleverly sending Dies a letter listing reasons why Daniel was best qualified to serve the district, he received an encouraging reply: "I note what you say about the candidacy of your son, Price Daniel, for state representative. As you know, Dr. Roark is related to my people and has been one of the best friends that we have ever had. He was very active for me in my race for Congress, and I hold for him the tenderest feelings. I could not take any part in this campaign which does not concern the duties of my office. In view of the fact that both you and Dr. Roark are my friends, I shall maintain a strict neutrality. I know that you will appreciate my position in this matter."[25] It was exactly what M.P. had wanted. He wrote the congressman on December 7: "Your very thoughtful statement that you will not take part in the campaign is extremely considerate, under the circumstances, and we greatly appreciate it."[26]

Daniel had no veritable campaign platform on which to run, or even basic dividing issues which are essential in most modern political races. Instead, he preached his own "honesty, hard work and courage in dealing with the people's business" and told how he would apply those qualities to the affairs of the state. He repeatedly echoed the sentiment of Thomas Jefferson that the country best governed is the country least governed. "It is my opinion that we have too many laws now," Daniel declared, "and that our lawmakers should give more time to correcting and changing some that we have, instead of spending so much of the State's time and the people's money in writing laws that our Constitution never intended for us to have." [27]

The race inevitably turned into something of a feud between Liberty and Hardin, each county monopolizing the support of its hometown candidate. And, with Liberty having a larger number of registered voters, the election was Daniel's to lose. But to Roark's credit, on election day he arranged to have Hardin County voters literally hauled to the polls in large numbers. Such tactics proved successful when the votes were tallied and Roark edged past Daniel by fewer than 100 votes. [28] Daniel had easily carried Liberty County, but had suffered from a very light voter turnout in comparison with that of Hardin County. Roark also won a large number of votes in the Cleveland area, which helped turn the results in his favor. [29]

The *Daily Courier* congratulated young Daniel for the "splendid showing made by him upon his maiden venture into the realm of politics.... Indeed, it was such a vote as would be gratifying to the most seasoned and able campaigner—a veteran in the art of 'corralling' votes... it was truly a remarkable and unusual political showing." And alongside the article, Daniel expressed his appreciation to the people of his hometown in a brief letter: "To know that 456 of my home people voted for me, in comparison to only 41 against, is one of the gratifications I have from the campaign. Such an expression of confidence in me by the people among whom I live is sincerely appreciated and will never be forgotten, and I shall ever strive to deserve that confidence." [30]

Commenting on his son's defeat, M.P. wrote to a friend in Saratoga: "The heavenly father knows what is best for each of us and Price's defeat has been taken with a wonderfully good spirit and will only help to mold him and make a better man of him." [31]

Daniel was naturally disappointed by his defeat, but would eventually point to the loss as an invaluable lesson which would benefit his career in years to come. Some time later, after having served his state as a United States senator and three-term governor, he conceded the naiveté of his first campaign for the legislature: "I think it was probably one of the best things that could have happened, looking back. Certainly not at the time did it appear good for anything. But looking back, I'm sure that it was good because it made me realize that you have to work a lot harder in politics. You have to plan. You have to know a little... a lot more about it than I knew at that time. And also it was good because it allowed me to get established in a law practice in Liberty which I would not have been able to do if I had been off in the Legislature." [32]

In an effort to recover from his narrow defeat, Daniel immediately immersed himself back into the law practice. Having adopted many of the same work characteristics as his father, he thrived on work and staying busy. He arrived at the office early each morning, worked continuously throughout the day, dashed home for a quick bite of dinner, then usually returned to the office and labored into the night. Hightower later referred to his young colleague as "one of the hardest working lawyers I have ever known. He just never did give up on anything he started until he finished it." [33]

In addition, Daniel meticulously dressed the part of a sophisticated big-town attorney. Commonly wearing wide-lapeled, double-breasted suits, heavily starched white shirts, bright striped ties, and freshly-polished shoes, complemented by his neatly trimmed and combed dark wavy hair, he made appearance a high priority. [34] In his opinion, clients would be attracted to a lawyer who paid attention to small details and was neat and orderly. His appearance, he reasoned, was their first impression of his capacity in this area.

Daniel and Hightower devised a plan to divide their casework evenly, but in a manner that allowed each to work primarily in his own area of expertise. Focusing on background research and legal specifics, Daniel was placed in charge of land cases. Hightower, with his numerous contacts and skills at questioning witnesses, handled the majority of criminal cases. The partners commonly appeared in court together and as a team quickly became regarded as one of the most prominent firms in Liberty. Pulling a monthly average of $75 apiece, quite good for that day, the partners were soon able to hire a full-time secretary. [35]

Since not all clients could afford to pay a reasonable fee for adequate legal representation, the partners would commonly work out other, more unusual ways of compensation. One case in particular, involving a local laundry owner, landed them complementary cleaning service. On another occasion, Daniel received a boat for his defense of a local client. One Liberty reporter described it as "a pretty good boat, and if the young lawyer has occasion in the near future to travel via the Trinity to the cities of Dallas or Fort Worth, his boat awaits with pleasure." [36]

However, the most memorable legal compensation the partners received came in a less manageable form—one cow, two goats, eight guinea fowls, a few pigs, and chickens. One morning they boarded an old truck and headed out to their client's farm to retrieve their breathing remuneration. When they arrived at the farm, it was clear that they would literally have to chase their fee around the yard. The guineas flew into some trees, forcing the men to roll up their sleeves and begin climbing. After a couple of hours of chasing birds, pigs, and goats, the exhausted attorneys headed back to town in search of an adequate storage facility for their latest prize. [37]

But despite his other involvements, Daniel's political aspirations only intensified with the passage of time. With the approach of the 1934 Texas elections, he developed a deep admiration for gubernatorial candidate James V. Allred, a Wichita Falls lawyer who had aspired to become attorney general in both 1930 and 1932. Allred advocated a decrease in taxes, strict control of lobbyists, creation of a Commission on Public Utilities, and the formation of a modern state police force. Daniel jumped at the opportunity of becoming his campaign manager in Liberty County, and quickly took to the streets to spread the message of his preferred candidate.

In fact, he opened a local Allred campaign rally by lambasting a *Liberty Courier* newspaper editorial which referred to the candidate as "the little boy with the big breeches." Daniel assured the crowd that the newspaper's endorsement of Allred's opponent, Tom Hunter, was inadvertently of great help to Allred. In the following morning's paper, the *Courier*'s editorial staff cleverly rebutted Daniel's charges by insisting that, at such a young age, even his leadership ability would be much preferred to that of Allred. "Price is a likable, dignified young gentleman," the article stated. "He has more sense in fifteen minutes than Jimmie Allred has in a full day. Right now, Price would fit into the governor's office much better than would little Jimmie Allred. Price has more personality, more brains, more native ability, and an altogether more impressive bearing. He would look, talk, and act more like a governor than would Jimmie Allred." And for the kicker, the editorial finished by claiming that Daniel would "get over his Allred fancy, and will recover from the shock of the defeat next Saturday of his 'hero,' Allred, just as a schoolboy grows up and forgets his high school sweetheart." [38]

James Allred did go on to win the governorship, but to Daniel's dismay, fell short in Liberty County by more than 100 votes. The *Courier* rejoiced in his defeat locally, and chided Daniel for having publicly doubted the power of their Hunter endorsement. "If the way the voters of Liberty County voted in the first primary may be pointed to as an indication of how the *Courier* helped," a subsequent editorial suggested, "it looks like somebody working for Allred might have given Mr. Hunter a good boost, too...." [39] Daniel was naturally disappointed that despite his tireless efforts, Allred had failed to carry Liberty County. But in the process of managing the local campaign, he made numerous contacts that would prove of immense worth a few years down the road and also received considerable positive media exposure throughout his district.

Daniel briefly considered entering the legislative race of 1936 but thought Representative Roark to be doing a credible job and decided to wait. He agreed to support Roark for reelection regardless of which other candidates were to enter the race. In return, Roark promised Daniel that he would hold the office for only one more term, leaving the position vacant for the election of 1938. Considering Roark's lucrative proposition, plus the benefits two years of preparation would provide for a campaign, Daniel readily agreed to bide his time. [40]

To assuage somewhat his political fever, he jumped at the opportunity of joining the Young Democrats of America. The organization was founded by President Franklin Roosevelt as a training exercise for future leaders and, of course, as a way to lure younger generations into the Democratic Party. Through Young Democrats, Daniel made invaluable contacts with a wide variety of people across the state. It was in this organization that he would meet for the first time a multitude of young men who would one day serve beside him in numerous public service capacities.

Daniel quickly advanced in the Texas branch of Young Democrats and was soon elected a member of the executive committee. In this capacity he worked to establish organizational clubs across the state and was responsible for keeping in touch with a wide range of pressing political issues. At the state convention in San Antonio in May of 1936, the delegates elected Daniel temporary vice-chairman and gave him the pleasure of addressing the gathering. He was honored to follow Governor Allred at the speaker's podium and took advantage of the moment to applaud the governor and the recent stands of the Democratic Party in general. Following the convention he was again asked to speak, this time at a special luncheon honoring Allred.[41]

Daniel was making considerable strides as a public speaker and was turning the heads of many influential men in his audiences. James A. Farley, postmaster general and New Deal strategist, asked him to join the Roosevelt-Garner Speakers Bureau in 1936 after the presidential duo was nominated for a second term. Daniel quickly obliged, and for the next three months addressed numerous groups on the president's behalf. The following year, the Texas chapter sent him to the national meeting in Washington as a representative to participate in both party and presidential festivities. The climax of his involvement with the Young Democrats occurred in 1938, when he led a delegation to greet Roosevelt in Wichita Falls. Along with other members of the group, he boarded the private presidential train car and was able to engage in a brief conversation with the president.[42]

It was around this time that Daniel's career as a lawyer shifted dramatically. Hightower informed him that he was leaving the practice of law to become a judge in Liberty County. Looking back on his years with Daniel, Hightower commented that he never once saw his partner unprepared or caught off guard. "Not only was he a good trial lawyer before a jury," he reminisced, "he was a fine lawyer in arguing the law before the court."[43] Daniel was now back on his own.

For the time being, still waiting patiently for his upcoming legislative race, he decided to immerse himself in local politics and in January of 1937 was elected president of the Liberty Chamber of Commerce. This enabled him to work on a project which to him had always been of utmost interest, the Trinity River. He looked closely at water rates, and learned that shell being transported to Liberty from Galveston was transferred by barge to Houston and then sent overland to Liberty when, he reasoned, it could instead come directly up the Trinity at half the cost. Upon further study, he received assurance that if the town could revive a once-flourishing barge line out of Liberty to the Gulf, Liberty would be the clearing point for a million barrels of oil piped to its port.

Local townsfolk were ecstatic at the far-reaching possibilities and pulled together to finance a $6,000 fee to remove sandbars and snag pockets from the river. As one reporter observed, "Liberty has taken on a new lease of life since the development of the Hardin oil field, and the promised development of the river. The latter is the chief subject of conversation on the streets and in offices, and has been in fact for several months."[44]

Daniel's efforts in reviving barge traffic prompted the Trinity Improvement Association to invite him to address its meeting in Fort Worth. In what a Dallas newspaper described as a "stout sermon," he told the gathering that the time had come to restore commerce on the lower reaches of the river. Back when Sam Houston practiced law in Liberty, Daniel explained, it was common practice for steamboats and stern-wheelers to carry freight, passengers, and mail between Galveston and Liberty. However, he reminded his audience, rates climbed when railroads replaced water travel. He proceeded to insist that people all along the Trinity prepare for the day when barges would run from Dallas all the way to the open sea.[45]

Everything seemed to be going Daniel's way. He had successfully rebounded from his legislative defeat to Roark, and had worked carefully in the years since to place himself in just the right position for the 1938 House race. But tragedy struck on December 7, 1937, when he received word that his father had passed away due to complications resulting from an enlarged heart. M.P. was only fifty-six. The loss deeply saddened the younger Daniel, and from that moment forward his full attention centered around his mother and her well-being. He would later look back with a trace of regret that his father never saw him elected to a single public office. "At least," Daniel reasoned in a letter to a friend, "he lived long enough to give me the best start that any boy could have had."[46] Indeed, M.P. had succeeded in making a positive, profound effect on his oldest son, and did live long enough to see him become the young man of character for which he had always hoped. There is good reason to believe, in fact, that Daniel never would have entered politics had it not been for his father's influence.

M.P. willed 9,000 acres of land in Liberty County, valued at

$100,000, to Baylor University in Waco and Mary Hardin-Baylor College in Belton, as a trust fund for the education of young men and women from Liberty and Montgomery counties.[47] Daniel did not inherit any money or property from his father, and would from that moment on be classified as a self-made man.[48]

As promised, Alf Roark announced in January 1938 that he would leave the Texas legislature and seek the judgeship of Hardin County. It was the moment Daniel had anxiously awaited for nearly four years, and as no surprise to any voter in the district, he immediately jumped into the race. By now, he had evolved into a much more refined and motivated candidate than the neophyte of 1933. This time out, he had a thorough grasp of the issues affecting his local constituents and better understood what it would take to motivate them to go to the polls on his behalf. In addition, during the several years that had passed since his loss to Roark, he had begun to formulate a personal political philosophy. The time had served him well. Until this period in his life, Daniel was attracted to public service for mostly glamorous reasons. He seemed to desire both the power and prestige that accompanied political life, and approached political races somewhat like popularity contests. After losing to Roark, however, he immersed himself for the first time in real issues and began to formulate opinions and ideas that would forever define his candidacies. For instance, having defended many indigent clients, Daniel began to resent any new taxation proposals that surfaced. He also picked the brains of local farmers who complained of poor farm-to-market roads. Moreover, as president of the Liberty Chamber of Commerce, he learned to appreciate the value of natural resources. And perhaps most significant, he devoted himself to learning and understanding many of the issues facing state legislators in Austin. This time around, he was much better prepared.

Since no other candidate had entered the race, many of Daniel's supporters contended that he was already known well enough in the district and advised him not to waste energy on a strenuous campaign. But he had learned from 1933 never to take any election for granted, and firmly believed that for a state legislator to serve his constituents adequately, he must have the full support of his district behind him. "I am at once beginning an active campaign," he declared in a letter to a local newspaper, "which, with the help of my friends, will be carried to every part of our district."[49] He made a personal vow to visit with as many voters as possible, and pretended that the race between him and his imaginary opponent would come down to the very end.

Daniel received glowing endorsements from the local media upon his announcement. One newspaper editorial insisted that "his actions in the past have already marked him as a champion of the people," and praised his outspoken support of "additional educational opportunities for every boy and girl in Texas, for conservation of natural resources, for better state highways and for adequate farm-to-market roads." [50]

Daniel would later recall a trip to Waco during this period to visit his brother Bill, then a student at Baylor. The two were eating lunch in a small diner on the edge of town when a few men walked in the front door with Hillbilly Flour signs on their backs and proceeded to change the records on the jukebox. Some young folks at a table nearby recognized one of the men as W. Lee O'Daniel, who had recently made public his plans to run for governor, and walked over to shake his hand. "I thought it was so silly that I didn't get up and go over with them to meet the man," Daniel would remember. "That was just a few months before he took the state by storm." [51]

O'Daniel did indeed take the state by storm, running an emotional homespun campaign that caught the fancy and the imagination of the people. It was vital to Texas, he proclaimed, to get rid of all of the politicians and clean house. As his daughter passed collection plates resembling flour baskets among the ever-growing crowds and his two sons played hillbilly music in the background, Pappy, as he came to be called from his famous "Pass the biscuits, Pappy" radio commercials, tagged himself a defender of "common folks" and called on the legislature to fund sizable old-age assistance payments. At first his odd and somewhat humorous campaign style was not taken seriously, but it became clear by mid-June that he was well on his way to a runaway victory.

O'Daniel's unorthodox campaign forced legislative candidates across the state to take specific stands on a variety of issues. Despite running unopposed in the 14th District, Daniel was no exception. He echoed Pappy's promises to oppose a state sales tax and any legislation which would raise the truck load limit on state highways. And in July, Daniel's hard work paid off at the Democratic primary when he polled 4,863 votes. After having been defeated in the same race five years prior, he had rebounded, persevered, and was finally headed to Austin to represent I ¨ ¬ty in the Texas legislature.[52]

At the same time, Daniel p. .ed victorious in another high-profile legal case. In November of 1938, after three trials, a jury acquitted a man named Blackie Fawcett on charges of killing an unidentified Italian ship officer and dumping his body in a roadside ditch just outside of Dayton. Daniel had represented him and, to the surprise of most onlookers, craftily discredited the testimony of the state's witnesses and cleared Fawcett of all suspicion.[53] Similar to the Pearlie Browney trial, the case received considerable media attention and introduced an even greater audience to the young legislator-elect from Liberty.

As Daniel prepared to step forth on the statewide stage in Austin, he was far different from the green young man who had returned home to Liberty from college almost seven years earlier. He had established himself as a successful lawyer. He had been disciplined in the mechanics of partnership by his years of association with Thomas Hightower. He had developed patience and perseverance as a result of his narrow loss to Alf Roark. He had been hardened by the untimely passing of his father. He had been honest with everyone. His dreams of holding public office had finally materialized, and unbeknownst to him at the time, a legendary career which would span over forty years had just begun.

CHAPTER 4

Look Out, Austin!

Precisely at noon on January 10, 1939, Secretary of State Edward Clark struck his gavel and called the 46th Texas Legislature to order. As the ferocity of the gavel striking wood echoed throughout the House chamber, Daniel's life had forever changed. No longer was he a dreamy-eyed youth, determined to sell the world on the grandeur of his future endeavors. His time had finally come, and he was well aware that many eyes were watching to see if the "cocky young rooster's" ability could match his broad ambitions. From this day forward, he would work tirelessly to prove to his colleagues and constituents that he was worthy of their trust.

Ned Price, Sr. of Tyler, a representative sworn into the Texas legislature the same time as Daniel, recalled the unusual air surrounding the new solon from Liberty who sat just a few seats up: "He gave the impression of being a clean cut young man in both his appearance and mannerisms, as well as the way he talked and acted. He was a young man of integrity and promise, the type of person you would want in your state government." [1]

The House readily agreed upon Emmett Morse as Speaker, and spent much of its first week in session speculating upon the governor-elect's undisclosed plan for funding statewide pensions. Pappy

O'Daniel had made it clear in hundreds of speeches that old-age pensions would top his list of priorities once in office but had never been forced throughout his campaign to explain where he would get the funds. Many predicted he would call for a straight sales tax, while others figured he would much prefer balancing a sales tax with a natural resources tax. Regardless, in the back of many legislators' minds was the fear that the governor-elect, being inexperienced in the complex world of politics, would place unreasonable financing demands on the legislature and trust public sentiment alone to champion his cause.[2]

As expected, Pappy kicked off his administration with a bang. Price Daniel was among the 50,000-plus who filed into the University of Texas Memorial Stadium to watch the governor-elect take the oath of office, and in turn witness what would prove to be an unprecedented inaugural celebration. Fifty bands participated in the festivities, which ended with Pappy leading the masses in a rendition of "Beautiful Texas," one of his original compositions.[3]

The following day, Governor O'Daniel went before the Texas legislature and finally spelled out his long-awaited plan for funding a statewide pension. He called for a constitutional amendment to levy a 1.6 percent business transactions tax which he boasted would provide every elderly Texan a monthly income of $30. In addition, he proposed the abolishment of the ad valorem tax, and suggested the use of state cigarette tax proceeds to reimburse the school fund. According to his estimates, this would bring at least $45 million annually into the state treasury, enough to ensure that his far-reaching programs would become reality.[4]

As expected, Pappy's transactions tax proposal became the dominant issue of the 46th Legislature. Only a month into the session, the governor had fine-tuned his amendment and was ready to present it to the House. But confusion surfaced as rumors concerning the details of his proposal circulated around the lower chamber, and as Daniel would recall, "Those who did understand it were opposed to it."[5] The misunderstandings prompted a number of legislators to investigate other tax proposals, and on January 30 a strong coalition in the House emerged with a major initiative of its own. Submitted by Rep. Grover C. Morris and forty-three colleagues, the Morris Bill, as it came to be called, proposed the taxation of natural resources rather than business transactions.[6]

The Texas Senate, however, was impressed neither by Pappy's

transactions tax nor the House's natural resources measure, and further confused matters by charting a course of its own. The Senate recommended a constitutional amendment, SJR 12, which would tax gas, electricity, telephone service, sulfur, natural gas, oil, and admission to amusement activities. By levying a two percent tax on all retail sales, the Senate estimated that SJR 12 could contribute more than $30 million annually to the state treasury.[7]

Despite encountering adamant opposition in both chambers of the legislature, Pappy at first stuck to his guns and insisted on the passage of his transactions tax. In weekly radio addresses, he urged Texans to write their representatives and express their support for his ailing amendment. But within a couple of months, he realized his transactions tax was nothing but a sinking ship and decided to jump aboard the Senate's amendment, SJR 12. Knowing that old-age pensions must be financed somehow, and seeking an excuse to abandon his own proposition, Pappy now hesitantly supported the sales tax measure.[8]

Daniel was not only disappointed in the governor's waffling but was also opposed to SJR 12. As a new legislator who did not know any better, he was at first somewhat receptive to the Senate's measure. But upon taking the time to read SJR 12 in its entirety and discussing it with his desk mate, Jack Langdon, Daniel made up his mind that he would never, ever consider voting for the proposed amendment. "It contained a lot of horrible provisions in addition to voting a sales tax," he would later explain. "One of the worst things... was the fact that it had a ceiling written in it assuring the natural gas-oil industry that no additional taxes would be levied for social security purposes in this state."[9] Believing that it would burden those citizens least able to pay, he and a large block of House colleagues formed solid opposition to SJR 12. For the next couple of months, the governor grew furious that the amendment continuously failed to gain the necessary two-thirds majority in the House.

On June 9 the House considered SJR 12 for the fifth time, and a group of fifty-six legislators, Daniel included, once again blocked its passage. O'Daniel was outraged and went on statewide radio to single out the fifty-six opponents. He demanded that the time had come for them to "yield," much like he had been forced to do with his transactions tax. But the more infuriated he grew, the more resilient the group of legislators became. And on June 15 and 21, when SJR 12 was presented a sixth and seventh time, respectively, the "Immortal 56," or so they came to be labeled by the press, firmly stood their ground.[10]

"You can never imagine the pressures that were brought to bear on those of us who were members of the legislature at that time," remembered Daniel. "In the first place, the speaker of the House, Emmett Morse, was for the measure and was bringing all the pressure he could. The majority of the members of the House were for the measure. The Senate had already adopted it. Then we had a governor who had a great following in this State at that time going on the air every Sunday morning, calling the names of all of us who voted against the measure. And, of course, he asked the people back home to write us letters and send us telegrams. He was able to drum up a lot of letters and a lot of pressure on all of the members of the legislature. It became, I suppose, the most heated fight that we've had in the legislature in my memory."[11]

In his support of the bill, Morse had continued to bring up SJR 12 for a vote, but after the eighth try announced that he would submit it once more and that would be the last chance. On the ninth and final vote, despite even heavier pressure and threats, remarkably, the "Immortal 56" again prevailed and the measure was dead. Daniel was proud of his association with the "56ers" and, as the years passed, his stern opposition to increasing consumer taxes, born in this early "SJR 12 education," would be a foremost conviction of his political beliefs.[12]

But SJR 12 was far from being Daniel's only concern in his freshman term. Having handled a large number of land cases in Liberty, he had grown concerned about what he termed the "vacancy racket," a scam in which greedy land seekers studied property boundary lines in attempts to purchase valuable mineral rights cheaply or gaps between the lines that owners were often unaware they possessed. Current laws declared that such vacancies were property of the public fund, and that a vacancy hunter could file a claim in Austin for the unbelievably low price of one dollar.[13] Daniel was puzzled about why it was so easy for a vacancy hunter to cloud a title, and, even more so, why a rightful landowner should be expected to travel all the way to Austin to defend his or her claim. After further investigation, he and Rep. Paris Smith of Bay City introduced HB 9, a bill which called for the original landowner to have first rights to purchase the land from the state, for increased filing fees on vacancy applications, and for all such cases to be tried in the county of original jurisdiction.[14]

In the following months, HB 9 became one of the most hotly contested bills in Austin. Of course, the landowners, who felt they had spent unnecessary time and energy defending claims which often were theirs to begin with, supported it. Even oil companies, which had to pay the state when vacancies were discovered and later seek reimbursement, readily jumped on board. But opposition to HB 9 erupted primarily from public school personnel, who feared a major loss in revenue if vacancy hunting was dissuaded.

HB 9 was Daniel's baby and presented him with his first real opportunities to speak on the floor of the House. He downplayed reports that the schools were opposed to the bill, claiming instead that the true resistance came in the form of a few Austin attorneys who were scared of losing business. HB 9 was indeed in the best interest of the landowners and oil companies, he insisted, and it would be a shame for client-hungry attorneys to block its passage.[15]

After a bitter fight in both the House and Senate, HB 9 was passed and sent to the governor's desk for a signature. Although O'Daniel had publicly supported the bill, SJR 12 was still on the table at that time and he figured a threat to veto it could possibly sway Daniel's mind on the governor's own pet project. Pappy sent Assistant Secretary of State Marlin Sandlin to retrieve Daniel from a House session and inform him that he doubted O'Daniel would sign the bill unless Daniel voted for SJR 12. Daniel was infuriated, and later recalled: "I cannot record here exactly what I told Mr. Sandlin, but I did tell him that he could tell the governor to take my bill and stick it where I would not be able to say here in this recording." [16] Pappy took notice of the suggestion, and on June 19 invited Daniel to attend an HB 9 signing party for the Liberty solon's first major legislative victory.

The 46th Legislature adjourned on June 21 with the pension funding dispute still unresolved. Much of the session had been an absolute nightmare for Governor O'Daniel, who repeatedly blamed the "Immortal 56" for his troubles and vowed to do all he could to begin the next legislature without a single "56er" remaining. But for Daniel, the session could be termed nothing less than an overwhelming success. The rookie legislator had not only fathered a major piece of legislation, but also earned a lasting reputation as an effective speaker and tireless worker. Recalled House colleague Ned Price, "He was always at his desk working on something, working his secretaries." [17] And such an impression prompted capitol correspondent Raymond Brooks of the *Austin Statesman* to write, "What about Rep. Price Daniel of Liberty?" when pondering a list of candidates for the 1940 gubernatorial race.

Commenting on his first term in the Texas legislature, Daniel later admitted: "I was a young man then and was not married, and I did give some attention to other things than legislation." [18] Often that attention to "other things" meant trips to Houston with friends to attend parties and dances. On one such occasion a man by the name of Johnnie Palmer, a fellow Young Democrat, suggested to Daniel that he might be interested in meeting his employer's daughter, Jean Baldwin. After all, Palmer reasoned, she was attractive, intelligent, and would be a wonderful attribute to a young man on the rise. Upon learning that she was doing secretarial work for a Houston law firm that he was currently opposing in an insurance case, Daniel was hesitant. Being a bachelor and nearing the age of thirty, he was frequently introduced to eligible women who were the friends of friends but never seemed to have much luck with such arranged meetings. However, for some reason Palmer's suggestion was different. Daniel was interested in meeting this young lady of whom his friend spoke. [19]

Jean Houston Baldwin was born February 13, 1916, into a prominent southeast Texas family. Her father, Franklin Thomas Baldwin, was a successful attorney for the Texas Company, and her mother, Jean John Baldwin, held the distinction of being a great-granddaughter of Texas hero Sam Houston. Jean excelled in school from an early age, and in 1933 graduated in the top ten percent from San Jacinto High School in Houston. She attended Rice Institute for two years, then transferred to the University of Texas, where for a time she slept in a linen closet while waiting for someone to drop out so that she could have a room in the Scottish Rite Dormitory. As a token of her hard work and determination, Jean graduated cum laude in 1937 with a major in English and a minor in French. She soon returned to Houston, took a secretarial position with a local attorney by the name of Larry Morris, and sat in the front office totally unprepared for who was about to walk through the door and into her life. [20]

One afternoon, while taking care of business in Houston, Daniel decided to drop by the Morris law office and meet the young lady about whom Palmer had spoken so highly. He walked in, engaged in brief conversation with Jean, then returned to Palmer with the surprising verdict of "not too impressed." However, thanks to some common acquaintances, Price and Jean met again a short time later in Houston and before long were seeing each other frequently.[21]

Daniel had continued his involvement with the Young Democrats throughout his freshman term in the legislature, and at a meeting in Dallas in May of 1939, delegates elected him president of the Texas chapter.[22] Soon thereafter a dinner was held in his honor in Beaumont, at which time the rising politico received congratulatory messages from a host of dignitaries, including President Franklin Roosevelt. When finally invited to the podium, Daniel confessed to the audience that the occasion was the first staged in his honor which he had not helped arrange.[23]

Daniel's new position forced him to articulate his views on national political issues. He had worked hard for Roosevelt in 1936, but was adamantly opposed to the president seeking a third term. Instead, he supported fellow Texan John Nance Garner. Like Garner, Daniel had grown disillusioned with the New Deal and opposed many large federal programs and policies that he believed sanctioned handouts. So when he received word that a large block of delegates wanted to endorse Roosevelt for a third term prior to the Young Democrats' 1939 national convention in Pittsburgh, even though the organization's constitution prohibited such action prior to the Democratic Party choosing its nominee, Daniel threatened to withdraw the Texas chapter. Tagged by one writer as the "leader of the dissenters," [24] he traveled to Pittsburgh to organize the Garner camp, and was successful in stalling attempts to endorse Roosevelt prematurely.[25]

In the summer of 1940, Daniel learned that he would be challenged for his legislative seat by a citizen from Kountze, Texas. R.A. "Red" Richardson's campaign platform closely resembled that of Governor O'Daniel. In fact, Richardson realized that his only chance of defeating Daniel was to echo Pappy's pledge to rid the state of every last "56er," and to ride the governor's popularity all the way to Austin.

Daniel was somewhat fearful of the governor's lingering threat and hoped that his brave stance as a "56er" would not jeopardize his promising career. To counter Richardson's charges, which in essence were truly Pappy's, Daniel opened his campaign standing in the back of a pickup truck in Cleveland, insisting that it was time to put the pension dispute on the back burner and focus on more immediate issues, such as the truck load limit. Besides, he claimed to have enough pledges from House members to pass his own pension measure and, even more impressive, the endorsement of many old-age applicants in the district. Also, he argued, the truck load limit on state highways should be of utmost importance to the local electorate. He said it must remain at 7,000 pounds, for if it were to get any higher, fewer trucks would be used and, as a direct result, local unemployment figures would rise.[26]

As could have been expected, Richardson accused Daniel of avoiding the issues in a futile attempt to save his own neck. By opposing SJR 12, Richardson argued, Daniel had helped block badly needed pension funds and, even worse, denied the citizens of Texas the right to vote on the impending issue. Daniel was indeed opposed to a public vote, figuring that with all the hidden complexities of the bill, the general public would view the referendum as more of a recommendation than anything else. "In that day and time," he later explained, "the likelihood is that they would have gone on and adopted the amendment, never knowing that it had these ceilings in there, or that it contained a provision forbidding the levy of any more taxes for social security purposes other than those set aside in this amendment."[27] As a result, he was stuck with a tough campaign position convincing voters that it was not in their best interest to make their own decision on SJR 12.

During the race, Daniel's relationship with Jean Baldwin intensified considerably, enough so that he invited her to Liberty to meet his mother. Trying to impress her with his country upbringing, he insisted that they go horseback riding into the woods. But as Jean later recalled, his law practice and legislative work must have prevented him from frequenting the back woods of the family ranch. "We got lost," she laughed. "It was like a big thicket, so I eventually had to get up on his horse. My sweater was torn, and he was desperate." Finally, much to the couple's relief, Daniel's brother and a friend soon passed by on the way to a hunt. Daniel told Bill they were lost, and that Jean had a date in Houston to attend a wedding.

"She has a date in Houston?" Bill whipped back in disbelief. He and his counterpart quickly kicked the hinds of their horses and disappeared into the woods, leaving the couple lost and alone.[28]

Daniel had no idea that Jean was a direct descendant of one of his Texas revolutionary heroes, Sam Houston, until one evening when he saw a bust of the general in the hallway of her home. "You folks must be admirers of Sam Houston," he commented. Needless to say, from that moment forward, when Daniel visited the Baldwin residence, history would be the main topic of discussion. In fact, Jean would often find herself virtually ignored as her boyfriend, parents, and grandmother, Mrs. Robert A. John, engaged in lengthy conversations on Houston, Texana, and current political affairs.[29]

Jean's brother, Thomas, had once told her, "You should marry a governor or somebody like that. You are so pretty you should be somewhere on display." But Jean wanted nothing to do with the public spotlight which was likely to come if her relationship with the presumptuous representative continued. Her parents, however, were impressed with her Liberty boyfriend, and at one point Mrs. Baldwin, a granddaughter of Sam Houston, mentioned that Daniel was much like the men in her family. Asked if she could one day see herself getting married to Daniel, Jean lashed back: "Don't be silly! I don't like politics and I don't like the country!" However, just a few months later, on June 28, 1940, at St. Paul's Methodist Church in Houston, Jean relinquished her maiden name and took Daniel's hand in marriage.[30]

Daniel won the lawsuit against the insurance company represented by Larry Morris, and the newlyweds used the $2,000 fee from the case to finance furniture and a honeymoon. Of course, with his campaign in full swing, Daniel could afford little time away from his legislative district. The couple made a whirlwind trip to Galveston, checked into the Buccaneer Hotel for one night, then raced back toward Liberty to continue campaigning. But on the way, the newlyweds were passing through Cleveland when Daniel informed Jean that he had to make an appearance at a rodeo in a neighboring town. Playing the part of a cooperative, devoted wife, she kindly suggested, "That's all right, I'll go with you." Much to her surprise, he told her that he would prefer she stay in Cleveland and pass out campaign leaflets. "He left me there," Jean would later fondly recall, "and I had never been to a country campaign before. So I spent my honeymoon campaigning."[31] Ironically, the girl who just a few months prior insisted that she disliked both politics and the country, was now married to a politician and living in the country.

Upon returning from his honeymoon, Daniel would soon see firsthand that Governor O'Daniel was serious in his attempts to get rid of every last member of that "disgraceful bunch of 56ers." Toward the end of a whistle-stop campaign trip around the state, he stopped in Liberty to make an appearance on the front steps of the courthouse. Attracting what Daniel would later refer to as "the largest political crowd I've ever seen" in Liberty County, Pappy, well aware that Price and Jean were in the audience, proceeded to blast the "56ers" and call for their complete ouster from office. "It made no difference that I was there," Daniel remembered. "I knew that I was in for a hard time.... He had the majority of the voters with him, and I knew I had to do something to overcome it."[32]

E.B. Pickett, Jr., a local attorney standing next to Daniel in the crowd, nudged his friend and suggested he get up on the podium and defend himself. "And if you don't think you should do it," Pickett insisted, "I will." But Daniel wisely resisted such temptation, reasoning that it would be detrimental to his cause to stand up in front of the governor's crowd and fight back with counterpoints destined to fall upon deaf ears. Instead, he knew that the only way to answer O'Daniel's charges was to organize meetings of his own and convey the true intentions of the "Immortal 56" directly to the people of his district. He was now forced to redirect his campaign strategy and knew that in order to retain his legislative seat he must address the pension funding issue head-on.[33]

Daniel sent personal letters to everyone in his district eligible for old-age pensions, inviting them to assemble at local schoolhouses to discuss his agenda. He printed up thousands of copies of SJR 12, and in red ink underlined what he considered to be the worst portions of the bill. At these meetings he would pass the copies around to each person in attendance and explain the complexities of the bill in terms they could understand. He made sure not to voice his personal frustrations with the governor, feeling it would alienate those present. Instead, he cleverly took the approach of saying that even though most of those in attendance were probably for Governor O'Daniel, "I think you will admit that any man can make a mistake at least once. And on this issue I differed with him; he was mistaken, in my opinion, and I want to tell you why I think so...."[34] After most of those meetings adjourned, nearly every person in attendance would surround Daniel and ask for campaign literature and cards.

"I made campaign workers out of those aged citizens," Daniel said, "because they could read for themselves. They knew that as the pension rolls increased, a ceiling on tax money for such purposes was certainly going to mean that their pensions would be reduced each and every year. And then I also got quite a few of O'Daniel's supporters who were friends of mine to put ads in the paper and go around and offset the Governor's work."[35]

Richardson's race against Daniel never drifted away from the O'Daniel platform, and after months of intense campaigning, the rising challenger from Hardin was still counting on the governor's popularity to carry him in the election. Richardson also maintained the support of truckers, who constituted a sizable voting bloc in a labor town such as Liberty and were angry at Daniel for having voted against increasing the truck load limit. In fact, as the election neared, someone drove a truck through several communities and scattered hundreds of leaflets which Daniel contended grossly distorted his record. Arguing that such charges should have been brought forward at an earlier date to allow time for proper discussion, he pleaded with the electorate to ignore last-minute mud slinging and concentrate instead on the central issues of the campaign.[36]

On July 27, despite the sizable reelection of the governor, Daniel trounced Richardson at the polls with 73 percent of the vote. The victory was most impressive considering the fact that Pappy kept his promise of dismantling the great majority of the "Immortal 56," who had so successfully opposed his passage of SJR 12. In fact, of the thirty-three "56ers" who braved seeking reelection, only a handful survived.[37]

Looking back on his ability to escape the decimation experienced by so many of the "Immortal 56," Daniel commented: "I think I was able, by a lot of hard work, to convince a majority of the people that the sales tax would have been wrong, especially at that time, before natural resources were taxed to the extent that they should have been taxed. To have had a sales tax at all, at that time, would have been bad. The merchants and the pharmacists and many other people were against the sales tax at that time. Although they would vote for O'Daniel because of other reasons, they disagreed with him on this issue when it was properly brought before them, and that's why I think it was possible for him to carry the district and at the same time for me to carry it."[38]

After the primary, Daniel wrote House members soliciting their support for his election as Speaker of the House, knowing good and well that Homer Leonard already had the votes sewn up for election to the office. "I did it only for the purpose of trying to see if we could not form a block of members of the House who would resist any further efforts at the sales tax and measures like SJR 12," Daniel later explained. "I quickly announced that I would not really run for the office after I found out just exactly how many members could be counted on to oppose the measure in the future. I made a strong appeal on that basis. But I did that solely for that purpose and not for the purpose of getting in line to run for speaker." However, most legislators had taken Daniel's bid seriously.[39]

Throughout the summer, Governor O'Daniel seemed to cool down somewhat on the pension dispute, possibly realizing that his hard-line approach during the last session had gotten him nowhere. As a conciliatory gesture he announced plans to make personal visits to the home of each legislator, and in September was greeted by Price and Jean at the Liberty train depot. The couple treated Pappy to a sizable lunch, then escorted him on a tour of the Trinity River developments. The conversation never exceeded small talk, but Daniel was impressed that the governor went out of his way to heal sore wounds.[40] Little did he know, however, that Pappy had no intention of changing his position on the pension issue. Instead, the governor hoped his whistle-stop personal visits would butter up legislators to view his proposals with more open minds.

Sure enough, with the advent of the 47th Legislature on January 14, 1941, Governor O'Daniel and the House immediately locked horns again on the pension funding dispute. Despite reliable polls which showed a majority of Texans favoring natural resource levies over a sales tax, Pappy retreated to his ancient 1.6 percent transactions tax proposal, which this time around he estimated would raise a whopping $50 million.[41] The proposal was rebuffed by a House committee, prompting Daniel and nineteen other frustrated legislators to offer a counter proposal, HB 8, which mirrored the old Morris bill by placing the heaviest tax burden on natural resources.

In desperation, Pappy eventually asked the legislature for an immediate appropriation of $26,820,000 annually from the general fund to finance the pensions. The House postponed his request, then on March 10 began lengthy debates on its own product, HB 8. From 10:00 in the morning until late into the night, Daniel and a host of colleagues argued once again that the tax load should fall most heavily on those persons who could afford to pay. By midnight HB 8 was passed. In the following month Pappy continued to push his floundering transactions tax, but much to the credit of Daniel and some determined House colleagues, his efforts were to no avail.[42]

With the death of United States Senator Morris Sheppard of Texas on April 9, 1941, Pappy's views on HB 8 shifted dramatically. Eying Sheppard's Senate seat, he knew it would be impossible for him to vacate the governorship without first resolving the impending pension dispute. So when the Senate passed an amended version of the bill in late April, it gave him the excuse he needed to sign the measure and once and for all end the funding feud. As a result, he dispelled rumors that he was unable to compromise with anyone of different belief, and in turn cleared the slate for his upcoming Senate bid.[43]

Daniel later conceded that the bill "would have never lived to see the light of day if it had not been for Morris Sheppard's death.... I certainly doubt that Governor O'Daniel would have allowed this bill to become law if he had not been interested in attending to this matter and getting it out of the way so that he could run for the United States Senate... but when he finally realized that it might be to his benefit to work more with the legislature and let the tax bill passed by the House become law, then he at least did get the money to pay old age pensions as he had promised."[44]

Ironically, many of Governor O'Daniel's biggest opponents in the House helped sponsor a resolution urging him to run for the United States Senate. Daniel called it "an obvious attempt to help get rid of the governor by pushing him into the Senate race."[45] Pappy responded to the call and in the special election squeaked past Lyndon Johnson by approximately 1,300 votes.

As would be the case in so many of the pivotal junctures in Price Daniel's political career, unsolicited supporters were working behind the scenes to plan his destiny. He did not know that a small, disgruntled alliance of legislators secretly met one evening at the

Stephen F. Austin Hotel to discuss possible changes they considered necessary in the House. Organized by Representatives Ned Price of Tyler and Durwood Manford of Smiley, the group was determined to elect a new Speaker, one who would allow younger members to wield more influence.[46] After surveying a list of possible candidates, the alliance soon agreed upon Daniel as its best hope for victory. The young Liberty lawmaker had exhibited strong leadership on many issues, they reasoned. But it also did not hurt Daniel's cause that he had written that letter to House members months earlier soliciting support for his election as Speaker. As a result, the search for possible candidates this time around pushed his name toward the top. He later said that it took some persuading to get him into the race: "In the first place, I didn't think I could win it. In the second place, I just really did not aspire to that office. I was more interested in other things." [47]

Indeed, Daniel never desired to be Speaker of the House and at the time was considering instead a possible bid for attorney general. However, the group continued to work behind the scenes to drum up support for his nomination, and soon presented him with a list of approximately thirty legislators committed to him. The list was quite impressive, considering that the current Speaker, Homer Leonard, had not yet indicated he would run for another term and that the six other candidates in the race were dividing the conservative vote and support of oil and gas interests among themselves. Daniel was encouraged by the numbers, and upon further prodding from Manford and Price, eventually agreed to run.[48]

Meanwhile, on June 8, 1941, Jean gave birth to the couple's first child, Marion Price Daniel, Jr. The arrival of the baby boy would mark the beginning of a pattern for the newlyweds over the next seven years as campaigns alternated with the arrival of children.[49]

As the session was nearing an end, whispers circulated around the House chamber that Daniel had racked up the most support in the Speaker's race. Responding to such reports, his six opponents held a special meeting in the Speaker's apartment, at which time they all agreed to throw their support behind Leonard for a second term. But their desperate attempt to maintain seniority control in the House quickly backfired, for many of the candidates' supporters were opposed to any House Speaker serving two consecutive terms, and as a result agreed to sign Daniel's petition. Consequently, when the session ended on July 3, Daniel claimed to have over eighty pledges of support, considered by some to be the most pledges ever received by a candidate for Speaker at the end of a regular session.[50]

Leonard faced two major obstacles in order to retain the speakership. First, he was closely linked to big-business interests and had been accused by many legislators of hand-picking House leadership that would faithfully vote the will of the powerful lobby. His voting record backed up the claim, showing he had consistently supported sales tax measures and condemned corporate taxes. And second, a growing consensus was emerging in the House that it was beneficial to rotate the speakership, thus providing different areas around the state the opportunity to claim the position more frequently. Daniel, on the other hand, was viewed by many as a refreshing change and made clear his intentions of holding the speakership for only one term.

Also to his advantage was new Governor Coke Stevenson's pledge to remain neutral in the race. The governor was a close friend and former House colleague of Leonard, prompting Daniel to concede in a May 21 letter that, should he ever change his mind, "I am in for a hard fight. But I am working my head off because I rely on the word of Coke Stevenson." [51] In addition, Daniel was encouraged upon learning that he would go unchallenged in the upcoming general legislative race. "Mr. Leonard's backers for the speakership did everything in the world to get an opponent out against me," he recalled. "And so I did not have an opponent, while Mr. Leonard did have an opponent. This left me free to campaign for the speakership while he was campaigning for reelection, which was a big help." [52]

Leonard claimed to have sizable support but refused to disclose a list of any backers. When Daniel received word that one of his workers had been offered a peek at the pledge list and refused, he dejectedly responded: "I wish you had accepted the invitation. Do so next time and . . . see who is on there we did not know about." [53] Even prodding from the *Houston Post* could not force Leonard to go public. Since both candidates claimed enough votes to win, the newspaper proposed the formation of a committee to question all House members, and the candidate who received fewer votes would at that time resign from the race.[54] Daniel agreed to the stipulations, now claiming ninety-six pledges. But Leonard, faced with growing doubt and a dwindling pledge list, still refused to disclose.

Daniel campaigned rigorously throughout the summer months, keeping his colleagues abreast of changing developments through scores of personal, handwritten letters. To one supporter he admitted: "I think that Homer will be surprised to know some of those who have quit his candidacy."[55] And to another, he more confidently declared: "I am going to win this speaker's race!"[56]

In spite of his campaign, Daniel found time to fulfill a childhood dream of becoming actively involved in the newspaper business. Following in the footsteps of his father, he became president of the Trinity Publishing Company and, a short time later, served in the same capacity for the Gulf Coast Press Association. In this position he was co-publisher of the *Liberty Vindicator* and the *Anahuac Progress*.[57]

In September of 1942, Jean gave birth to the couple's second child, a daughter named Jean Houston Daniel. With the onslaught of new responsibilities, Daniel was forced to relinquish his role as president of the Texas Young Democrats, the post he had proudly held for nearly three years. But regardless of other duties, he would always make time for the Trinity River and was reelected president of the Trinity Barge Line.[58]

Meanwhile, his support in the Speaker's race continued to grow. Leonard soon realized he would not be able to defeat his young opponent and, shortly before Christmas, told Governor Stevenson that he was going to withdraw from the race. But as a special provision, he requested that Stevenson advise Daniel to retain two of the Speaker's faithful employees. "I had a call from the governor," Daniel remembered. "In the meantime, I had found out about what was going to happen and so was prepared for it. And Governor Stevenson told me what Mr. Leonard had told him and told me that he would like to have these two employees retained; and although I was unable to make any promise, I certainly said that I would give the request every consideration."[59] On January 2, 1943, just two weeks before the session was to open, Leonard formally withdrew from the race.

The Daniel camp was ecstatic. One legislator expressed his excitement in a brief note to the future Speaker: "The rent is free at the Governor's Mansion… also at the White House! Let's go!"[60]

But Daniel had little time to gloat over the victory, for the following week he found himself hounded by legislators seeking different
committee assignments. Such a hectic schedule prompted
Associated Press correspondent Dave Cheavens, Daniel's former
newspaper boss at Baylor, to describe his old cub reporter as the
"busiest and most bedeviled man in the capitol." [61]

CHAPTER 5

Running the House

One of the best perks of the Texas House speakership was the spacious apartment located in the majestic State Capitol building. For years the quarters had been made available for each Speaker's family while the House was in session. Daniel, however, refused to move his own family into the apartment until a law which prohibited anyone from living in the Capitol was changed, despite the fact that previous lieutenant governors and Speakers had been living there for many years. He approached Speaker Homer Leonard, whose family was currently residing in the Capitol. "Now, Homer, so that it will not appear that I'm doing this as a dig to you," he intimated, "I wonder if you wouldn't sponsor the bill to take this old law off the books?" Leonard graciously agreed to do so, and in his next speech before the House confessed that he had been "living in sin" and that in order to make it lawful, would need the legislature's help in changing the law. After the matter was settled, the Daniels moved into the apartment in the towering granite structure. "This made it quite convenient," Daniel later recalled, "with your office and your apartment being there." [1]

World events had changed drastically since the Texas legislature had last convened. The United States had entered World War II on December 8, 1941, following the bombing of Pearl Harbor. The Atlantic was infested with German submarines; England was falling victim to murderous air bombardment; Nazi armies had entered Russia and were pointed eastward toward India to form a decisive link with the Japanese. But the most irreparable damage had taken place in the summer of 1942. Japan had conquered Guam, Wake, Hong Kong, the Philippines, the Dutch East Indies, New Britain, and the Solomon Islands. Nazi subs had sunk eight million tons of Allied shipping in the North Atlantic and their armies had swung south and entered Stalingrad.[2]

In the midst of such uncertainty, the 48th Texas Legislature convened in Austin on January 12, 1943. Vacant seats were scattered around the House chamber, each belonging to a legislator who was currently adorning a military uniform. Daniel was unanimously elected Speaker within a few minutes after the session began and immediately declared that the first aim of each lawmaker should be to help defeat the Axis powers by backing President Roosevelt. Furthermore, he insisted that their efforts assist the overall needs of the country and underscored the importance of the session adjourning at the end of the 120-day constitutionally allotted period.[3]

For some time, Daniel had felt a greater calling to be overseas in combat. At the outbreak of the war, he had written to a colleague: "We have too many important things to do without spending much of our time on selfish things."[4] To some degree he resented his legislative exemption from the war and felt an obligation to risk his own life, as so many others were doing, for the principles and liberties he was defending in the safe confines of the House chamber. Surely he also took into consideration the political benefits of serving in the war. He made up his mind that as soon as the legislature adjourned, he would immediately enlist in the army and fulfill what he described as a "greater obligation" to his country.[5]

Colleagues soon challenged Daniel's devotion to the war effort by accusing him of already orchestrating his next political step, possibly the office of attorney general or even governor. But he shunned such suggestions and insisted that he would join the army and eventually return to Liberty to continue his law practice. When one friend wrote him and announced plans to save vacation time so that he could one day visit him in the Governor's Mansion, Daniel replied: "You had better take your vacation with me now because this is about as close as I will ever get to the Mansion." [6]

He had been careful not to promise any legislator specific committee assignments, fearing that it might be misinterpreted as a promise for a vote. Therefore, he did not have any outstanding obligations and was free to choose the people he felt were most capable of performing specific committee assignments. Surprising many colleagues, he proved his determination to treat all members fairly by appointing some of his most outspoken opponents to prominent positions. Most unexpected was the selection of Representatives Jimmy Phillips of Angleton and Jack Love of Fort Worth, two brusque critics, to all five committees each had requested. "And they were two of the most surprised people you ever saw in your life," [7] Daniel remembered. It was a bold attempt at bridging the gap between party lines and, at the same time, demonstrating that he was above holding grudges. Having been determined to appoint some of his opponents to these positions, however, he was forced to overlook some of his ardent supporters. The bipartisan appointments would eventually prove successful, but prompted him to admit to colleagues that his popularity had probably sunk to an all-time low in his own camp. [8]

Daniel knew this session would be much different from those to which he was accustomed. The House gallery was almost ghostly quiet compared to just a couple of years prior, when Pappy was hammering his transactions tax proposal down the throats of outspoken legislators. But with the Morris natural resources bill resolved and a promise from Governor Coke Stevenson not to challenge the existing structure of the state's administrative machinery, the stage was set for a low-profile session, one which Daniel was determined could be extremely productive. In fact, if the legislature took advantage of the lack of fanfare and concentrated on the mechanics of state government, such as measures to deal with the ill-fated Texas economy, many politicos predicted it might result in one of the most important sessions in decades. [9]

It also helped that Daniel had a warm working relationship with the governor. Stevenson, conservative in political philosophy and personal behavior, was willing to work with him to ensure a smooth session. Having presided as Speaker himself for two terms in the mid-1930s, Stevenson had much experience on which Daniel could draw.

Daniel took his role as Speaker seriously and occasionally went to the extreme to guarantee that order was maintained. For instance, he banned secretaries from the House floor unless they were running specific errands for legislators or taking dictation, and also instructed wives of lawmakers to remain outside the floor railings at all times. Offended by such a request, several of the wives authored a resolution demanding the placement of a row of chairs along the House walls for their use.[10] And when Daniel felt that a certain legislator was wasting the House's valuable time by letting his personality or showmanship dominate the discussion, he ordered him to curtail giddy remarks and return to the central issues. He later described his rigidness as having been "not too popular at first, but I think that everybody saw that it was a good thing and that we didn't want any foolishness or disorder or cluttering up of the floor when we had a lot more serious things going on outside of Austin."[11]

Perhaps it was the calamity inflicted by war that caused him to rule the session with such a stern hand. Or maybe his clinched fist was a direct result of a young and anxious solon being quickly elevated to a position of such prestige and power. But regardless, on some occasions, Daniel's sardonic humor was much too dominant to be suppressed even by his own strict House rules. For instance, when he received word that a constituent had given Representative Sam Hanna of Dallas a large quantity of deer meat—the likes of which Hanna had previously insisted should be made illegal to store and, because of domestic shortages, made readily available to the public—Daniel pulled a butcher knife out from behind his Speaker's podium amid loud laughter and suggested that all members should receive a fair share. And when another legislator spread reports that a labor union executive had accused legislators of working only a few days each week while receiving pay for seven, Daniel responded: "I hereby appoint you to whip the author of the statement." The lawmaker quickly reminded Daniel that he was the official representative of the House and should thus perform such actions himself. "No," Daniel laughingly replied, "the speaker carries out all of his work through committees."[12]

This was one of the best times in Daniel's life. Having achieved the position of Speaker at such a young age, his stock in Texas politics was quickly rising. For the first time, he was placed in a position where he could exhibit leadership abilities on a large scale. "I enjoyed the service as speaker of the House as much as any other service that I've ever had in public life," he later recalled. "And there are many reasons for this. You're close to the people who elected you. It's not like getting out on the ballot and having a lot of people vote for you who know you, but many more who do not know you. In this case, you're elected by the vote of a majority of those within a group of a hundred and fifty people, all of whom know you quite well, or have heard about you, or have learned to know you. And you're close to these people. You have to run the session. You have to appoint the committees and get things organized to where they'll run. And I would say that it is indeed one of the most powerful offices in state government. I enjoyed the work." [13]

The major theme of the 48th Legislature quickly became "no new taxes." Faithfully following the lead of Daniel, Jo Ed Winfrey, chairman of the House Revenue and Taxation Committee, helped form a stern blockade against new tax proposals. "We were at war, and we had just passed a big tax bill," Daniel recalled, "so I advocated that we not have any new taxes. . . . I appointed a Revenue and Tax Committee that would not let a tax bill out of committee." [14] On March 4, much to his liking, the committee struck down five proposals for higher taxes and, despite further attempts, Winfrey and his colleagues never allowed such measures to reach the House floor.

It was during his tenure as Speaker that Daniel first engaged in lengthy conversation with his future Senate colleague, Lyndon Johnson. Johnson had paid a couple of visits to the House chamber during Daniel's previous terms, but the two men had yet to meet. This time, however, accompanying U.S. House Speaker Sam Rayburn for a speech he would deliver to a joint session, Johnson made himself available to Daniel and began laying the foundation for a friendship which would mature as years passed. [15]

It was also while serving as Speaker that Daniel sponsored what he would later describe as his most embarrassing piece of legislation. Unaware that the issue would one day come back to haunt him, he became concerned that some state officials could hold one office while running for another and sponsored a bill for election reform aimed to stop such practices. In front of the House

Committee on Privileges and Elections, he testified that public officials could, under current law, campaign on state time and use the power and prestige of their elected positions to raise funds. In his opinion, no politician should be paid by the state to perform one job while seeking another. The bill passed both houses of the legislature and was signed by the governor. It was later declared unconstitutional by the Texas Supreme Court, however, eventually allowing Daniel to attempt one of the most notable jumps from one office to another in the state's history.[16]

Much to the credit of Governor Stevenson, the proceedings of the 48th Legislature were among the most harmonious the state had ever witnessed. Contrasting Stevenson's performance to that of his predecessor, Daniel later reasoned that Stevenson "handled his approach to the legislature in an entirely different manner. Having been a member, he knew how to work with the legislature, and Governor O'Daniel did not.... And it was easy to work with Governor Stevenson because he respected the presiding officers of the House and the Senate.... He used to come over and visit in the House a lot, and I'm sure he did in the Senate. But, we couldn't have asked for a better relationship than existed during that time."[17]

As the 120-day adjournment deadline rapidly approached, Daniel encountered resistance to his plan to end the session on time. In fact, on May 11, the very day he had hoped to adjourn, a group of determined House members made public their intentions of maintaining sizable appropriations for the Liquor Control Board. Fearful of bootleggers overrunning Texas and what they termed the inevitable crippling of the state's law enforcement ability, they resisted the efforts of several senators to reduce drastically such expenditures in conference committee. But Daniel was well aware that much more was at stake than merely the finances of the Liquor Control Board, for unless a settlement was reached, the session would end with major questions concerning the whereabouts of funds for forty-eight state agencies and departments.[18]

Late in the evening, realizing that both sides were unlikely to give way and fearing the possible consequences of a special session, Governor Stevenson jumped to Daniel's aid. He presented the lawmakers with a compromise, one which would allocate an appropriation a little higher than some senators had originally desired, plus produce additional funds to be drawn from a separate source. But as the night wore on, the legislators stubbornly clung to their all-or-nothing positions. While Stevenson walked back and forth between the House and Senate chambers, Daniel implored his colleagues to come to their senses and accept the governor's compromise. "You will live to see the day when you regret your stand," he warned.[19] And by dawn, as the struggle continued, a frustrated Daniel paraded the aisles of the House chamber and pleaded in a demanding voice for certain members to get "prejudices and pride out of your hearts" and do instead what was best for the people of Texas. "Haven't you ever been whipped on a thing before?" he asked desperately.[20]

Nearing 11:00 A.M. that same morning, Daniel's preaching paid off as a majority of legislators finally agreed to accept the compromise and adjourn. Described as "the worst sparring in the memory of veteran observers," the session-end deadlock resulted in a $23 million departmental appropriation bill, which, with other major appropriations—higher education, eleemosynary institutions, judiciary, rural school aid, and vocational education—brought authorized state spending for the next biennium nearly $11 million under the existing appropriations.[21]

Having lasted a mere 121 days, the 48th Legislature would go down as the shortest and least expensive session in modern Texas history. But in that brief time it accomplished what no legislature had been able to do in the last decade by cutting appropriations below those of the previous session. For the first time in more than forty years, the legislature refused to pass a single tax bill. And much to Daniel's credit, necessary funds and legislation were created to carry the state through the remainder of the war. Governor Stevenson praised lawmakers for their work, which he boasted would pare state expenses almost $8 million over the next couple of years.[22]

Daniel received much praise for his performance as Speaker. The *Austin Statesman* and *Houston Chronicle* hailed him as one of the best in the state's history,[23] and even bitter opponent Jimmy Phillips revealed: "He's made a whale of a good speaker, and I wouldn't be much if I didn't admit it."[24] In a congratulatory letter, another colleague wrote: "You have been a good speaker fair to everyone, and that is a task. A splendid record has been made and you deserve much credit."[25]

But with his speakership at an end, Daniel had only one thing in mind. Having faithfully executed the duties of his office, he now wasted no more time in joining the war effort. Within two months, he enlisted as a private in the U.S. Army and awaited word of his first assignment.

Before charting this new course, Daniel received a letter from Virgil McPhail of Abilene containing the following advice: "Don't give up your future in politics in Texas. Get your name on the ticket for some office even if you are overseas on duty and let's keep our eye on that Governor's Mansion in the years to come." [26]

Daniel would heed the advice.

CHAPTER 6

Humble Soldier

Daniel packed a small diary in his bag as he headed off for military service, but ended up making only a few entries. He wrote of Jean and his sister Ellen driving him to the military office on the morning of July 17, 1943: "I didn't want them to come to the bus—too many tears for me and them." [1] The bus pulled out at 9:45 and reached the Induction Center at Old City Hall in Houston at 11:15. There the group underwent physicals. Wrote Daniel: "Stripped off naked and went through a plenty long line of doctors and psychiatrists. Of course, so many doubted my ability to pass the physical except for limited duty that I was worried about it myself. But much to my surprise, I passed everything, even vision without glasses in the top flight, and was okay for any Army or Navy assignment. What a thrill this was! I could hardly put on my clothes for crying, especially when so many were rejected on all sides of me." [2]

Indeed, out of the 250 examined, only forty-five were sworn in and accepted for the army, and just another thirty made the navy cut. In his diary, Daniel concluded that 50 percent of passing the test depended on the individual's desire to go into the army or stay out. If a man wanted to stay out, he reasoned, he could simply tell them about enough ailments to get turned down. "But if he wants to go in," Daniel wrote, "he will keep quiet about ailments unless pointedly forced to mention some, and even then he can minimize them like I did my occasional stomach trouble. It hurt me even when the doctor pressed hard on my old adhesions and lower stomach, but I said nothing and made no motion or sign of any sensation therefrom."[3]

Daniel was sworn in at 4:30 that afternoon by Lt. Robert J. Understeller and promptly wired Jean a telegram bearing the good news. Along with thirteen other new privates, he marched down Houston's Preston Avenue to Union Station and boarded the Santa Fe for San Antonio. "What a train!" he scribbled in his diary. "Changed at Milano Junction... chair cars all the way and a dirty train if I ever saw one!" Upon his arrival at Fort Sam Houston the following morning, he was assigned to Co. B, Barrack 5, Serial No. 38,541,074, was allotted $72.00 per month for Jean and the two babies, and received a $10,000 insurance policy, for which $7.30 per month would be deducted from his salary.[4]

Despite being at least ten years older than most of the privates, Daniel was quick to make friends at the fort. Because he was the only Liberty County man not to have taken a seven-day furlough, he had to start from scratch building relationships. He adjusted well to the rigorous schedule and learned to deal with the physical demands placed upon him. The most difficult task he faced, however, was his separation from Jean and the children. He phoned home as often as his schedule allowed, and wrote long letters complimenting the food at the fort and the "excellent treatment" the privates received from their superiors. In fact, his only complaint was that he had to be addressed by his first name exclusively, "Marion."[5]

For some time he had succeeded in keeping his identity unknown. But in early August a Houston reporter followed a lead and telephoned Fort Sam Houston asking the whereabouts of the former Texas House Speaker. After receiving word that no private was at the base with the name of Price Daniel, he stepped up his investigative work. Calling both Liberty and Austin and learning that indeed Daniel had recently enlisted, he pleaded with the public relations officer at Fort Sam Houston to recheck the camp rolls. A short time later the officer summoned to his office a recruit with a similar name and asked, "Are you Marion P. Daniel?" The private nodded his head as the officer stepped closer. "Are you the son of Price Daniel?" The recruit, relatively unknown at the camp to this point, took a deep breath and replied, "I am Price Daniel."[6]

The news that Private Daniel was among the new recruits sent shockwaves around Fort Sam Houston. Daniel had valiantly attempted to keep his identity a secret, preferring instead not to receive any preferential treatment. Upon arrival at the base he had been regularly assigned walking guard and K.P. duty and underwent strenuous exercise and drill training beginning each morning at dawn. But one sergeant, upon learning the true identity of one of the recruits he had been giving such a hard time, exclaimed: "And to think that I have been bossin' around the speaker of the Texas House!" Another observer who had been impressed with Daniel's performance at the fort remarked: "You could have pushed me over when we found out who he was!" The local media was equally impressed by his modesty, suggesting that he probably would have been eligible for a commission but instead revealed a perspective that was "quite refreshing" by doing it the hard way.[7]

Although Daniel longed to fight in the war for patriotic reasons, he was also surely mindful of the political consequences that could result from not enlisting in the service. In postwar elections, he knew it would be hard to compete against a candidate with a strong record of military service if he, too, had not made a personal sacrifice.

In August 1943, upon completing basic training at Fort Sam Houston, Daniel was assigned to the Security Intelligence Corps. Since most of his assignments were of utmost secrecy, such as investigation of the loyalty of persons applying for commissions in the military or seeking employment at munitions plants, his work was conducted in civilian clothing. He spent the fall of 1943 and the following winter covertly gathering information, living for brief periods in Pine Bluff, Arkansas, Amarillo, Texas, and Baton Rouge, Louisiana.[8]

Daniel grew somewhat frustrated with his prospects for advancement. Although having kept his identity unknown when enlisting in order to avoid special treatment, he wrote a letter to U.S. House Speaker Sam Rayburn in early 1944 asking for assistance in getting into Officer Candidate School.[9] In a February 23 reply, Rayburn assured Daniel that it would not be long before he was admitted.[10] Sure enough, two months later, Daniel was enrolled in the OCS at Ann

Arbor, Michigan, and became a member of the largest class ever admitted. He brought Jean and the children along and rented a small house but, to his surprise, was informed upon their arrival that wives were not allowed. It would be the first time Jean recalled seeing her husband break down. He pleaded with the officers to make an exception on his behalf and eventually was granted some consolation. His family could remain but, as punishment, he would not be able to graduate as a first lieutenant.

Daniel accepted the decision and immediately began working to obtain an assignment overseas.[11] The Allied forces were beginning to take control of the war, and for both patriotic and political reasons he desperately wanted to participate in combat while time allowed. But he was too late. Within two months after his arrival in Michigan, on June 6, 1944, Allied forces landed on the beaches of Normandy. Paris would soon be liberated as the Allies pushed to Berlin.[12]

In the midst of these dramatic events, Daniel was commissioned a second lieutenant and assigned to Washington and Lee University in Lexington, Virginia, where he taught officer candidates for one year. It was there that Jean gave birth to the couple's third child, Houston Lee, on July 1, 1945.

Only six weeks later, the war having ended, Daniel finally received a pass overseas. He was assigned by the Marine Corps to help establish a training school in Japan and in early September traveled to Washington for final instructions.[13] Upon arrival in Sasebo, Japan, he worked as executive officer on the staff of "V Amphibious Corps, Special Services School." The school's mission was to furnish proper training for special services officers and men of V Amphibious Corps units, and operations were set up in the former Japanese Naval Academy Building. From October 31 to November 15, Daniel and nine other staffers taught courses in all phases of marine, army, and navy special services, including courses in education, personal affairs, recreation, and athletics.[14] His tour of duty in Pearl Harbor, the Johnston Islands, Iwo Jima, and Japan opened his eyes to the horror and destruction that resulted from the war. He walked among the charred remains at Nagasaki, and was approached by destitute children seeking basic necessities.[15]

Upon his return to Lexington, Daniel spent the early months of 1946 contemplating his future in Texas politics. Without his knowledge, some of his legislative friends back home had begun promoting him for the attorney general's post. "We got together and agreed that we were going to run this fellow for attorney general," one recalled. "We began to write him and call him long distance... he never solicited it at all." [16] In late March, when incumbent Attorney General Grover Sellers announced his retirement, Daniel received a letter from former governor and Baylor president Pat Neff, Sr., suggesting he consider seeking the post. [17] Having become interested in the race, Daniel wrote several personal letters to friends back home assessing his chances and requested their active support in their respective counties if time permitted. He returned to Austin on April 8 to attend a campaign strategy session at the Driskill Hotel and, upon conclusion of the brief conference, was immediately touted as a probable candidate for attorney general by the statewide media. [18]

Daniel refused to make an official announcement of his candidacy while still in uniform, and returned to Lexington after his Austin visit. Anxiously awaiting his release from the service, friends back home filed his name for candidacy on April 30 by submitting a petition bearing the signatures of more than 1,000 Texas voters and, at his prodding, established a campaign headquarters at the Driskill. Then on May 9, leaving behind eight wooden crates of belongings to be forwarded later, Daniel was formally discharged from the army at Fort Sam Houston with the rank of captain. Immediately he returned to Austin to embark on a last-minute, whirlwind campaign which would take the state by surprise. [19]

CHAPTER 7

I'm Not Afraid of Anybody

The letter Daniel had received from Pat Neff suggesting he run for office upon his return to Texas proved ironic, for little did the former governor know that Daniel's opponent would be Neff's very own son, Pat Neff, Jr. The younger Neff had all intentions of becoming the state's next attorney general and had spent a considerable amount of time and energy spreading his message to the Texas electorate. Daniel's campaign, however, was forced to work against the clock as a result of his late army release, but he found a way to use that effectively as an issue in the race. "Although my opponent has had two years compared to my two months to plan and make his campaign," he said on a July 20 KTHT radio broadcast in Houston, "although he has an old political name and the backing of the old time politicians of the state, I tell you that down the homeward stretch the people of this state are backing Price Daniel for a victorious finish on July 27." [1]

As if being behind in public opinion polls and having only sixty days to catch up were not enough of a disadvantage, Daniel also had to compete against the junior Neff's rich political heritage. His father, considered one of the greatest orators in Texas history, had spent the past five decades building a thick file of political supporters on which his son was free to call. The senior Neff, a publicly avowed teetotaler, had served as Speaker of the Texas House, governor, railroad commissioner, and president of Baylor University. Though fond of Daniel, he was more determined to help his son get elected.

Cleverly, Daniel managed to turn the tables by making his own modest upbringing an asset. "Like most of you within the sound of my voice tonight," he would say, "Price Daniel has no old political name to run on. I am running on my own name and my own record just like you or your son, brother, or father would have to do. I find a warm response in favor of the man in this race who stands on his own feet and runs on his own name and record." [2]

Daniel's make-do campaign stood on five basic planks, each of which he told voters would spell out what he stood for and what he would accomplish if elected. First, he vowed to make the public's interest and welfare a top priority, and expressed his unwillingness to yield to the interests of political action committees; second, to stand up to intolerance and persecution of minority groups; third, to fight the federal government's claim to valuable riverbeds and submerged lands off the Texas coast; fourth, to "work in every way possible to bring about harmony between industry and labor in Texas"; and, last, to establish a mainstream veterans' desk with a full-time assistant to handle veterans' affairs. "I will put the full influence of the attorney general's office behind a fair deal for veterans and lend all assistance possible under the law to break bottlenecks, red tape, and down-right discouragement that now face many veterans who want to establish small businesses, or obtain materials to build homes," he promised. [3] As a veteran himself, he not only sympathized with the men returning home from war, but also realized that support of their causes could prove helpful in the upcoming election. And large numbers of young boys from the Corps responded to Daniel's interest in them by knocking on doors and actively campaigning for him.

Daniel formulated a stringent campaign schedule which had him behind a podium from early morning until late in the evening. One day in particular, he delivered a 10:00 A.M. speech to a large crowd in Waxahachie, then addressed voters in Hillsboro, spoke twice in Temple, made appearances in Belton, the public square at Georgetown, and capped off the day with a 10:30 P.M. address to an after-movie crowd in Round Rock. In a press release following the busy day's activities, campaign coordinator Booth Mooney wrote: "Daniel will resume travels Monday. Will spend part of week in San Antonio area, attending state bar convention, campaigning among South Texans. Thursday will head into East Texas, then swinging up to North Texas, over to West Texas."[4] In addition, Daniel managed to secure at least one dedicated volunteer in each of the state's 254 counties, thus establishing an invaluable networking system through which to spread his message.[5]

Leading a small caravan of campaign workers and family, Daniel crisscrossed the state speaking on courthouse squares, in drugstores, courtrooms, barber shops, and wherever else a crowd could be gathered. On the stump he often removed his suit coat and, looking through wire-rimmed glasses and wearing a tie and long-sleeve white shirt, punctuated his speeches with a clenched fist and well-timed hand gestures. He sparked crowds with his relentless vigor. "Some may say that Price Daniel is just back from the service all fired up with youthful enthusiasm, idealism, and the hope of helping to solve the problems of the state," he exclaimed at a South Texas rally. "To this I plead guilty. I am young, and I do have enthusiasm for justice and progress in our state and nation. As attorney general, I have faith and hope that I can contribute something toward making our glorious Texas an even better place in which to live."[6]

In a July 22 radio broadcast piped from KWBU radio in Corpus Christi, he told listeners: "I have been out of the army only six weeks. Like your own sons and daughters, brothers, sisters, and fathers, I am mighty glad to be back home. Upon my return last month, I found things quite different from the day I left Texas for the army. Things are so much better that many people act and feel like the job is over and our patriotic duty is done. But my friends, the job is not over, our patriotic duty to Texas and to our great country, and especially to American boys who gave their lives and sleep beneath the soil of every land in the world, is never done. We have many evils and many problems facing this world today. Yes, they face our great state of Texas, and they require our interest as individuals in public affairs, government and politics."[7]

The hard work paid off for Daniel in the primary. He surpassed

Neff by 13,580 votes and was unopposed in the November general election. But his victory celebration came to an abrupt halt the day before his inauguration. Word came that both his mother and sister were seriously injured in an automobile accident en route to Austin for the gala ceremony, so he canceled the celebration at the Capitol and requested the chief justice meet him at the hospital. The following morning, January 1, 1947, Daniel placed his left hand on his personal Bible at his mother's bedside and became the youngest attorney general in the United States. Both women would later fully recover from the accident.[8]

More than any other official in Texas government, the attorney general, in his regular duties, reflects a combination of law and politics. He enables government to adjust to changing policy demands through flexible interpretations of rigid constitutional and statutory decrees. The external pressures upon his office are great, but so are his delegated and discretionary powers to act in the areas of his particular competence. The amount of work he undertakes is determined by federal legislation and court decisions, increasing awareness of ecological and natural resource management problems, the growth of the state's economy, and competition for the best available legal talent. Each attorney general responds to these pressures differently, and each combines his resources and applies them in different ways. During Daniel's tenure nearly all of the forestated factors would come into play, making him one of the most active attorneys general in state history.

Daniel assembled one of the largest law offices in the South. With an organization of some seventy-five people, including more than forty attorneys, he quickly set the rules. Many prior attorneys general had used the office as a stepping stone, pushing issues to build a strong political base from which they would eventually launch a statewide campaign. Daniel, however, made known his desire for the sanctity of law to override political considerations in his administration. Recalled Joe Greenhill, who would eventually be promoted to Daniel's first assistant, "His instructions were to me, 'You get the law right, and I'll worry about the politics.'"[9] In fact, Daniel parted with one of his top assistants early in his administration whom he suspected of using the office as a political springboard.[10]

Upon the conclusion of World War II, Texas consumers were left without protection from hungry corporations eager to cash in on the postwar vulnerability of a free-market economy. In July 1946, with the abolition of such wartime cost regulators as the Office of Price Administration (OPA), prices soared as manufacturers were suddenly free to test the limits of capitalism. Despite the fact that Texas law strictly forbade the practice of price-fixing, gasoline rates quickly skyrocketed, as did the cost of basic survival commodities such as milk and bread. Furious citizens demanded that legal action be taken against such corporate antitrust violations and thus laid the groundwork for Daniel's first challenge as attorney general.[11]

The issue was well suited to his crusading style. He promptly assigned twenty of his assistants to investigate possible corporate antitrust violations, assuring the public that his office was looking into the alleged price-fixing of over twenty commodities. Within three months he was appalled to discover that, as a result of high prices, numerous companies had reported profit increases of 100 percent and had flagrantly disregarded Texas laws in the process. Vowing to do all his office could to protect the Texas consumer, he promised to seek prosecution against all guilty parties. He forewarned barbers in Dallas, dry cleaners in Odessa, and pediatricians in Corpus Christi that if their proposed price increases were enacted, government regulatory action could result. And in late October, when crude oil prices uniformly increased significantly, he attracted statewide support by sharing statistics of how oil company profits had suddenly escalated from 100 to 350 percent at the consumers' expense.[12]

At the same time, Daniel was thrown head-first into one of the pivotal cases of the civil rights movement. In February of 1946 a young black man by the name of Heman Marion Sweatt had been denied admission to the University of Texas Law School on the basis of race, and in turn filed suit in the 126th District Court. He insisted that the inability of qualified black students to gain entry to any law school in the state of Texas was a direct violation of the Fourteenth Amendment and, in turn, that state laws upholding segregation in public schools were unconstitutional. The NAACP had been laying the groundwork for a lawsuit for some time collecting finances and studying both state laws and the university's admission requirements. Locating a qualified student who would agree to attend the school proved to be a difficult task, however. In fact, the association was close to giving up its search when Sweatt stepped forward and volunteered to serve as the plaintiff.[13]

The NAACP attorneys intentionally targeted Texas for their landmark lawsuit, a state where racial hostility was somewhat less intense than states in the Deep South. As one astute observer noted, "Texans, unlike white Mississippians, have little cause to be obsessed about the Negro." With low black percentages, growing cities, and rapid industrialization, Texas was seen as the vanguard of the newly developing South.[14] These factors, combined with the fact that not a single black law school existed in the entire state, made Texas especially appealing to the NAACP. Furthermore, the association's chapter in Texas, which would be responsible for the cost of litigation, was both numerically and financially sound. Once the attorneys had chosen Texas as the most advantageous state for their litigation, the University of Texas, with its strong financial base and the prominence of its law school, was a logical choice for a specific suit. The NAACP attorneys figured it would be virtually impossible for the state to improvise hastily a comparable facility for black students.[15]

Daniel's predecessor, Attorney General Grover Sellers, had already made the state's position on the Sweatt case quite clear, declaring that "Heman Marion Sweatt will never darken the door of the University of Texas."[16] When university president T.S. Painter had sought a ruling on whether Sweatt could be admitted, it was Sellers who had declared that Sweatt was not entitled to enroll "at this time," but must be admitted if equal educational opportunities were not provided within the state in a reasonable time. Sellers concluded that racial segregation in education was well defined in Texas. His ruling was based on a 1945 state legislative act which stipulated that the directors of Texas A&M College should establish, upon demand, courses in the professions at Prairie View College, a state school for blacks. The same act raised Prairie View to university status.[17]

Sweatt took his case to the federal district court at Austin in May. Sellers argued that Sweatt should have applied to A&M, which would provide for his legal education at Prairie View. The following month Federal Judge Roy C. Archer granted Sweatt an interlocutory writ for admission to the University of Texas, but suspended it for six months to give the state an opportunity to establish a law school for blacks.[18]

To the surprise of Sweatt and his attorneys, various campus organizations began to express support for his admittance to the law
school. Just one month before Daniel's inauguration as attorney general, sixty students representing the Canterbury Club, Wesley
Foundation, Lutheran Students Association, Baptist Student Union,
American Veterans Committee, YMCA, and several other organizations held a rally in support of the NAACP's fight.[19] Growing support
for Sweatt, however, only stiffened the defiance of the University of
Texas Board of Regents. Predicted Regent Orville Bullington in 1944,
"There is not the slightest danger of any Negro attending the
University of Texas regardless of what Franklin D., Eleanor, or the
Supreme Court says, so long as you have a Board of Regents with as
much intestinal fortitude as the present one has." [20]

Daniel would have preferred not to have inherited the contentious issue, one that was far from resolution. He was, however,
particularly qualified for his new role as defender of the state's segregated educational facilities. He had grown up in the shadow of the
East Texas Jim Crow system and as an attorney was familiar with
many of the historical legal precedents that had systematically upheld the South's racially segregated society. This background certainly helped shape his beliefs and actions as attorney general. After
all, segregation was an accepted way of life. Daniel never questioned
it, but always justified his position by saying that the purpose of
segregation in the South was to keep public order, not to support
any belief that one race was superior to another. Perhaps this was a
politically convenient explanation for his actions. Regardless, the
pressures of upholding Texas segregation laws probably led Daniel
to defend Southern racial practices beyond his true convictions.

In a time when blacks in Texas were banned from state parks
and required to enter many restaurants through separate doors,
Daniel felt that separate quality educational facilities would serve a
noble purpose—providing opportunities for blacks that had never
existed before. After all, of the 7,726 lawyers in the state, only
twenty-three were black and all of them were forced to receive their
legal education outside the state.[21] Many Texans also agreed that
something needed to be done. In a poll conducted in January of
1947, a majority of both white and black Texans voted in favor of
the establishment of a separate university system.[22] Even Heman
Sweatt supported the concept.[23]

Once in office, Daniel immediately pushed for the creation of a comparable law school for blacks, warning state university officials that failure to comply would very likely lead to Sweatt's admission to the University of Texas. As a result, the 50th Texas Legislature appropriated $2,750,000 and a transfer of the land and facilities of Houston College for Negroes to create a new institution, Texas State University for Negroes.[24] Unable to get the university facility operational by the court's deadline, however, the legislature authorized a temporary facility in Austin to be called Texas State University for Negroes. The University of Texas leased the basement of a building from a petroleum firm and, using an emergency appropriation of $100,000, began to piece together a law library. The basement school was to share certain members of the university's faculty. In fact, the dean of the University of Texas Law School was to serve as the part-time dean of the temporary facility.[25]

When the Sweatt hearing convened in May 1947, the makeshift basement law school had failed to attract any students even though it had been open for registration for three months. Although several black students had made inquiries, the NAACP had dissuaded them from applying. Even Sweatt, who had received a personal notice concerning the school's opening, chose not to attend.[26] The five-day hearing proved to be the highlight of the Sweatt case. Overflow crowds of onlookers and law students, many of whom had been dismissed from classes to attend, witnessed Daniel and his staff go head-to-head with NAACP lead attorney Thurgood Marshall.[27] George Washington, Jr., a black activist who later become one of the first Texans to benefit from the *Sweatt* outcome, recalled peeking through the windows in the Travis County Courthouse to watch Marshall press the case to conclusion.[28]

Marshall argued that the newly founded university was far inferior to the University of Texas Law School and thus failed to provide the level of equality in education required to meet the existing Supreme Court standards. He called Robert Redfield, chairman of the anthropology department at the University of Chicago, to the stand to testify that blacks were not inferior to whites intellectually and that segregation not only intensified distrust between the races but also hindered the learning process for African Americans.[29] Daniel countered by calling two professors from the University of Texas who testified that black students would actually benefit from small classes by having a better opportunity for intensive training.[30] He argued that the African-American school was "substantially" equal, prompting Marshall to reply, "You either have equality or you don't. It's either equal or it isn't."[31]

In rebuttal, Daniel focused his argument on the contention that Sweatt would have refused entering Texas State regardless of the level of education the university could provide, and thus moved that the case revolve solely around whether or not separate schools were constitutional. Under this argument, he cited previous Supreme Court decisions which had upheld the constitutionality of separate but equal schools. The Texas Constitution permitted such facilities, he contended, and Texas State was ready and waiting for Heman Sweatt.[32] While Marshall wanted to use the case to scrutinize the broader issue of racial segregation, Daniel focused exclusively on Sweatt and the rights of Texas. "This is not a class suit to review the history of education for Negroes in the United States, its merits and demerits," he reasoned. "The sole question remaining in the case is the State's power under its own Constitution to provide separate publicly supported colleges and universities for its Negro and white students."[33]

Claiming that at least seven black students had expressed interest in enrolling in the temporary facilities but suddenly changed their minds, Daniel tried to prove that the NAACP organized "a concerted program to boycott" the temporary school in Austin in order to break down Texas segregation laws. One of his witnesses, whose testimony was later ruled inadmissible, said that he had considered entering the school and had attended a "Negro meeting" in Dallas two days before the school opened.

"Did you announce at that meeting that you would not attend the school?" Daniel prodded.

The witness shook his head.

"But didn't you tell me—"

Sweatt's attorney rose to his feet. "We object to his arguing with his own witness," he said.[34]

Daniel told the court that he was trying to establish a chain of events to show bad faith by Sweatt in refusing to attend the temporary school while Texas State University for Negroes was being established in Houston. With Sweatt on the stand, Daniel asked if he would attend a separate law school if he considered it equal to that of the University of Texas.

"You build your assumption upon something that I can't agree with," responded Sweatt.

"Well, assume it," Daniel persisted. "You still would not attend it, would you?"

"I would not," admitted Sweatt.[35]

After sustaining objections from Marshall to this line of questioning, the Court ruled that even though Sweatt said at first he would be satisfied with separate but equal facilities, he still had the right to change his mind on the matter.[36] An editorial in the *Negro Labor News* claimed that the attorney general "had either overrated himself and his case or had underestimated the brilliancy of Sweatt's attorneys." Almost everyone present at the weeklong hearing, the editorial proclaimed, "expressed the fact that Sweatt's attorneys proved to be too much for Attorney General Price Daniel and his assistants. With all cards on the table and Sweatt holding a good hand, the eyes of the nation are again on Texas to see if Texas will again step out and lead the Negroes of the South into an era of freedom of study." [37]

Judge Archer eventually refused Sweatt's request for a mandamus to grant him admission to the University of Texas, citing the requirement for segregation of whites and blacks mandated by the Constitution of Texas. To the surprise of no one, the NAACP immediately gave notice of appeal to the Texas Court of Civil Appeals.[38] The Texas media was complimentary of Archer and the state's attorneys. One reporter in particular complimented Daniel for keeping the case clean: "A man with demagogic instincts could have made something altogether ugly of the fight to keep a Negro out of the university. If there was a single emotional appeal to bias or baiting, we didn't hear it." [39]

In February 1948 the Court of Civil Appeals also ruled against Sweatt, citing the state's effort to build an equal educational facility for blacks. But the matter was still not over. The following year Sweatt received surprising news that the U.S. Supreme Court had agreed to hear his case. Fearing that a ruling in favor of Sweatt could lead the Court to declare segregated schooling unconstitutional, Daniel moved quickly to drum up public support in his favor. He pleaded with southerners to defend their educational system however possible, asked several southern states to submit testimony on behalf of Texas to the high court, and publicly attacked a group of

188 northern law professors whom he contended "have tried to tell us how to run our schools." [40] Texas officials in the meantime intensified efforts to develop Texas State University for Negroes in order to strengthen the state's upcoming case before the Supreme Court.

Segregation proved to be one of the few issues in Daniel's political career that made him appear timid and self-conscious of public perception. Sensing that some had interpreted his support of separate but equal facilities as knee-jerk racism, he found some comfort in explaining that it was his duty to uphold the laws of Texas, regardless of the merit of those laws. In truth, this explanation provided him an opportunity to appease both sides. To the segregationists, he could boast of his staunch defense of segregated schools. And to civil rights advocates, he could explain that, regardless of personal convictions, he was bound to uphold state law.

While many critics were accusing him of discriminating against Sweatt by upholding what they believed to be archaic Texas laws, Daniel was hard at work making sure the Ku Klux Klan was aware it was not welcome in Texas. He had learned that the Klan had set up operations in Georgia and threatened to spread throughout the entire South. "I will use every legal resource at my command to prevent this unlawful organization from coming into this state," Daniel promised, "and this is my means of advising all law abiding citizens that the law prohibits such operations." He went on to stress the immorality of the Klan and its destructive influence upon the democratic system. "There is a right and a wrong way to fight for the principles of local self-government embodied in our Constitution. Open and above-board discussions and actions within the framework of our constitutions and laws is the only way that justice will prevail. Secret under-cover groups which thrive on prejudices, hatred, and fear, and advocate enforcement of a law of their own will only retard the day of understanding, justice, and government by constitution and law." [41]

In April 1948 the Daniels ushered in their fourth child, John, who was named for his maternal grandmother's family, the Johns. The Daniels had purchased a large house in Austin on a corner lot with plenty of room for their children to play, and the attorney general went out of his way to be at home as much as his hectic schedule would allow. In fact, it was rare for Daniel not to be at home for three meals each day. [42] "His top priority, with the exception of God, was always his family," one colleague would recall. "It did not matter what was going down at the Capitol, it was never as important as his wife and his children." [43]

For some time Daniel had been hoping to find a place in the country where he and his family could occasionally retreat and where he could try his hand at ranching. One day, while aboard a train, he was scanning a newspaper and noticed some property for sale just north of Liberty. Within a short time he had bought several acres, moved a small-frame house from an abandoned oil camp at Sour Lake, built a dam that turned a creek into a lake and, because of an abundance of holly trees, named the place Holly Ridge Ranch. The Daniel family was soon spending weekends camping and picnicking at Holly Ridge, and in the years ahead would expand both the house and land holdings as Daniel bought cattle and fulfilled his dream of becoming a rancher.

Meanwhile, he continued his crusade against antitrust violations. In fact, by the end of January 1948, he had already come close to breaking a state record for such investigations. He targeted eight wholesale milk dealers in north central Texas alone for price fixing and, in addition, even sought legal action against distributors. In April he obtained a temporary restraining order in an Austin courtroom against four bakeries and two grocers, claiming they had entered a mutual agreement to keep the retail price of bread at twenty cents per loaf. In June he unveiled a six-man investigative committee organized to probe possible antitrust violations in building material and household appliance industries. By December he combined a number of large milk industry cases into one suit in Austin's 98th District Court, where Judge Charles Betts issued a permanent price-fixing injunction against ten milk companies and assessed fines totaling $75,000. [44]

Some were already tagging Daniel as one of the biggest "trust-busters" in Texas history. [45] His office had filed fourteen antitrust lawsuits against thirty firms and twenty-three individuals for price-fixing and restraint of trade, losing not a single case and assessing more than $115,000 in penalties. He also had obtained temporary injunctions against twelve loan agencies for charging exorbitant interest rates and filed suit against another 1,701 corporations for delinquent tax payments, yielding the state $244,769 in fines. In his first term alone, Daniel's staff made final disposition of more than

2,500 cases, of which only thirty-three judgments were adverse to the state. In turn, Texans became so impressed by their attorney general that he was granted two more terms without opposition.[46] In the 1948 primary he polled 1,231,881 votes, more than any candidate in Texas had ever received running for a state office.[47]

On occasion Daniel could not resist commenting on issues which surpassed his powers as attorney general. Most notable was his concern with postwar conditions at home and abroad. Speaking before the American Legion, he remarked: "The power and size of our Army and Navy and Air Corps are being diminished daily while we are sending both steel and oil to Russia, the country which keeps its army and air corps at full strength and blocks practically every move we make to peacefully settle the problems of this world. We hope and pray for peace and understanding with Russia, but until the day comes when we do have an understanding with that country, we must keep our powder dry and our armed forces strong and powerful enough for any eventuality. And we must let no Henry Wallace talk our government into sharing the secrets of the Atomic bomb with Russia. The safest thing for America would be to keep our Atomic bomb at home and send Russia Henry Wallace."[48]

Daniel soon became immersed in one of the biggest issues of his career. Not long into his second term (1949) he was disturbed to learn that bookies were thriving in many of the state's cities. Believing that any public investigation would give the lawbreakers a chance to escape prosecution by temporarily closing shop, he discreetly sent several assistants and their spouses across the state to visit numerous locations that he suspected were engaging in illegal operations. Much to his satisfaction, they returned with the proof he needed.[49] On August 15 he sent troops of Texas Rangers to raid undercover operations simultaneously in Fort Worth, Galveston, Odessa, and Beaumont. The raids were a success for the most part, with numerous Western Union machines used for horse-racing information uncovered. In Galveston, however, an advance warning gave the illegal operators time to hide their equipment and escape prosecution.[50]

Daniel soon made public his intentions to "declare war" on the illegal gambling operations, promising quick and productive lawsuits. On August 20 he disclosed that a national organization based in Chicago with local headquarters in Houston was connecting Galveston, Beaumont, Port Arthur, Fort Worth, Stafford, Odessa, and Houston to a racing network. The following day he filed suit in Austin's 126th District Court against the Western Union Telegraph Company and A.G. Coggins of Little Rock, Arkansas, whom he claimed had arranged a special deal with Western Union to transmit racing information to Texas bookies. Following a little persuasion, he was granted a temporary restraining order against both parties.[51]

Despite numerous attempts from attorneys representing Western Union to persuade Daniel to drop the suit, the hearings proceeded as scheduled. The defendants grew worried as the emphatic attorney general unloaded impressive evidence he had managed to obtain, including a tape with actual racing information which had been transmitted to a bookie shop in Houston. His argument was sharp and direct, with each accusation reflecting careful reasoning and analysis. When Western Union attorney John Miller rose to his feet in objection to one of Daniel's questions, warning that Galveston could be a dangerous place and that a reply from his client might subject him to bodily harm, Daniel responded: "I'll take that responsibility. I'm not afraid of anybody."[52] After further prodding, he managed to squeeze information out of Miller's client that indeed Galveston was an organized gambling hotbed and that one of his own Western Union tickers operated at a local grill. As a result of Daniel's efforts, the Court issued a permanent injunction against Western Union, forbidding it from any further transmission of race information and results.[53]

Meanwhile, Daniel was pulled into another issue concerning minorities. House Speaker Sam Rayburn pleaded with him and the state legislature to abolish the state poll tax, which he argued had worked to silence minorities for generations. In a letter from Washington, Rayburn wrote: "I am opposed to a poll tax as a prerequisite to voting, but I cannot vote for the abolition of the poll tax here as I think it is a matter pertaining to the states and localities and should be handled by them."[54] Although a supporter of segregation, Daniel wanted to keep radicals from coming down even harder on blacks. In a speech given while campaigning for attorney general, he had promised to "offer the protection of the office in every way permitted by law against intolerance and persecution of minority groups. What we need is more harmony, love and cooperation among our fellow men if our great state is to progress as it should down through the years to come."[55] He eventually pushed for the submission of a constitutional amendment that would abolish the poll tax in Texas, but the measure was defeated by the 1949 state legislature.[56]

In January 1950, just months before the Sweatt case was to go before the Supreme Court, New York attorney Charles Tuttle requested that Daniel consent to his filing a brief for the Federal Council of Churches of Christ supporting Sweatt, declaring segregated schools unconstitutional even if the separate facilities were equal. Daniel said he would consent to the brief being filed only if Tuttle would insert "a disclosure of the fact that the religious denominations represented by the Federal Council maintain separate churches, separate church schools, separate denominational colleges, and separate congregations for white and Negro citizens in Texas and 14 other Southern States." Reasoned Daniel, "On the point you seek to cover as to 'necessity and desirability' of separate facilities in this state, your practice is equally as important as your preachment."[57]

Daniel and Thurgood Marshall argued the Sweatt case before the United States Supreme Court on April 4, 1950. With Assistant Attorney General Joe Greenhill by his side, Daniel told the Court about "troubles" some people warned would happen when races were intertwined. But Marshall responded: "It's just beyond reason" that if one black student were admitted to a law school the "whole state would be in bloodshed."[58] Daniel told the Court that the new law school had now met the standards of both the American Bar Association and the American Association of Law Schools, that it had already graduated one student who now had his license, and that if Sweatt had really been interested in obtaining a legal education he already could have done so at Texas State. Daniel's 127-page brief cited nine Supreme Court rulings holding that separate schools were constitutional and pointed to similar holdings by lower federal courts in thirteen cases and by the highest state courts in fifty-eight cases.[59]

While Daniel focused on preserving the status quo, Marshall challenged the Court to pave a new path by declaring public segregation unconstitutional. "Qualified educators, social scientists, and other experts have expressed their realization of the fact that 'separate' is irreconcilable with 'equality,'" he argued. And while the University of Texas Law School obviously had more tangible facilities, Marshall and his colleagues contended that intangible facilities were equally as important. The University of Texas Law School was recognized as one of the leading institutions in the state, he said, and how could such immeasurable qualities as "prestige" and "reputation" be equal for a separate institution?[60]

On June 5 the Supreme Court ruled unanimously in favor of Sweatt. Texas State was not an equal educational facility, said the Court, and Sweatt's Fourteenth Amendment rights had been violated. Hence, Sweatt was to be admitted to the University of Texas. "Whether the University of Texas Law School is compared with the original or the new law school for Negroes," wrote Chief Justice Vinson, "we cannot find substantial equality in the educational opportunities offered white and Negro law students by the State."[61] As a result, the University of Texas would become the first major southern collegiate institution to drop all racial restrictions for enrollment.[62] It was a monumental victory for Marshall, who considered the Sweatt decision the first substantive break in the wall of segregated public education.[63] Although the Court fell short of repudiating the "separate but equal" doctrine, this decision suggested that it was only a matter of time.

"We had quite a friendly fight," Daniel later recalled. "He [Marshall] said after it was over that he had been treated better here in Texas in the courtroom by us than he had been in any other state that he'd appeared, and he had been in many making the same fight to declare segregated schools unconstitutional. Then after we argued the case in the Supreme Court he asked Joe [Greenhill] and Jake Jacobsen and me to come out and have a picture made with all the lawyers."[64] Years later, echoing Daniel's sentiments to a reporter, Greenhill said that "it was an honor and a privilege [to argue against Marshall] and, quite frankly, I'm glad he won. This nation could not have survived the segregated society."[65]

The ruling met mixed reactions in Texas. Some accepted the decision, while others blamed Daniel for allowing the collapse of segregated education. One Daniel assistant wrote to a supporter: "The students have accepted the Negroes quietly. However, we are getting lots of letters from people back in the forks of the creek who don't like it at all."[66] But Daniel was satisfied with his efforts. "I think perhaps you know that I have done everything I humanly could to uphold the provisions of the Texas Constitution that separate schools should be provided for Negro and white students," he wrote to a supporter. "I worked on the case myself and had five other lawyers in my office working with me to be sure that no stone was left unturned." [67]

The Court's decision was monumental in that for the first time the quality of education was weighed against hardware such as desks and blackboards to determine whether equality existed. The mere physical presence of a separate school for Negroes was no longer sufficient if the opportunities for learning and development were not comparable to white facilities. In *The New York Times,* columnist Arthur Krock predicted that the Court's decision would soon affect primary and secondary educational facilities as well, thus dooming segregated public education altogether. [68] Following the ruling, Daniel met with the president of the University of Texas and other officials to devise a policy that would meet the new legal requirements. "Perhaps they even faced the task with a trace of relief," speculated historian Michael Gillette. "The brief attempt at 'separate but equal' professional schools had been an expensive, embarrassing, and bothersome experiment for dignified, intelligent men to have to implement." [69] Heman Marion Sweatt did enter the University of Texas Law School four years after his original application but dropped out after two years of poor grades. He went on to earn a master's degree in social work from Atlanta University and eventually became assistant director of the National Urban League's southern region. [70]

Daniel ran unopposed in the 1950 Democratic primary and breezed to a third term as attorney general. [71] Gambling would soon top his list of concerns, especially considering the fact that Texas led the nation in total number of slot machines, reportedly greater than 10,000. Determined to launch a campaign equal in vigor to his last, on March 19, 1951, he summoned prosecuting attorneys from all over the state to Austin to discuss organized gambling. The group assembled at the Driskill Hotel, where Daniel furnished them with the name and address of every person in every county who had paid taxes the previous year on slot machines. "Within a week let's have them gone and out," he insisted. [72] His confidence in what a united front could achieve so inspired the attorneys, they unanimously supported proposed legislation to ban not only slot machines but also punch cards and football lottery cards. Daniel was pleased by the results of his hard work when the Texas legislature in May outlawed not only the manufacturing, ownership, and leasing, but even the mere storage of slot machines. The legislature passed a lottery act and prohibited punch cards altogether.[73]

Despite Daniel's impressive crackdown on organized gambling, one major hurdle still remained—Galveston. Tagged the "bawdy house of Texas" by newspaper editor E.M. Pooley,[74] Galveston had managed to fall through the cracks of Daniel's investigations. Many attributed this to the ability of city leaders to gain insider information on who was currently being investigated and when. Others thought the problem was due to the layout of such clubs as the famed Balinese Room, which was equipped with roulette wheels, slot machines and dice tables. To enter, visitors were required to walk down a hallway, called Rangers Run by locals, which stretched 300-feet from the shore out over the Gulf of Mexico. Thus, by the time Texas Rangers raced from the building's entrance to the actual Balinese Room, all traces of gambling equipment could be hidden.[75]

It was no secret that the Maceo Syndicate, a slick, family-run organization, was the heart of the Galveston gambling scene. Daniel was confident that its demise would bring an end to large-scale gambling in Texas. In less than a week after forcing disclosure and investigating financial records, he had representatives of the Maceo Syndicate in an Austin courtroom scratching their heads. He told Judge Jack Roberts that the Maceos had five local gambling setups equipped with betting counters and race results posted on the walls, each of which transmitted information through Southwestern Bell. By midafternoon Roberts issued an order forbidding Southwestern Bell any further involvement with the Maceo Syndicate, and the telephone service was terminated immediately. Much to Daniel's credit, within just six months of his crackdown, Galveston was for the most part free of gambling. Rid of more than 1,000 slot machines, the city became a gambling excursion destination only for the elite.[76] While the state would not be completely rid of gambling until the 1960s, Daniel had succeeded in crippling the underground industry.

Impressed by the positive results of his hard-nosed gambling crackdown, Daniel's colleagues elected him vice president of the National Association of Attorneys General, which convened in Seattle in August 1951. At the conference he received national attention. Chairing a panel discussion with Tennessee Senator Estes

Kefauver, who at the time was in charge of a major national crime investigation, Daniel reported that Texas had almost rid itself of syndicate-controlled gambling. In fact, only 127 of the reported 10,000 slot machines were still known to be in service.[77]

Over the years, in addition to his other responsibilities, Daniel worked to compile laws relating to newspapers and public notices for the use of his office. The Texas Press Association believed that such a collection should be made available for public use and, in 1951, sought permission to publish and distribute his compilation in the form of a book. Once assured the project would be executed as a public service without cost to the state and without profit, he agreed, and the book was made available at the actual cost of printing and distribution. Included were several chapters of textual material written by Daniel himself from his unique viewpoint as both a lawyer and publisher.[78] "The attorney general of Texas often is required to give legal advice to certain county and state officials concerning publication of legal notices," he wrote. "For the use of this office, all constitutional provisions, laws, and court rules relating to newspapers and legal publications were compiled, indexed, and annotated with leading cases and opinions of prior attorneys general. At the request of the Texas Press Association, I have edited this compilation and herewith make it available for publication." [79]

In Daniel's six-year tenure he disposed of more than 5,000 lawsuits; handed down 2,500 legal opinions; served on twenty-five state boards and agencies; composed over 2,000 bills for the Texas legislature; successfully defended more money and land claims against the state than any previous attorney general; and won the largest number of antitrust suits filed in state history (none lost). He also was praised for putting an end to natural gas waste in state oil fields and for muscling numerous anti-pollution suits.[80] In the meantime, Daniel was also in the process of leading one of the largest legal battles in Texas history.

CHAPTER 8

The Tidelands

resident Woodrow Wilson once wrote that "almost every great internal crisis in our [national] affairs has turned upon the question of state and federal rights."[1] In the twentieth century, where that fine line should be drawn was rarely debated more clearly than in the case of tidelands ownership.

Almost since the establishment of the Union, each state had exercised dominion over the beds of its respective navigable waters. The seaward boundaries of most coastal and Great Lakes states extended three miles out from shore. Some, however, like Texas and the Gulfward side of Florida, ran three leagues (nine marine miles) from shore. The submerged lands were viewed not merely as a possession of individual states but, even more, as an actual part of them. In fact, for more than 100 years and in more than 52 opinions, the U.S. Supreme Court had held or confirmed that states owned the submerged lands within their respective boundaries.[2] However, with the discovery of vast pools of oil off the California, Texas, and Louisiana coasts in the late 1930s, federal officials began to take note. Over the next ten years these states, seeing the submerged lands as valuable sources of revenue, began selling leases to oil producers.[3]

Even though Interior Secretary Harold Ickes had already ac-knowledged that these submerged lands belonged to the states and not the federal government, federal officials began to assert claim. At the prodding of President Truman, United States Attorney General Tom Clark filed an original action in the Supreme Court against the State of California in the summer of 1945, declaring that the United States owned or had paramount rights to all lands and minerals from the low-water mark three miles out to sea. Several coastal states, in-cluding Texas, followed the developments closely, aware that their coastal waters could be in jeopardy of federal takeover.[4]

Advocates of state ownership, including deep-pocketed oil pro-ducers, immediately sought help from Congress. By July 1946 a measure quitclaiming "right, title, interest, or claim" to submerged lands within the three-mile limit had passed both houses of Congress and was sent to the desk of President Harry Truman. However, claiming that he did not want to interfere while the Supreme Court was still deliberating the matter, Truman vetoed the quitclaim bill.[5]

Since the onset of the tidelands issue, no attorney general out-side of California had been keeping closer watch over these devel-opments than Price Daniel. He knew that a lot was at stake for Texas. With four wells, the state averaged approximately a $20 per acre bonus on 350,000 acres of tidelands. The annual return to the state's school fund from this lone source, not including revenue from rentals or royalties, was well in excess of $7 million.[6] If the federal government was planning to file a similar motion against Texas, Daniel was going to be prepared. To his dismay, the Supreme Court abruptly reversed the federal government's relationship with the states in June 1947, ruling that the federal government, not the State of California, had "paramount rights" over coastal property for national defense and international affairs.[7] The repercussions were sure to hit coastal states hard, most of which, like Texas, were using these lands as a major source of revenue.

This issue held all the right ingredients to interest Daniel. It not only summoned and mobilized his penchant for crusading, but also drew on his love and knowledge of Texas history. This was an attack on his beloved state; an outside power was threatening to take what rightfully belonged to Texans. Surely he also realized the political benefits.

Daniel came out fighting. He called a press conference the morning after the Supreme Court reversal and insisted that if a similar suit were filed against Texas, he would ask the Supreme Court to uphold the property rights of his state as they had existed "when we lowered the Lone Star and raised the Stars and Stripes on February 16, 1846." He promised a "last-ditch" fight against federal seizure of land and mineral rights and denounced the Court's ruling as the greatest blow against property rights of the states since the Civil War.[8]

Texans responded to Daniel's battle cry. The Texas Bar Association, agitated by the ruling, named a special committee to assist Governor Beauford Jester and Daniel in trying to get Congress to overrule the decision and confirm state ownership.[9] Jester called the Court's decision a dangerous threat not only to submerged coastal lands in Texas but to inland submerged lands and to "private lands, over all of which the federal government has the same power of National defense and international affairs." He traveled to the national Governors' Conference in July of 1947, where he sponsored and obtained passage of a resolution placing the governors behind the desired congressional action. "Congratulations to you and the Governors' Conference on adoption of resolution," Daniel telegrammed Jester at his Salt Lake City hotel. "I believe this will be the beginning of a victory in Congress."[10]

When California requested a rehearing of its case, the National Association of Attorneys General (NAAG) prepared a brief on behalf of California and chose Daniel to argue it orally before the U.S. Supreme Court. It was a huge honor for someone who was still the youngest attorney general in the nation.[11] Before Daniel began his argument to the Court, Attorney General Tom Clark came down the aisle and put his arm around him. "Well, Price," he said, "at least you got a good trip to Washington out of this, but that's all you'll ever get out of it because I've just issued a statement saying that Texas is different and this Court decision will not apply to Texas." Clark handed him the release that he had just given to the press. It was an all-out statement that Texas would not be sued, that the state's title was retained when it entered the Union.[12] Clark's assertion sent Daniel's confidence soaring. In arguing the brief, he stressed to the justices that their recent decision in the California case would affect not only coastal waters but inland as well. He also pointed out that the doctrine of "paramount rights," if unrestricted, could lead to federal control of all natural resources.[13]

Returning home, Daniel labored indefatigably to organize an aggressive tidelands campaign which attacked on every front. In December 1947 he wrote to Governor Jester that "the success of our submerged land legislation depends largely upon what can be done with Mr. Truman, and, I believe we have made a mistake in not working on him directly before this date. To say the least, we should map out some kind of strategy to get the viewpoint of the states, the justice of our claims, and the political implications before President Truman before he makes up his mind definitely to submit a message against our viewpoint." To accomplish this, he suggested that Jester get a group of Democratic governors and other leaders to request a conference with the president.[14]

Daniel's leadership in the tidelands fight caused his political stock to rise dramatically. When rumors circulated that Governor Jester was considering a run for the Senate, many Texans considered Daniel a top candidate to replace him as chief executive. "One sure thing," prophesied the *Beaumont Enterprise* in September 1947, "the campaign between Mr. Shivers and Mr. Daniel is already an actuality with the latter given the edge on Mr. Shivers for the present because Mr. Daniel, being attorney general, has more chance to keep himself on the front pages. He is conducting investigations in Texas now of items popular with the common man—meat, bread, milk and some 20 other items. [He] is said to have a flare for making news wherever he appears. He recently had three stories about himself—all legitimate news—when he attended a convention in Dallas and other stories when pumping hands in Fort Worth."[15]

The newspaper proclaimed that "the Daniel forces are already highly organized and are out working counties. The nucleus is the group of Young Democrats who became a tightly welded clique while Price Daniel was their leader back in 1941. They are conducting several polls in the state. One evidenced in north Texas appeared to be financed by a Dallas lumberman." The article went on to quote one unidentified leader of the Young Democrats as saying, "We started to get Price in office not yesterday but eight years ago."[16]

Daniel, although privately flattered by the speculation, was quick to squash rumors of any immediate plans for higher office. At this time, his entire being was engulfed by the tidelands crusade. He publicly chided anyone who accused him of using the issue for his own political gain. "I had rather win the tidelands case than to hold any public office that exists, and if it becomes necessary for me to remove myself from unsolicited speculation on the political scene in order to maintain united support on this case, I shall do so without hesitation," he declared.[17] But Daniel knew that should he prove victorious in the tidelands fight, his political future would take care of itself.

Despite Attorney General Clark's assurance that Texas was immune from prosecution, Daniel received contrary news on October 13, 1947. The Supreme Court refused to reconsider its previous decision, and thus denied California a rehearing. This meant that Texas was still at risk of having federal action taken against its offshore lands. A determined Daniel promptly began working with several other attorneys general to bring the battle back into the legislative arena. He also asked House Speaker Sam Rayburn to take the lead in Texas' claim to the submerged lands. Rayburn was split between the interests of his nation and home state, but, after a convincing argument from close friend Tom Clark, decided to support the Court's decision. In July, Rayburn had written Daniel: "Sometimes it is better to let sleeping dogs lie as it is doubtful whether we could pass a bill through the Senate and the House here declaring what we think would be Texas' rights."[18]

Undaunted by the Speaker's decision, Daniel's group introduced a new quitclaim bill in Congress in January 1948 and made another urgent plea to Rayburn, this time begging him to use his leverage with President Truman to help defend the state's contention. "When you demonstrate your personal interest and the political implications," Daniel wrote, "I am sure Truman will agree for you to sit in on further consideration of matters pertaining to this issue."[19] Rayburn rejected the suggestion, but had already arranged a January 15 meeting between Daniel and Truman.[20] Joining Daniel at this White House meeting were Texas Senator Tom Connally and Robert Lee Bobbitt, chairman of the Texas Bar Association's Tidelands Committee. The trio was granted assurance from Truman that should Congress pass the bill, a similar meeting would be arranged before the president would make any veto decision.[21]

Beginning in January 1948, Curtis Morris, a friend of Governor Jester who classified himself as an "unofficial representative of Texas business people," began sending confidential reports to both

Jester and Daniel from Washington, updating them weekly on tide-lands events on the Hill. In his first such report to Jester, Morris suggested that "we all should plan our campaign on the basis of a presidential veto. While that's a big hill to climb, it can be climbed." Morris reminded the governor that Congress had passed the Taft-Hartley Act over a veto, which he contended to be as controversial as the tidelands matter.[22] In coming months both Jester and Daniel relied on these Washington reports for inside information that could be obtained nowhere else.

Daniel actively lobbied on behalf of the new bill and was opti-mistic about its chances when fellow attorneys general selected him to help manage the February Senate hearings on the measure. Before leaving for Washington, he suggested that Governor Jester "stir up some of the Coastal governors" by writing each of them and calling attention to the fact that "the bill purports to cover all Coastal States, and is an attempt to assert title and the rights to lease their lands without giving any of the states, except California, a day in Court." Daniel also provided a list of governors whom he recommended that Jester should urge to personally attend the up-coming sub-committee hearings "in order that they may become fully acquainted with the legislation and try to help the states in ob-taining its passage."[23] As he would do many times, Jester complied with Daniel's request and, two days later, sent personal letters to the governors via Western Union.[24] For eighteen days Daniel sched-uled witnesses on behalf of state ownership.[25]

In March, Tom Clark announced that the government was preparing legal action against Louisiana and possibly some other states. Because of his assurances from Clark following the California decision, Daniel was not alarmed. He refused to believe that the Justice Department would move against Texas and grew more confident on April 30 when the House overwhelmingly passed the quitclaim measure.[26] In May a jubilant Sam Rayburn in-formed Daniel that "the Submerged Land Bill turned out, in the House, as well or better than could be expected. Now, if the Senate will go ahead and do their job, this Bill should become law before long, even without the President's approval."[27] Months later, President Truman bolstered Daniel's confidence by declaring in an Austin campaign speech that when it came to ownership of sub-merged lands, Texas was "in a class by itself."[28]

But Daniel's hope that Texas would escape a legal confrontation with the federal government was suddenly shattered on December 21, 1948. Attorney General Clark announced that a recent Supreme Court decision had left him no choice but to reverse his pro-Texas position. Clark, himself a Texan, issued a statement from Washington declaring that the Justice Department was filing suit in the Supreme Court against both Texas and Louisiana. Daniel had become so emotionally involved in the tidelands crusade that tears fell from his eyes as he received word of Clark's announcement by telephone.[29] He immediately released his anger at federal officials, publicly claiming that the United States government would not treat even an enemy nation with such disregard. He pledged to fight with the spirit of legendary Texans who led them to "win these lands by blood and valor at San Jacinto."[30]

Governor Jester, also stunned by the news, began urging fellow Texan Sam Rayburn to use his influence in Washington to strengthen Texas' claim. "The recent developments and the things that may yet transpire as a result of the efforts that will be made by those who are wrongfully and unlawfully wedded to the ideology of federal ownership of the tidelands make me realize all the more that you, in your position, are the one strong bulwark and force who can turn back the tide of tidelands ownership by the Federal Government," Jester wrote to Rayburn on December 23. "I realize that you still hold a strong hand and position and can, at the time of your strategic choosing, endeavor to get from [President Truman] the agreement not to include this item in his message and get his agreement to leave this matter to the decision of Congress and, if the Congress passes a state ownership bill, not to veto it."[31]

The Court had granted Texas a two-week period to contest the federal suit, during which time Daniel dropped all other responsibilities and worked expeditiously around the clock to prepare a brief. He canceled his family's Christmas vacation and began assigning staff members to research different aspects of the case. Wary of his chances to change the opinions of the same justices who had ruled against California in 1947, he encouraged his staff to formulate original arguments that might work to shift the battle into Congress.[32] On January 15, 1949, the long hours of studying, writing, and editing came to an end as he officially filed the brief with the Supreme Court on Texas' behalf.[33]

In the meantime, Daniel continued to exhaust all other avenues to keep the case out of the courts. Congress, he maintained, was the proper battlefield for this matter. But Daniel grew somewhat frustrated that Washington politicians did not share his urgency. "Price, the pace here in Congress is slow," warned Curtis Morris on February 3 in one of his regular confidential reports from the Hill. "Seems somehow that the Democratic leadership isn't sure of itself—doesn't know what to schedule. The Republicans are showing a lot of bounce. Southern Democrats for the most part seem to me to be taking a wait-and-see attitude." [34] Weeks later Morris assured Governor Jester that "time is playing into our hands" and that "patience may well be worth while for a time yet." [35]

In early March, Daniel urged Lyndon Johnson to help draft a bill that would grant Texas all of the lands within its original limits as well as a portion of the revenue within the state's extended boundaries. He also asked Johnson to seek a postponement of the court date in order to allow Congress time to work something out. [36] Johnson offered no assistance in changing the court date but did express hope for some sort of bill. "If you and Tom [Clark] and some other able and reasonable attorneys could sit down in an office together," Johnson replied, "such a solution could be arrived at." If Daniel was interested in the idea, Johnson promised to participate in the talks. [37]

In late March, Daniel was disappointed to read a half-page editorial in the *Fort Worth Star-Telegram* that favored a compromise and urged Texans "to look at the tidelands issue from a practical standpoint, appraising their chances of winning dispassionately and what would be the result if they do not." The newspaper said that "Texans should realize the risk involved in a no-compromise attitude," and that Texas officials who carry responsibility in the matter "might do well to consider whether they will serve the state's best interest by following a 'shoot the works' policy or whether they can put on their trading clothes and make a deal that in the long run might prove more profitable to Texas." [38]

Daniel understood the importance of public opinion and on occasion resorted to inflated rhetoric to rouse support from Texans who thus far had appeared indifferent on the tidelands issue. "The seizure of the Texas tidelands will go down in history as the blackest page in all this era of centralization and lack of morality," he told a crowd of onlookers on the front lawn of the McLennan County Courthouse in Waco. He virtually accused an editor of the University of Texas newspaper, *The Daily Texan*, of being a communist for advocating federal control of the tidelands. "If private and state ownership of property is morally wrong, then our whole system of government has been a great mistake, and your editorial writer is the only one who has been brave enough to openly advocate a change to the socialistic or communistic theory of national ownership of all property," wrote Daniel in a scathing letter to editor Bob Hollingsworth. Hollingsworth responded that "Daniel seems to be under the impression that anyone who doesn't string along with states rights is advocating communistic theories. If so, then Harold Ickes, Tom Clark, and six justices of the United States Supreme Court are doing the same thing. This writer thinks he is in excellent company." [39] Nevertheless, Daniel's public relations campaign proved effective. According to a 1948 statewide poll, the tidelands controversy was ranked as only the sixth most important issue. However, a similar poll conducted the following year placed the tidelands crusade above all other issues in Texas, including segregation, housing, and the economy. [40]

On May 9 the Supreme Court heard oral presentations from both Texas and Louisiana attempting to stop the federal suit. Governor Jester wrote personal letters to selected members of the Texas congressional delegation urging that they attend the oral arguments. Most of the delegation complied, prompting one congressman to write Jester days later explaining that he put in his appearance "for whatever effect it might have and found the courtroom so crowded it was not possible to obtain a seat." [41] Missing from the Texas delegation, however, was Lyndon Johnson. He explained to Jester that his absence "was wholly because of my longstanding belief that it is quite improper to intermingle any evidence or hint of 'influence' with proceedings of any court." The presence of the entire delegation, he reasoned, "would have been a very obvious display, the implications of which would have been inescapable and would have hurt the cause rather than helped it. At the proper time and in the proper place I shall certainly use all the influence that I can muster and I know, as you know, that the entire delegation here will continue to champion the fight here with vigor, vigilance, and tenacity." [42]

Daniel argued his case before the Court for two hours, insisting that Congress should ultimately resolve the dispute. He reminded the justices of how Texas, under the state's annexation resolution, was granted all the vacant and unappropriated lands lying within its limits and told them that until recently neither party had disputed a boundary extending three leagues into the Gulf of Mexico.[43] But his arguments fell on deaf ears. On May 16 the Supreme Court decided that the federal government could indeed sue both Texas and Louisiana for ownership of their offshore lands.[44] Daniel was sulky. He now believed more than ever that his political future was irrevocably linked to the success of Texas' tidelands claim.

Back in Texas, speculation was circulating about a compromise between Texas and the federal government. "That compromise was hatched up by a couple of oil company lobbies," Daniel later explained. "They figured that it would just not be possible to get the bill signed by President Truman and... that the oil company was getting hurt in the fight so they felt there should be this compromise."[45] Jester called a meeting of the School Land Board at the Mansion and invited the oil company representatives to present their reasons for supporting the compromise and urged the board to do likewise. The board, including Jester, unanimously rejected the proposal, however, stating that it failed to recognize the treaty by which Texas had entered the Union and, without vesting title, would not prevent the proposed revenue split from being revoked or changed by a subsequent Congress.[46]

"They couldn't get any of us to support the compromise, but they evidently did get Mr. Rayburn sold" on the idea, Daniel speculated. "And they were able to sell then Lieutenant Governor Shivers on the idea. He was the only one they were able to get on the state level to go to Washington, discuss the matter, and come out for the so-called compromise."[47] Indeed, Shivers made a special trip to Washington and returned home insisting that Texas should be practical on the matter, that it had already lost some legal skirmishes and could lose more. By compromising, he reasoned, Texas would gain more revenue "in the long run."[48]

Rayburn, who had twice supported the state ownership bill but feared another Truman veto was imminent, soon put forth his own plan which would allow Texas, Louisiana, and California the right to two-thirds of the oil and gas within a 10.35-mile limit and one-third from there out 125 miles. This arrangement would allow the federal government to keep one-third of the rights within the 10.35-mile limit and two-thirds of the rest.[49] Many proponents of state ownership welcomed Rayburn's plan, believing the retention of some of the oil and mineral rights was better than nothing. Daniel viewed Rayburn's proposal as a compromise of principle, however, and frustrated many states'-rights activists for stubbornly clinging to his all-or-nothing claim. He pleaded: "The few Texans who are publicly advocating a tidelands compromise and doubting our chances to win either in the Court or Congress are not expressing the opinion of the elected officials who bear the legal responsibility for the lands." He labeled the federal action a giant step toward "nationalization" of public property and declared that "the fight has just begun!"[50]

Still determined to reach some sort of solution, Rayburn invited Daniel, Giles, and other interested parties to a series of meetings in his office. Despite his resistance to a compromise, Daniel made the trip to Washington to discuss what he termed "this so-called compromise" with Tom Clark and the assistant attorney general handling the tidelands.[51] "That was the most nebulous proposal," Daniel recalled. "We found that they just weren't as strong for it as it had been represented and by that time Giles was all the way for the compromise. In any event, Mr. Rayburn said to come on back and present a bill that would accomplish what they thought might be workable. That bill was never brought back by the Justice Department, so when the books say that there was a proposal offered to us that we turned down, actually there was nothing ever proposed in writing on this compromise by the Justice Department on just anything they would support. There were proposals by Mr. Rayburn. There were proposals made by former Governor Shivers, when he was Lieutenant Governor, and by the oil folks. But really there was nothing that you could say that we could have had that we walked away from."[52]

Public opinion soon shifted in favor of Daniel's uncompromising stance, and thus Texas was perched in a position to win or lose the tidelands completely. Rayburn feared the outcome and predicted that the Supreme Court would once again rule in favor of the national government when Texas had its day in court. As he wrote to a supporter shortly before the decision, "I am still very fearful that the Supreme Court will hold in other instances as they held in the California case."[53] He also began to believe that Daniel was merely using the tidelands as a political issue on which to gain popularity. He later expressed his frustration with Daniel for not supporting his plan: "I realized that he didn't want a settlement—he wanted the issue to run for office on. He wanted to demagogue it. So, it couldn't be settled."[54] But Daniel felt strongly that Texas should not have to compromise, that the tidelands were truly a possession of Texas under its admission to the United States. For him to let ownership of these lands be lost on his watch as attorney general would be unforgivable.

At Daniel's prodding, Governor Jester had been successful in keeping the Texas delegation in Congress and most all state officials behind the fight for state ownership. Because Daniel and Lieutenant Governor Shivers did not see eye-to-eye on the tidelands compromise, the attorney general was banking on continued support from Jester.[55] Perhaps Jester's beliefs about the matter were best expressed in a May 30 letter to Rayburn in which he boldly confessed that he was not sold on the Speaker's compromise plan. "Frankly, Sam, I must tell you again that I can never go along with any sort of trade, deal or compromise," he wrote. "The principle involved far surpasses in importance the financial aspect. Simply and bluntly put, the question is one of states' property rights versus nationalization of property. It is contrary to my political philosophy, my personal convictions and my sense of right and justice to accede to any scheme that would contravene the states' property rights and ownership doctrine and open the door to nationalization of vital natural resources. The Congress, which is the branch of our federal government that negotiated the terms of the admittance of Texas into the Union, is the proper branch to uphold the annexation agreement."[56]

Just a month after that letter was written, however, the hierarchy of Texas government suddenly changed. Governor Jester, who on July 10 held a post-legislative-session party for his staff at Lake Austin, where he swam and played ball, boarded a train that evening for a routine physical examination to be conducted in southeast Texas. The next morning, at age fifty-six, he was found dead in his Pullman berth. The victim of a heart attack, Jester became the first Texas governor to die in office.[57]

Shivers was visiting his family farm in Tyler County when a Houston newspaper reporter informed him of the governor's death. Having been with Jester only a few days earlier, who appeared healthy and in high spirits, Shivers was stunned by the tragic news and the revelation that he would now assume the role of chief executive. Jester's body, after lying in the Senate chamber, was flown to Corsicana for burial. Three days after Jester's funeral, on July 16, 1949, before a crowd of approximately 2,500 people, Shivers was administered the oath of office at his log farmhouse. Jester's widow, Mabel, moved to an Austin apartment complex to make way for the new governor.[58]

Daniel had greatly admired Beauford Jester and later expressed uneasiness that Jester's role in the Texas tidelands fight had been minimized and often overlooked by historians. He actually felt guilty that both he and Allan Shivers had received most of the credit. "It was [Jester] who first carried the issue to a national Governors' Conference and to a Democratic National Convention," Daniel would later write. "He had established a firm record on which state officials could continue to build their defense of the Texas tidelands in the U.S. Supreme Court and in Congress."[59]

On the political front, Jester's death was quite significant in Daniel's life and career. No longer were he and Allan Shivers on an equal playing field, ready to compete for the state's highest office. With Shivers suddenly elevated to the office of chief executive and possessing the power of incumbency, Daniel knew his gubernatorial aspirations would have to be put on hold for some time.

As governor, Shivers became one of three powerful Texas School Land Board members, along with Land Commissioner Bascom Giles and Daniel, who supervised tidelands revenues. With Giles leaning toward a tidelands compromise, Shivers now had the deciding vote in his pocket. "Shivers and Giles were inclined to accept the plan as a good deal for Texas," Speaker Rayburn later surmised.[60] All of a sudden, Daniel found himself the only high public official in the state who did not favor a compromise.[61]

The new governor's differences of opinion with Daniel had already been well documented by the press. One newspaper featured a cartoon depicting Shivers and Daniel arguing in front of the Alamo, one waiving a "Compromise!" flag and the other hoisting a banner proclaiming "Never!"[62] Notwithstanding, Daniel tried assiduously to get Shivers to change his mind and even hinted that should he and Shivers not ultimately agree on the Texas position, he might challenge the governor in the upcoming election. Shortly afterward, Shivers walked into Daniel's office unannounced and said he would like to discuss the matter before issuing any further public statements. Daniel made his case to Shivers as meticulously as he had before the courts, arguing that the only viable solution would come with congressional quitclaim legislation. If Shivers were to allow a compromise, Daniel promised that such a settlement would always be subject to change by the federal government.[63]

Daniel's tenacity proved effective. When the Texas School Land Board met on July 22, 1949, Shivers had surprisingly changed his position and, much to Daniel's delight, voted against a compromise. The board, as well as the governor, had now shifted sides in support of Daniel's "all or nothing" stance.[64] Shivers said his change of heart came as a result of his attempt to avoid "a conflict in the Texas position or an open conflict between the Texas officials."[65] But, more likely, he had sensed the growing lobby of Texans who were coming out in support of the state's uncompromising stance and feared the political consequences of being on the downside of public fervor. He also knew a pro-ownership stance would thwart Daniel's political momentum as an opponent in the upcoming election. His new-found determination to resist compromise resulted in a crucial alliance between himself and the powerful Texas oil-and-ranch faction of the party, a group which had few expectations of him at the time of his election.[66]

In the few months leading to his day in court, Daniel undertook a massive research effort. He rented the entire second floor of an old office building near the Capitol to serve as his headquarters. Equipped with wooden chairs, desks, filing cabinets, and scores of books, the office soon became a temporary home to four stenographers who would labor day and night shifts. Daniel also enlisted seven full-time assistant attorneys general, a research assistant in Washington, a former University of Texas professor who drew up charts and maps for visual aids, as well as a staff of linguists to translate Spanish documents and law books.[67] "President Truman, the Department of Justice and Interior, and particularly Justice Black of the U.S. Supreme Court and others are expected to feel the lash of this Southeastern Texas boy before he is through," predicted the *Beaumont Enterprise.*[68]

In March, Daniel announced with pleasure that some of the top legal names in the country had come to his aid, such as Roscoe Pound, former dean of the Harvard Law School, Judge Manley O. Hudson, chairman of the United Nations International Law Commission, Joseph Walter Bingham, professor emeritus of international law at Stanford University, and James William Moore, a foremost authority on federal procedure.[69] In this second-floor hideout Daniel spent countless hours pouring over law books, court decisions, and documents in order to meet the Supreme Court deadline.

Granted $100,000 by the Texas legislature to defend the tidelands, Daniel sent assistants as far as Chile and Spain to gather evidence.[70] To better his chances of persuading the court, he assigned his wife, Jean, to study biographical accounts of the justices so he would know what "struck home" with each of them. She was delighted to discover that Chief Justice Fred M. Vinson was a Sam Houston buff, knowing full well that no one was better at talking Houston than her husband. Daniel and Vinson had at least that much in common.[71]

Daniel soon received word that the Supreme Court would hear the Texas case on March 28, one day after Louisiana. In order to buy some uninterrupted time for rest and last-minute preparation, he chose to travel east by railroad. As the train pulled away from the Austin depot on the morning of March 24, Daniel, with a tidelands map clutched firmly in his hand, waved farewell to a crowd of supporters.[72] The young attorney general was determined to return home victorious. He felt much pressure to disprove his critics who had warned him that Texas was in danger of losing its entire claim to the offshore lands. Having been the only state official at one point who resisted a compromise, he feared returning home empty-handed.

As the proceedings began, Daniel was surprised and frustrated to learn that the Supreme Court would not allow him to submit evidence. The justices insisted on making a judgment based solely on the pleadings, following the same guidelines they had used in the 1947 California case. Daniel implored them to reconsider, highlighting the sharp contrasts between the 1947 California claim and that of Texas. California did not have to introduce evidence, he contended, because no basic facts were in dispute with their claim. Texas, on the other hand, had a completely different argument and should be warranted a full, fact-gathering trial. Without the opportunity to admit evidence, he was left no choice but to argue the framework of his case the best he could. "All we claim," he maintained, "is the property ownership which we have exercised for more than 100 years."[73] Attempting to sway Vinson, he made frequent references to Sam Houston. In particular, he spoke of Houston's part in the negotiations which led to the annexation of the Texas Republic by the United States.[74] And prior to the case, Vinson was reminded of the fact that Jean was a great-great-granddaughter of the Texas hero.[75]

When the proceedings ended, Daniel and his supporters were optimistic about the outcome. Robert Lee Bobbitt said afterward that, based on his thirty-year experience before appellate courts and the Supreme Court, never had he seen a case presented with such "ability and effectiveness." Another onlooker called the brief the "best prepared" and "most extensively researched" land suit in history.[76] The press was equally supportive of Daniel. One reporter noted how the usually unfazed Washington correspondents had seemed impressed with the Texas brief.[77] And the *Houston Chronicle* praised the attorney general, declaring that whatever the Court's decision may be, the best interests of all Texans had been "capably defended."[78]

In the end, however, Chief Justice Vinson remarked that he was swayed more by his old buddy Harry Truman than an interest in Sam Houston. His proved to be a crucial vote.[79] On June 5, 1950, as Rayburn had predicted, the Supreme Court handed down a 4–3 decision declaring that the federal government, not the states, had "paramount" rights to the tidelands. The Court majority was persuaded by the "equal footing" clause of the joint resolution by which the Texas Republic had entered the Union, under which Texas was admitted "on an equal footing with the existing states."[80] Expressing the majority opinion, Justice William O. Douglas wrote, "When Texas came into the Union, she ceased to be an independent nation. She then became a sister state on an equal footing with all other states." Concerning the claim that Texas maintained the rights to the lands under its annexation agreement, Douglas explained that Texas' admission to the Union "concededly entailed a relinquishment of some of her sovereignty."[81]

The three dissenting justices, however, were adamant in their support for the state's claim. "The needs of defense and foreign affairs alone cannot transfer ownership of an ocean bed from a state to the federal government any more than they could transfer iron ore under uplands from state to federal ownership," wrote Justice Stanley F. Reed. "In my view, Texas owned the marginal area by virtue of its original proprietorship: it has not shown to my satisfaction that it is lost by the terms of the resolution of annexation." And according to Justice Felix Frankfurter, the Court "now decides that when Texas entered the Union she lost what she had and the United States acquired it. How that ship came to pass remains for me a puzzle." [82]

Daniel was understandably frustrated by the decision. "As far as I am concerned, the fight has just begun," he declared. "I still believe this land belongs to the Texas public school fund. We will ask the Court to at least hear all the evidence before finally deciding this case. The close decision of 4 to 3 indicates that it might be helpful if the Court allows the evidence to be fully developed." [83] He noted that this case was the first time in history that the Supreme Court had denied a state an opportunity to introduce evidence in a contested lawsuit. [84] The Court did not rule that the federal government owned the submerged lands outright, but rather that the federal government had "paramount rights" to them. Nor did it rule against Congress taking the initiative to enact legislation which could permanently grant the lands to either the United States or Texas, an avenue that Daniel came to believe was imminent. [85]

Daniel's office was flooded with letters, telegrams, and phone calls from Texas and abroad urging him not to give up the fight. He promptly filed for a rehearing, assuring Texans that should the Supreme Court deny his request the state would still prevail. "Congress would never treat Texas that way," he said to a crowd in Temple on his fortieth birthday. "Don't, above all, be willing to give up the fight." He reminded voters of a state ownership bill pending in Congress which, he boasted, had strong support in the House and had been endorsed by more than thirty senators. [86]

Daniel would soon be left with no other choice but to use Congress as a means to prevail, for on October 16, 1950, the Supreme Court denied his request for a rehearing. In December, the Court issued a final decree, requiring Texas and Louisiana to account for all tidelands royalties acquired since June 5, 1950, and refused to consider the matter any further. The ruling angered Texans, who viewed the oil-rich lands as an essential revenue source for their children's education.[87] Sentiments were so strong, in fact, that 200 citizens of Nocona, Texas, demanded the state's secession. Prominent figures such as Railroad Commissioner Ernest Thompson and Congressman Lloyd Bentsen, Jr. seriously recommended that Texas exercise its unique right of dividing into five states in order to produce ten senators in Washington committed to the state's tidelands claim.[88]

Daniel sent his able assistant Dow Heard to Washington to help organize a Texas-style bill. As a result, Texas Congressman Ed Gossett introduced legislation that would grant coastal states undisputed title to the tidelands. By this time even Rayburn was convinced something had to be done and, declaring that "this is the psychological time for the House to move," responded by working in favor of the state's claims in the House. Lyndon Johnson did likewise in the Senate.[89] A bill eventually passed both houses of Congress, but, like the one before, was rejected by President Truman, who denounced it as "robbery in broad daylight." This second veto caused many Texans to ponder leaving the national Democratic party and led some prominent Washington elites to blame Rayburn for not winning the president's support.[90]

For Daniel, the tidelands crusade had become more an issue of principle than a matter of mere fiscal concern. Addressing the Texas State Bar Convention, he insisted: "Principles of government and... property law are involved in this conflict which are far more important than the land and the money involved. New and revolutionary principles of law have been written into the tidelands decisions which should never be allowed to stand as the law of this land." [91] His frustration soon increased. The state of Mississippi announced in August 1951 that the Gulf Refining Company and the Mebbin Oil Company of Pittsburgh had leased 800,000 acres of its tidelands and had guaranteed to drill within a year. The five-year lease promised Mississippi $50,000 the first year, $80,000 each year thereafter, and approximately one-eighth royalty on all oil drilled. Daniel's cries of "discrimination" were heard all the way back to Washington.[92]

He was not upset at the state of Mississippi, but rather at the federal government for allowing some states, and not others, to collect on tidelands oil leases. Since the Supreme Court's ruling a year earlier, millions of dollars from tidelands oil income belonging to Texas, California, and Louisiana had been pouring into federal coffers. The Court ruling applied to all the other twenty-one coastal states, but until the federal government filed individual suits against each of them, the states were allowed to continue collecting marginal belt revenue. Daniel also pointed out that the state of Maine was profiting from tidelands kelp beds; Florida from sponges and mineral leases; and that states such as Connecticut, Delaware, Rhode Island, and Maryland all sold shellfish cultivation leases the same way Texas had once done with oil leases prior to the Supreme Court's ruling.[93]

More frustrated than ever, Daniel was now convinced that he would have a much better chance of pushing Texas' claim by attaining higher elective office. He and Shivers had been upset with the state's senior senator, Tom Connally, who made the mistake of suggesting that a powerful tidelands oil lobby did not exist. Unknown to him at the time, that "non-existent" lobby was quietly offering Governor Shivers its support if he would challenge Connally in the upcoming election.[94] Daniel thought Shivers would jump at the opportunity to challenge Connally, thus leaving the governor's chair vacant.

In November 1951 Daniel approached Shivers in front of the Capitol and asked him point-blank if he was considering a run for the Senate.[95] Shivers expressed a lack of desire to do so and later recollected that Daniel, with tears in his eyes, urged him to challenge Connally, telling him that only he could defeat the longtime senator. Shivers replied that most anyone could beat Connally because he had failed to keep his fences mended.[96] Oblivious to Daniel's reasoning, Shivers surprised both Daniel and Lyndon Johnson by avoiding the Senate race and seeking another term as governor.

CHAPTER 9

I Like Ike!

Upon Allan Shivers' decision to run for reelection, a strong lobby quickly shifted its support in favor of Daniel for senator. Shivers also encouraged Daniel to enter the race, feeling that he had a good chance of defeating Tom Connally.[1] But Daniel was reluctant. Even before his politically ambitious college days, he wanted nothing more than to govern the state in which he was raised. Washington, D.C., on the other hand, was distant both geographically and structurally to the nature of traditional Texas politics. If only Shivers had chosen to challenge Connally, he mused, his dream of becoming governor very well could have become reality.

But upon weighing his options, Daniel began viewing a seat in the Senate not as a second choice but rather a grand opportunity to serve Texas in a greater capacity. The Senate, he came to believe, would provide him with a place to push the tidelands legislation in which he so strongly believed. So, with an abundance of statewide support and a mission in mind, he entered the race.

Tom Connally was no easy opponent. Somewhat of a legend in Texas, the seventy-four-year-old senator had chaired the Senate Foreign Relations Committee during World War II, played a vital role in the process of the United States joining the United Nations, and led the way for American entry into the North Atlantic Treaty Organization (NATO). But as time passed, he inherited a mounting list of vulnerabilities. Having served in Washington since 1917, he had let his political organization back in Texas grow decrepit. In fact, it was discovered that some people listed as Connally's county leaders were deceased. He also suffered from his close association with the Truman administration and was consequently linked by many Texans to multifarious charges of corruption in government and lenient policies toward communism.[2]

Taking these factors into consideration, Daniel liked his chances against the elder senator. On January 21, 1952, he broadcast his intentions with a thirty-minute paid spot on two Texas state networks. Introducing him was Judge Robert A. Hall of Dallas. "Good evening, fellow Texans," he began. "It is a sincere pleasure and privilege to introduce to you a true champion of the people of this state, the Honorable Price Daniel. During his five years as attorney general, Daniel has risen to the ranks of great Texans because of the way he has fought the battles of Texas in the courts and legislative bodies of our state and nation. I know Price Daniel to be a Christian gentleman, a devoted husband and the father of four children. He is a man that places the welfare of our state and nation above all personal and selfish interest. It is with pride that I present to you Price Daniel, attorney general of the state of Texas."[3]

Daniel leaned into the microphone across the studio from Hall. "I thank you, Judge Hall," he said, clearing his throat. "It is in a spirit of sincere humility and with high purpose that I come to you, the people of Texas, tonight. You have honored me with confidence in the past; you have given me your confidence three times in electing me to fight your legal battles as attorney general of this state. In these critical times, when there are even greater battles to be fought at the nation's capital, I am asking you to extend the measure of confidence that you have placed in me. Believing that there is a desperate need for a change in the direction in which our country has been going since World War II, and believing that the change can be hastened by one who has no obligations to present federal officials, I, Price Daniel, hereby announce my candidacy for the Democratic nomination for United States senator from Texas." He offered change, declaring that Washington needed "a thorough housecleaning to purge it of the over-concentration of power, greed and corruption" which he felt threatened the very foundation of democracy. He urged listeners who were interested in helping him organize a statewide organization to answer his call.[4] Within a few weeks he had received more than 50,000 letters of encouragement.[5] In fact, one Liberty correspondent observed that not since Sam Houston had the county "blazed with such enthusiasm."[6]

Senator Connally tried unsuccessfully to hide his discomfort with the level of support Daniel had been able to generate so quickly. "When I came home to look into my prospects, friends told me that Price Daniel had got word from Shivers to run against me," reflected Connally. "Shivers had promised him the support of the state Democratic organization, and for insurance Daniel had gone ahead to organize his forty deputy attorneys around the state as his local campaign managers against me. I also found out that Lyndon Johnson had been over to talk with Shivers and promised to support Price Daniel."[7] But Daniel did not pressure Johnson to choose sides. "I do not believe that I talked it over with Senator Johnson," he later stated. "I knew where he would stand. He would have to support his colleague in the Senate. But the feeling throughout Texas was that Tom Connally was full-time chairman of the Senate Foreign Relations Committee and wasn't a senator from Texas at all."[8]

Connally had leveled some sharp jabs at Daniel over his handling of the tidelands controversy, asserting that the "Texas" case should never have been confused with those of California and Louisiana. Because Daniel had bungled the case, Connally implied, many senators no longer backed Texas' tidelands claim.[9] Daniel counterpunched, insisting that had the senator paid more attention to news coming out of his home state, he would be aware that Daniel had indeed asserted Texas' unique claim at each and every opportunity. The bickering only intensified, finally prompting Daniel to send Connally a telegram: "Let's work together. It is more important for Texas to win this fight than for either of us to win this race."[10]

Many factors began causing Connally to doubt his chances of defeating the resourceful attorney general. His closest friends and advisers warned him of Daniel's growing statewide popularity as a result of his leadership in the tidelands fight, as well as his having successfully linked the senior senator with many of President Truman's unpopular policies. Even more ominous, Connally mailed a campaign advisory to his long list of supporters, but received disappointing results. A large portion of the letters had come back marked "addressee deceased" or "addressee moved—no forward address." [11] Fearing that his long and prosperous career would be scarred in the end by a bitter defeat, he chose to retire. In one last desperate attempt to derail Daniel's candidacy, Connally telephoned Shivers and urged him to run against "that young whippersnapper." [12]

Indeed, upon Connally's withdrawal, Shivers began to receive telephone calls from friends and supporters urging him to change his plans and announce as a candidate for the Senate. On April 14, Shivers squashed the rumors by issuing a statement from Austin declaring that "my answer has been that I have no plans to change my present intentions." [13]

Connally later explained the reason for his departure. "Some reporters told me that Lyndon wanted me out of the Senate so that he wouldn't have to be called the 'junior Senator from Texas' in floor debate, but I preferred to believe that Shivers had made him shiver," said a frustrated Connally. "I finally concluded that renomination would not be worth what a state campaign would cost me and my friends in money, toil, and in the tax it would impose on my strength and health. So after being in Congress since 1917, I announced my retirement." [14] As a result, Johnson telephoned Daniel and pledged his support. [15] At Daniel's request, Johnson also made calls to some prominent newspaper friends who had sided with Senator Connally, such as Amon Carter of the *Fort Worth Star-Telegram*. [16]

Following Connally's departure from the race, the Texas media was quick to back Daniel. "Had Senator Tom Connally stood for reelection, [we] would have supported him to the limit," editorialized the *Houston Post*. Now, the editors announced, "we are for Price Daniel to succeed him. He has the makings of a great U.S. senator—one who will maintain the high standard of statesmanship set by his predecessors. The *Post* heartily endorses his candidacy." [17] In northeast Texas, *The Longview Journal* prophesied: "Others may seek the post, now that the old master has announced his retirement, but there is none in sight in Texas of the stature of Price Daniel." [18] Editors of *The Sherman Democrat*, also shifting their support from Connally to Daniel, wrote that "Texas need not fear for its voice in Washington so long as a man of Price Daniel's caliber is available to plug the breach."[19]

Daniel expressed great admiration for Connally. "He was the first candidate that I ever campaigned for," he later explained. "As a boy I tacked his signs up over at Liberty for my father and Mr. E.B. Pickett, who were his campaign managers. The senator was kind to me through the years. I regretted to announce against him, but I really felt that the time had come, that he was paying more attention to Dean Acheson and to the State Department and some of the things they were doing than he was to Texas and the interests of our state. I felt that if the senator was going to be defeated anyway, which I felt positively he would be, I decided it would give me an opportunity to go on to Washington and at least try to get this four million acres of land back to Texas. That was what really interested me."[20]

As a top priority in his campaign platform, Daniel stressed the need to eliminate political corruption in Washington. He favored a "non-partisan house cleaning" which would rid his constituents of all "graft, dishonesty and disloyalty which may exist in any agency of the Federal Government." He spoke of the need to expose, eliminate, and punish those who had violated public trust and, with no obligations to any federal officials, billed himself as the best man available to push for such action. To be successful, he argued, the cleanup would have to be removed from the hands of departments, appointees, and cronies who themselves may have been under suspicion or attack and instead be assigned to a non-partisan commission. "Our country must be morally and spiritually strong before we can be physically or militarily strong," he declared. "Nothing can be successfully accomplished by our government without loyalty, moral integrity and honesty on the part of public officers and employees."[21]

Of next importance on Daniel's campaign slate was the need to increase the country's economic strength by eliminating what he called wasteful and unnecessary government spending. "Our country is taxing its people beyond all reason and spending itself into bankruptcy," he argued. "These programs must not be allowed to weaken and destroy our economic strength or reduce us to financial ruin." He then linked internal financial and moral weaknesses which he believed caused many great nations' downfall to the fear of external communist aggression which was sweeping the country in that day: "Both Lenin and Stalin have written that it would never be necessary for Communists to conquer our country by force of arms. Instead, they said they would make the United States spend itself into bankruptcy and destruction; and that is exactly what we are doing." He pointed to the country's $260 billion debt, which was more than twice as large as the combined national debts of all the countries to which the United States was sending financial aid. Furthermore, he faulted Harry Truman and his secretary of state, Dean Acheson, for much of the problem.[22]

Daniel's opponent in the Democratic primary was an East Texas congressman by the name of Lindley Beckworth, who, little known apart from his district, decided to enter the race after two White House meetings with President Truman. "Lindley got encouragement from Mr. Truman, I think, and it was a surprise to me for him to do it because we had been friends through the years," Daniel later admitted. But perhaps more surprising was the fact that Beckworth was risking fourteen years of seniority in the House and a very important committee assignment for what one historian opined was "almost certain defeat."[23] During the campaign, Daniel accused Beckworth of being a tool of the CIO and charged him with pushing such issues as spending, taxing, socialized medicine, as well as being lax on the tidelands.[24] Beckworth traversed Texas with his family, often speaking to small handfuls of voters at town squares. A dramatic orator, he would routinely remove his coat, roll up his sleeves, and accuse his opponent of being driven solely by selfish interests.[25] But Beckworth had trouble negating Daniel's charges and could do little to counter the snowball effect of his popularity.

Nevertheless, Daniel put himself on an even more grueling campaign schedule than he had undertaken during his attorney general races. He rode countless city streets in a decorated Chevrolet with a loudspeaker on top. Delivering more than ten speeches a day, he could be heard on street corners, in churches, cafes, auditoriums, and even courtrooms, urging voters to reject "Trumanism" and demand the cleansing of big government.[26] "We must get our country back to God and our government back to the people," he would routinely say.[27] On one occasion, having promised to deliver the main address at the annual Variety Club dinner in Dallas, a strictly black-tie function, Daniel stepped down from a Pullman car wearing a brown suit and matching shoes. "Did you remember that this was to be a 'black tie' affair?" asked Dallas campaign manager Robert Hall. Daniel began fishing through one of his bags. "I brought one," he responded, holding up an old, wrinkled black bowtie. Hall took the attorney general by the arm and hurriedly escorted him to the nearest tailor for a complete head-to-toe makeover.[28]

As in most elections, fundraising was the essential element of a winning campaign. In that realm, Beckworth was no match for the attorney general. The oil and gas support Daniel received in the election was nothing short of impressive, taking into account that he was facing a little-known candidate on a shoestring budget. Hugh Roy Cullen pitched in over $5,000, Humble Oil lobbyist Walter Woodul and family donated $3,600, El Paso Natural Gas president Paul Kayser, $3,500, oil lawyer Palmer Bradley, $2,500, and oilman George Strake, $2,500, just to name a few.[29]

When the votes were tallied, Daniel won with ease. Beckworth carried all eight counties in his district, but Daniel still managed to secure a solid 72 percent of the total votes. In fact, he collected more votes than Governor Shivers.[30]

Meanwhile, Republican presidential contender Dwight Eisenhower was catching Daniel's ear by delivering campaign speeches that echoed his tidelands sentiments. In New Orleans on October 13, 1952, Eisenhower stated: "The same administration that claims to give everything also claims to take a lot away. The attack on the tidelands is only a part of the effort of the administration to amass more power and money. So, let me be clear in my position on the tidelands and all submerged lands and resources beneath inland and off-shore waters which lie within historic state boundaries. As I have said before, my views are in line with my party's platform. I favor the recognition of clear legal title to these lands in each of the forty-eight states. This has been my position since 1948, long before I decided to go into politics."[31]

But despite Eisenhower's pro-tidelands position, Daniel debated with his conscience whether he could support a candidate from the party that he, his father, and grandfather had so adamantly opposed. He felt obliged to give Democratic nominee Adlai Stevenson a chance to plead his position on the tidelands and sent him a packet on August 12 containing a legal brief outlining the Texas case along with some questions of his own. He understood how important it was for Stevenson to carry Texas if he were to have a chance of defeating Eisenhower, but was also mindful of the nominee's frequent remarks condemning state efforts to claim the tidelands. For the candidate to change his position now would be seen as nothing more than a last-minute compromise of principle to capture Texas' twenty-four electoral votes. After Stevenson avoided the issue for some time, Governor Shivers decided to pay him a visit in Springfield. On August 23, after four hours of intense conversation about the Texas tidelands, the governor returned home declaring that he would not vote for Stevenson.[32]

Upon hearing Shivers' account of his meeting with Stevenson, Daniel publicly called on fellow Texans to take drastic action. On August 25, claiming that party loyalty was less important than principle, he summoned Texans to revolt against the national Democratic Party, which he said "ignores our views" and "tramples our Annexation Agreement." To facilitate this, he vowed to devise a way whereby Texas Democrats could vote for a set of electors under the Democratic column who would support a presidential candidate favoring Texas' claim to the tidelands. That way voters could choose between state and national party electors.[33]

Daniel was fully aware that he was placing his political career on the line. Not only was he sharply criticizing Harry Truman and the national Democratic Party, but he was urging Democrats to support a Republican nominee. If voters did not feel as strongly as he that principle outweighed party loyalty, he realized that his political career could come to an abrupt end. In an interview some years later, Daniel would concede that he thought at this point in his life he would never win another elective office in Texas.[34]

The Texas Republicans had some tricks up their own sleeves. At their state convention in late August, delegates voted to support the full slate of Democratic nominees for state office. They realized that support for Eisenhower in Texas was growing rapidly and that their election chances would improve if Democrats were not drawn to the polls by state contests. Therefore, to his dissatisfaction, Daniel would also appear on the Republican ballot. It was an unprecedented action, one which blurred state party alignments almost beyond recognition.[35] Daniel did not wish to have the support of the Republican Party and, unlike Governor Shivers and John Connally, both of whom would later switch party affiliations, he would remain a registered Democrat throughout his career.

On a rare family vacation in Colorado Springs, Daniel received a telephone call from Shivers. The governor asked him to address the Texas Democrats at the state convention in Amarillo and, within a few hours, Daniel boarded a train and hurriedly prepared his speech en route to the convention.[36] To a large, enthusiastic audience, Daniel scolded national party leaders, whom he insisted had long taken Texas for granted. And, after claiming that he had no worries about possible reprisals against him from national Democratic leaders, he was greeted with thunderous applause. Television spotlights swept across the auditorium as spectators proudly waved Texas flags.[37]

By the end of the convention, delegates passed a resolution placing Stevenson and Sparkman on the ballot, while at the same time urging Texans to vote for the Republican nominees. Knowing Daniel's ability to drum up public support, Shivers urged him to announce publicly for Eisenhower. Consequently, Daniel was persuaded to introduce Eisenhower in Houston on his upcoming campaign swing through Texas.[38]

Grateful for the Texan's support, Eisenhower had his train stop in Liberty on the morning of October 13 to pick up Price and Jean. En route to Houston, the Daniels helped the president celebrate his sixty-second birthday by sharing a piece of cake and discussing strategy.[39] A few hours later, Daniel stood in front of 15,000 people gathered outside the Sam Houston Music Hall and boasted that he was a Texas Democrat who was going to vote Republican. Eisenhower then took the podium amidst vigorous applause and praised Daniel for his valor in the tidelands struggle. "He thinks the Texas tidelands ought to belong to Texas," Eisenhower professed. "So do I." [40]

The following day, after a private conference with Harry Truman, National Democratic Chairman Stephen Mitchell, from the steps of the White House, produced a picture of Eisenhower and Daniel together. He insisted that Daniel's support of the Republican candidate would ultimately bar him from Democratic patronage. Not intimidated, Daniel responded: "I may return to Texas without any patronage, but I promise you I will return with my principles." [41]

The battle was about to grow even hotter. The following week Stevenson made a campaign swing through Texas lambasting both

Daniel and Shivers for defying the party. As Lyndon Johnson and Sam Rayburn sat quietly behind him on the speaker's platform, Stevenson accused Daniel and Shivers of disseminating false propaganda about the personalities involved and the issues at stake.[42] Angered by what he felt was unjust criticism, Daniel responded four days later in a statewide radio address branding Stevenson's charges not only erroneous and misleading but also a grave insult to the integrity of all Texans.[43] Johnson and Rayburn, fearing that a revolt could lead Democratic congressmen from inland states to desert the tidelands battle in Washington, continued to support Stevenson. But that explanation was only given in public. Behind the scenes, they were more concerned with holding the party together and winning the presidential election.[44]

More so than Johnson, Rayburn was infuriated at Daniel and Shivers. He urged them to reconsider defying the party. "Granted that Stevenson is wrong on this question," Rayburn would plead, "does that make Eisenhower and the reactionary-isolationist Republicans right on every other issue?" Indeed, Daniel had gambled his entire political career on a single issue, but considered Rayburn's stern beliefs about party loyalty a reflection of the attitudes of his generation. Born in 1882, the future House Speaker was reared in a time when the Civil War was still fresh on southerners' minds. In fact, his father had been a member of the Confederate army.[45] Daniel later described Rayburn as a "real southern gentleman," but conceded that the Speaker "could clam up and be pretty rough at times, too." He recalled the chilly reception he received from Rayburn at a black-eyed-pea dinner in 1952—the first time the two had seen each other since Daniel had endorsed Eisenhower. Rayburn exhorted, "Get out of my way. I don't want to see you. I want to see Jean." He stormed past Daniel and began to engage in conversation with Jean, who happened to be a distant cousin.[46] Although Rayburn was having fun, Daniel believed that to some extent the Speaker's behavior was driven by deep-seated resentment.

Rayburn's appeals did not prevent Daniel from using his rising popularity to help carry Eisenhower by 132,750 votes in Texas. He had gambled and won, for if Stevenson had been victorious, the Texan may have jeopardized his Senate career.[47] Daniel, with virtually no opposition in the general election, received a whopping 1,895,142 votes. He had helped buck not only his own party, but a

regional tradition dating back to the Civil War. Only one time before, in 1928, had Texas voted Republican in a national election.[48]
Years later, Rayburn would privately concede to Jean that had he
been attorney general of Texas, he probably would have followed
the same course as Daniel regarding the tidelands. Johnson would
also sympathize with Daniel, telling him that he could "always be
proud of supporting Eisenhower."[49]

CHAPTER 10

Washington

A s a member of the Senate's freshman class of 1953, Price Daniel stood to gain from the timely nomination of Lyndon Johnson as minority leader. Johnson, who put the revitalization of the ailing Democratic Party atop his list of priorities, worked hard to convince the party's steering committee to ease up on its traditional seniority rule. He felt that the seniority system, by which the longest-serving Democratic senators (usually southern conservatives) would be appointed to more prestigious committees, was preventing both the nurturing of fresh ideas and party cohesiveness. "We have old members who have everything, and want more, and the younger, abler men sit under the trees and do nothing," he told Adlai Stevenson. "We are opening up nine to ten committee assignments for the younger men." As a result, Hubert Humphrey of Minnesota and Mike Mansfield of Montana landed seats on the powerful Foreign Relations Committee; Russell Long of Louisiana on Finance; Albert Gore, Sr., of Tennessee on Foreign Commerce; George Smathers of Florida on Interstate and Foreign Commerce; John F. Kennedy of Massachusetts on Labor and Public Welfare; and Price Daniel on Senate Interior and Insular Affairs.[1]

There was some unfounded speculation about which party

Daniel would line up with upon his arrival in Washington. Legally, because he was nominated by the Republican Party, he could have registered as a Republican. The Senate was almost evenly divided between both major parties, so his decision had a great effect on the balance of power. Prominent Republicans tried to persuade him that since he had supported Eisenhower he might as well vote with them to organize the Senate, but Daniel registered as a Democrat.[2]

He openly described himself as a "Texas Democrat," as opposed to a "National Democrat," but at the same time made obvious his intentions to remain as independent as Sam Houston,[3] who had effectively renounced all organized political groups and claimed to have confidence only in the people of the United States. The remark no doubt turned heads in the Capitol, but also expanded the popularity of Daniel back home.

The national media was also lured to the Texan. A post-Senate election edition of *U.S. News and World Report* described Daniel as a "strapping, breezy, round-faced politician. Nearly everything about the Truman regime has received a lambasting from Mr. Daniel in recent months: China, he thinks, was given to the Communists on a platter, and Secretary Acheson should resign."[4] *Newsweek* called the senator a "big, breezy Texan who can blow a turkey gobbler's head off at 100 yards with a rifle and writes learned treatises on tidelands oil."[5] And Paul F. Healy of the *Saturday Evening Post* wrote, "Nobody could be more Texan, in heritage and thinking, than Daniel." In fact, because of the tidelands issue, Daniel was receiving more news coverage than any other freshman in Congress.[6]

Daniel's slap at the Democratic Party over the tidelands apparently did little to scar his relationship with his new senior colleague in Washington. "Senator Johnson had plenty of friends who supported Eisenhower in 1952," remembered Daniel. "He was and is a great man to try to heal any breaches or misunderstandings and to forgive and meet anybody halfway or more than halfway. So he never chided me about it at all, about supporting Eisenhower."[7]

"When I went to Washington, there was no office space left for me because one of the senators who was having to move hadn't moved," Daniel later recalled. "So Senator Johnson gave me a desk in his office and the free run of his staff. The day that the Democratic Caucus met, he asked me to go with him, and I entered the door with his arm around me." Johnson was happy to introduce his new colleague around the Senate chamber. Sam Rayburn, however, was not as quick to forgive Daniel for defying the Democratic Party. "I had committed the unforgivable sin," Daniel recalled. "He was peeved at me for several years, but he finally got over it." [8]

In order to bring proper attention to the tidelands issue, Daniel was determined to get on the Interior and Insular Affairs Committee, which was going to handle the bill. He wisely enlisted Lyndon Johnson's assistance. "I was at his [Johnson's] house when the campaign was being put on to elect him majority leader," reflected Daniel. "I remember him telling several senators, or them asking him, about me and whether or not I might want to be on the committee." [9] Thanks to Johnson, Daniel earned a position on the powerful committee.

Now perched in a prime position to make noise, Daniel immediately resumed his tidelands fight. He personally drafted a bill similar to the one President Truman had previously vetoed which guaranteed all states outright ownership of submerged lands within their boundaries. Needing the support of someone with procedural experience and considerable influence, he was pleased when Senator Spessard Holland of Florida agreed to act as a co-sponsor. During the next few weeks the two men worked together to organize support for SJR 13, as it came to be called, by circulating the measure to several colleagues for their signatures, as well as having a brief White House visit with President Eisenhower. When SJR 13 came before the Interior and Insular Affairs Committee in mid-February, Daniel appeared as a witness and garnered support by utilizing the debating experience he had gained during his Baylor and courtroom days. Facing more than three hours of intense cross-examination, mostly from Senator Clinton Anderson of New Mexico, he articulately countered every argument against his resolution with both legal and historical points. His persuasiveness won the support of many committee members who before had been inadequately informed of the merits of SJR 13 and who would have influence once it reached the Senate floor. [10]

Herbert Brownell, President Eisenhower's new hand-picked attorney general, attempted to throw a knuckle ball at Daniel's plans. He proposed to the committee that the bill should include a map that delineated the exact boundaries. The map would have given the three-league limit to Texas and the west coast of Florida, and three miles to the other Gulf states. Instead of restoring the property rights, Brownell claimed that Texas wanted merely to reap the benefits. "His testimony was very disappointing," Daniel recalled. "I never shall forget Senator Guy Gordon told me at lunch after Brownell had testified that he never heard such a damn-fool presentation in his life. I remember that the day after his appearance is the day that I had lunch with President Eisenhower. The President asked me if Brownell had split his britches before that committee, and I told him that I certainly thought he had. I said, 'He did not testify for what you had committed yourself for—outright ownership being restored.'" [11] Brownell's testimony notwithstanding, the tidelands bill cleared the committee unscathed.

Most first-term senators were expected to spend the majority of their time watching, listening, and trying to learn the routine of that unique legislative body. However, the first major item on the agenda was the tidelands bill—a perfect opportunity for the rookie to get his feet wet.[12] Someone with Daniel's lack of experience in the Senate could expect this to be an incredibly difficult task. But he had the Senate Democratic leader on his side, offering advice and strategy to better his chances for the bill's adoption.[13]

A relatively large number of senators were present the day of Daniel's maiden speech on April 8, 1953, some of them no doubt interested in seeing if the presumptuous Texan could hold his ground. Since his desk was hardly visible in a side wing, Daniel received permission from Senator Harry Byrd to speak from his, located near the center of the chamber. He held the floor for more than four hours, delivering a twenty-six-page speech and fielding heated questions from a slate of emphatic tidelands opponents. But more importantly, for the first time he was allowed to present evidence he had been collecting. He reviewed the argument that the needs of the federal government "are paramount to 'bare legal title' and transcend the right of a 'mere property owner,'" and concluded that such a theory would lead to further nationalization of property and increasing centralization of government. "If this rule is followed to its logical conclusion," he predicted, "the federal government could take any land—public or private—within the entire country." [14]

Daniel narrowed his argument to seven points, which he presented in the form of an outline:

First. All 48 states not merely 3 coastal states, and not merely 21 coastal states, but all 48 states—have lands beneath navigable waters within their historic boundaries, title to which would be confirmed or restored by this legislation. Second. All of the 48 states have held and possessed their submerged lands, both inland and seaward, under the same rule of law, recognized for more than 100 years by the Supreme Court of the United States. Third. It would be rank discrimination against the coastal states to exclude their marginal sea lands from this rule of state ownership while continuing its application to the far greater bodies of lands beneath inland waters and the Great Lakes. Fourth. The rule of state ownership of lands under inland waters and the Great Lakes grew from the common law rule of state ownership of the lands under the marginal sea. Fifth. The coastal states have been in complete good faith in their possession and ownership of the sea bed within their historic boundaries for more than 100 years. Sixth. Under such circumstances, restoration of these lands to the states will not be a gift but an act of equity and justice. Seventh. Texas has a special claim under its annexation agreement with the United States which should be confirmed by this legislation.[15]

Senator Paul Douglas of Illinois, an outspoken opponent, told his colleagues on the floor that Daniel was probably the greatest legal expert on the tidelands issue in the country. Daniel smiled and replied: "I thank you for the compliment. Now I'm waiting for your blows." Douglas, responding to the invitation, accused the Texas senator of pushing legislation that was too generous to Texas. "We are being more generous to Texas than to my own state," Douglas complained, referring to the fact that Texas would be granted more land beneath inland waters than Illinois. Daniel did not miss a beat with his quick response: "Isn't it true the Lord was generous to Texas, not the Senator from Illinois or the United States Senate?" And when Senator Hubert Humphrey of Minnesota lashed out at Daniel's reasoning, the Texas senator accused the Minnesotan of inconsistency. How could Humphrey claim the federal government owned the rights to coastal states' waters, yet at the same time argue that Minnesota and other inland states should retain submerged water revenues? "You're in the same boat with Louisiana and Texas and you just don't know it yet," he proclaimed.[16]

Humphrey, one of Daniel's staunchest opponents, admitted afterward that "the senator from Texas almost persuaded me. His arguments have been remarkable, and I say that in all seriousness."

Another of Daniel's opponents, Senator Herbert Lehman, referred to what he had heard that day as "brilliant." And Walter George, the elder statesman of Senate Democrats, called Daniel's work one of the greatest maiden speeches he had ever heard.[17]

The Texas media was also highly complimentary. An article in the *Fort Worth Star-Telegram* stated: "Reporters and other observers were impressed by Daniel's apparent knowledge of his subject. As an opponent of the legislation would ask a question, Daniel would come back almost immediately with a quotation from a past decision." [18] And the *Houston Post* was equally flattering: "It was a masterly address, eloquently compelling in its logic. Senators Lyndon Johnson of Texas, Long of Louisiana, George of Georgia and others rose spontaneously on the Senate floor to praise it. If any disinterested senators were sincerely undecided as to the merit of the senate bill confirming the state's title to their offshore lands, Senator Daniel's presentation of documented facts and logic should have convinced them." [19]

While some praised Daniel's maiden speech, others were ready to debate. Senators Humphrey, Douglas, and Anderson waged an around-the-clock filibuster in a last-ditch effort to kill SJR 13. But none could match Wayne Morse of Oregon, who spoke continuously for over twenty-two hours, setting a new Senate filibuster record.[20]

Daniel and Holland responded to the call, taking the floor for twenty-seven consecutive days in stout defense of SJR 13. "Senator Holland and I were on the floor all during the twenty-seven days, but we were on the floor day and night around-the-clock for a period of about a week," Daniel remembered. "One of us would sleep while the other stayed on the floor; one of us would go back to the cloakroom and get a little sleep." The around-the-clock sessions were actually the idea of Johnson, who worked closely with Senator Robert Taft of Ohio to ensure that Daniel held the feet of his opponents to the fire throughout the filibuster. Eventually, the opposition surrendered.[21]

On May 5 the pro-Texas tidelands legislation passed the Senate by a vote of 56 to 35, ending the longest congressional debate in more than fifteen years. Daniel, who had occupied the floor as a leader for more than a month, could finally enjoy the fruits of his labor. The bill now moved to the House. But he had to be sure the House did not amend the measure. "If the House had passed an amendment just dotting an I or crossing a T, that would give the Senate an opportunity to have a filibuster on concurrence. So we never wanted that bill to get back to the Senate," Daniel recalled. "We got busy with the House leaders and keyed them in on the situation and got them to agree that they'd pass the bill." [22] They did. All the bill lacked then was the promised signature of the president. The May 22 issue of the *Hubbard News* declared: "Undoubtedly, the happiest man in the nation's Capital this week was Texas' U.S. Senator Price Daniel who, in the seventh year of his long fight, could see victory near in the effort to restore Texas' off-shore submerged lands to the State Public School Fund." [23]

Daniel received word from Press Secretary James Haggerty that Eisenhower wanted him to be present and receive a pen at the bill's signing. Upon arriving at the White House, however, amidst a large crowd of spectators, Daniel was forced to stand near the back of the room and was unable to witness the finalization of a project he had nurtured six years. Acknowledging the oversight, Eisenhower invited him back to the White House the following day for a private ceremony at which the president signed a special copy of the bill and presented Daniel with a pen. [24]

This was a defining moment in Daniel's career. Although the tidelands fight would later resurface, the major battle was over. Back home he was hailed as a hero, a fresh overachiever in the Texas tradition. He had accomplished in his first year in the Senate what others had tried and failed, a feat he would refer to in later years as his greatest political achievement. Having resisted a compromise plan despite immense pressure from the state's most powerful leaders, Daniel had proven his critics wrong. Any doubt about the young senator's ability to get the job done existed no longer. Success in Washington had made him overwhelmingly popular in Texas, as would soon become evident. [25]

Carrying the pen Eisenhower had used to sign the bill, Daniel made a special trip to Austin, where, after being greeted by a large crowd, he proudly donated the pen to the Texas Memorial Museum. [26] His overall performance in handling the case had increased his stock even with colleagues from other states. In fact, expectations were so high for the freshman senator that Jean once felt compelled to ask, half jokingly: "Price, this is wonderful, but what will happen when they find out this is all you know?" Daniel looked at her with amazement, then began to smile. "Well," he replied, "maybe if I could get prepared on this subject, I could get prepared on another." [27]

Despite passage of the tidelands legislation, Attorney General Brownell refused to abandon his attempt to litigate whether the Texas boundary was three miles or three leagues. At one point he had an assistant, Bill Rogers, call Daniel at his ranch in Liberty and read him a release outlining the attorney general's intention of filing suit against Texas to roll the boundary back to three miles.

"Bill, this won't do," Daniel quipped. "Why does he want you to read it to me?"

"Well," Rogers responded, "he just wanted you to know about it and see if you had any comment." Daniel seized the opportunity: "My comment is, 'Don't dare do it!' I'll be in Washington as quick as I can get there by plane!" [28]

After getting word to the president, Daniel flew up to see Brownell and dissuaded him. "What made him finally decide he wouldn't file it was when I told him very casually that Senator Johnson had told me that he was going to put me on the Judiciary Committee the next session of Congress. Well, the man nearly jumped out of his chair being friendly then, because that committee handles all of his appointees. So he said, 'Well, okay, we'll put this off.'" [29] Daniel had silenced Brownell, at least for the time being, but before long their agendas would clash again.

According to the *Saturday Evening Post,* not a single Democratic senator seemed to hold animosity toward Daniel for supporting Eisenhower in the previous election. [30] On one occasion, however, the junior senator could not resist making fun of his unusual predicament. Early in his term, Senate Democrats honored Harry Truman with a luncheon upon the former president's return to Washington for the first time as a private citizen. Daniel, having strongly opposed the Truman policies in his 1952 campaign, was for obvious reasons asked by fellow Democrats to stay behind and keep an eye on the session. But he had other plans. After patiently listening in the chamber for a while, he exited the Senate floor and entered the nearby room where the luncheon was being held. When introduced to Truman, he smiled and said, "I guess I'm the rebel. Some people thought I wouldn't show up today, but, after all, if it wasn't for you I probably wouldn't be here." [31]

Daniel's heated feuds with Senator Humphrey over the tidelands issue were eventually forgotten as a new controversy swept the 83rd Congress. Both men became interested in resuscitating a bill introduced by Senator John Butler of Maryland intended to curtail communist activity in the United States. Seeing merit in Butler's idea, Humphrey asked Daniel to co-sponsor an amendment that would be more specific than Butler's and have a better chance of being upheld by federal courts. Daniel obliged, and before long the two submitted an amendment which, in effect, outlawed the Communist Party in America. After a few days of debates, both houses of Congress overwhelmingly passed the measure and the president signed it into law. For pushing what became known as the Communist Control Act of 1954, Daniel and Humphrey had successfully blunted Republican charges that Democrats were soft on communism.[32]

It was during this crusade to expose the evils (real and imagined) of communism that Daniel had an opportunity as a public servant to voice his own spiritual beliefs. In late March, speaking at the climax of an all-day "Democracy in Action" program at Howard Payne College, he pleaded: "We must make a fearless comparison throughout the world between our spiritual and religious principles and the godless teachings of Soviet Communism. We must know that democracy, as in Christianity, begins with the individual and recognizes the infinite worth of individual man." The senator continued: "The Communists teach that there is no God—that man owes his existence to the state. It is the only way that they can justify complete government control of the activities and rights of their citizens. Here we have one of the greatest conflicts between communism and American democracy. It is the weakest point in the armor of communism and the strongest shield in the armor of Americanism."[33]

A much more outspoken opponent of communism in the 1954 session, however, was Joseph McCarthy of Wisconsin. For five years McCarthy had been investigating what he called subversion in the ranks of government employees and officials, and many began to believe the senator was going overboard. At a county women's Republican club in Wheeling, West Virginia, McCarthy claimed to hold in his hand the names of a number of Communists who were working in the State Department. That remark ignited a controversy which would leave deep scars in the American political body.

As chairman of the Senate Government Operations Committee, McCarthy held nationally televised hearings throughout the spring and summer of 1954 in which he leveled serious charges against the United States Army. Mostly, he accused the army loyalty program of being lax. He also arranged a private "treaty" whereby certain Greek shipowners agreed not to trade with Red China. Furthermore, he used his powerful influence to drive four or five senators out of office who had spoken against him. As a result, both public and congressional disapproval was rapidly mounting against the Wisconsin senator.[34]

Some would insist, however, that the most ironic commentary on McCarthy's Red Scare crusade was that he had actually strengthened the Communist cause as a result of his actions. One French newspaper editorialized: "Far from being a formidable foe of communism, he also is fast becoming the precious ally of communism."[35] Indeed, he also began to attract fanatical support from many hate groups across the country. They distributed McCarthy speeches and materials and, before long, even notorious racist publications were giving the senator rave reviews. Conde McGinley, once called a "hate-mongering editor" of *Common Sense*, wrote: "Those Americans who wish to live as free men and enjoy Christian worship as they see best, should thank our good Lord for such a man as Joe McCarthy."[36]

Daniel followed the McCarthy developments closely. Like most senators, he was embarrassed by the negative publicity McCarthy was bringing to the Senate proceedings and knew it would only be a matter of time before the kettle whistled. Sure enough, on July 30, 1954, Republican Senator Ralph W. Flanders of Vermont formally introduced a resolution to censure McCarthy. Daniel, feeling strongly that senators should follow proper rules of procedure since McCarthy himself was being accused of neglecting such rules, took the Senate floor on July 31. He was concerned that the Flanders resolution did not specify charges against McCarthy, nor did it allow for any evidence to be introduced. He claimed that certain senators who had charged McCarthy with violating principles of due process were supporting a document which in itself was guilty of the same offense. Daniel called for patience, reason, and fairness when considering what actions to take against McCarthy. Above all else, he was alarmed that his colleagues would set a reckless precedent by supporting the Flanders resolution. Daniel knew that throughout the years many senators had been equally guilty of using inflammatory remarks against their colleagues and others. A quick judgment against McCarthy made in haste, he reasoned, could become a razor's edge sure to cut freedom of speech in the Senate chamber on future controversial issues.[37]

The swelling controversy soon led to the formation of a seven-man select committee to investigate the charges against McCarthy. Recognized by many senators as a legal authority on procedural matters, Daniel acted as a mediator for the committee. Along with Senator Barry Goldwater, he was asked to meet with McCarthy in a last-ditch effort to end the highly publicized matter peacefully. He assured McCarthy that senators would drop all censure efforts if he would simply retract some of his accusations and publicly admit having acted improperly.[38] Much to the dismay of Daniel and Goldwater, however, McCarthy would not give an inch. His refusal to back down accelerated the downward slide, and further losses in his popularity were reported from his home state of Wisconsin, where "Joe Must Go!" had become a popular chant.[39] Despite the road blocks, Daniel continued to search for some means by which a censure vote could be avoided.[40]

This controversy was extremely stressful for Daniel. For years he had denounced communism, long before the rise of McCarthy. From every indication, his hostility to this form of government stemmed not just from political considerations, but also from a genuine belief that its godless nature rendered it both wrong and fatally flawed. He knew well the danger of appearing to be weak against communism, but he also realized that McCarthy was becoming a separate issue, an embarrassment not only to those who opposed communism, but also to anyone who cared about the dignity of the Senate.

On November 8 the select committee formally recommended censure. McCarthy was outraged and went so far as to call the committee's chairman "stupid" and the committee itself nothing more than the "unwitting hand-maiden" of communism.[41] Daniel was now in a position where he could no longer ride the fence on censure, for a vote was certain to occur before the 83rd Congress ended in December. On one hand, he firmly believed that McCarthy had brought dishonor upon the Senate by making reckless charges against his colleagues and did not want to condone such intemperate behavior. On the other hand, he was in favor of continuing investigations into subversive activities and feared a vote against McCarthy would be interpreted back home as being soft on communism.[42] Hundreds of letters from constituents arrived at his Washington office, trying to sway him one way or the other.[43] This was one of the few moments in Daniel's political career when a decision did not come easily.

Daniel shared an affinity with the three major anti-Communist groups that had organized in Texas to deal systematically with fear of communism. There was the American Legion, an existing organization of which Daniel was a member, and two new groups: the Committee for the Preservation of Methodism, a coalition of several conservative Methodist churches, and a Texas chapter of the Minute Women of the U.S.A., Inc., a mobilized group of conservative women who had strongly supported Daniel in his tidelands crusade. Unlike Senator Johnson, Daniel had been very accommodating to the Minute Women's requests for background information of persons selected as targets for attacks. He instructed his staff to check House Committee on Un-American Activities files to determine if an individual had been named by the committee or by someone testifying before the committee.[44] His cooperation in these matters was much appreciated by the state's Red Scare activists, and he assured the groups of his "continuing efforts against communism and all subversive elements that may be found in our government departments."[45]

Daniel received heavy pressure from these pro-McCarthy groups with which he was closely associated, but like so many other times in his career, refused to allow political alliances of any kind to influence his decision-making. On December 1, to the surprise of many, he stood before a packed gallery in the Senate chamber and announced his decision to vote for censure. He had come to the decision, he explained, only because McCarthy had violated the decorum and dignity of the Senate. In Daniel's opinion, the censure resolution should be amended in such a way as to allow investigations into Communist activities to continue unabated.[46] The measure was altered sufficiently for Daniel's support, and as finally proposed condemned McCarthy only for his conduct before the select committee. Consequently, on December 2, 1954, the Senate voted 67-

22 to censure Joseph McCarthy.[47] As one biographer later noted, the condemnation ultimately "destroyed McCarthy's spirit, accelerated his physical deterioration, and hastened his death."[48]

In the end, Daniel had found an acceptable compromise that allowed him to stand firm against the threat of Communist subversion and, at the same time, condemn McCarthy's methods. He was able to support McCarthy's cause without supporting him.

It was also during this period that Daniel became a leading advocate of the "commonwealth" amendment to the Hawaiian statehood bill. "The argument we are making for commonwealth status as an alternative is not idle talk," Daniel insisted. "It is not simply an effort to try to defeat statehood. If the people of Hawaii could really understand the advantages of commonwealth status, as the people of Puerto Rico understood them when the newspapers were willing to write about the subject, and if they could understand what Puerto Rico does to attract business to Puerto Rico, how much more local self-government the people of Puerto Rico have, and the advantages in the tax situation, while they still enjoy the national defense protection of the United States without contributing any money, they would see that it would be a pretty good thing for them."[49] Despite his arguments, Hawaii was eventually granted statehood on August 21, 1959.

Much like the tidelands controversy, the "separate but equal" school debate also followed Daniel to Washington. Years earlier he had watched as Thurgood Marshall attempted to reverse the *Plessy vs. Ferguson* decision of 1896 in the Sweatt case. Not until May 1954, in the famous *Brown vs. Topeka Board of Education* decision, did the Court finally declare "separate but equal" facilities unconstitutional. It meant that Congress, after nearly a century of evasion, could no longer avoid the most highly charged legal and moral issue confronting the country. For Price Daniel the landmark decision demanded great adjustment, which he accepted reluctantly but with philosophical resignation. One day after the ruling he took the floor and urged compliance among senators who were attacking the decision and predicting mass violence. He rejected the view that the Court's decision would ultimately destroy public education and urged lawmakers to set an example of compliance for the nation.[50]

The tone and content of Daniel's speech surprised many. He refused to criticize the Court's opinion. Those in the gallery who expected to hear a bitter denunciation of the ruling instead heard a call for tolerance on all sides. "It is unfortunate that there are any prejudices left; that there is even one person of the white race or of the Negro race who would still cause trouble when commingling in public places, but we might just as well face the facts," he said. "There has been trouble in the past. I hope we may not have it in the future." [51] After the speech, some tagged Daniel as the "new Southern lawmaker" for his seemingly newfound tolerance on this issue.[52] He still supported segregation, but imperceptibly, perhaps even to him, his lifelong public position on the most crucial domestic issue of the age was beginning to shift. Times were changing, and he sensed the need for a new outlook, in himself and the South.

The Supreme Court's ruling especially infuriated many southern senators, who in turn felt great pressure to adopt a common position. Several gathered in Senator Richard Russell's office to draft a document accusing the Court of acting illegally. They secretly circulated the document, which had already been revised several times, and soon received support from nearly every southern colleague. But when the document reached Daniel by way of Senator John Stennis of Mississippi, he refused to sign. The group's intemperate language would encourage disobedience of the ruling, Daniel reasoned, adding that the Supreme Court had not in any way acted unconstitutionally.[53]

Daniel's reasoning swayed many of the document's supporters, such as William Fulbright of Arkansas and John Sparkman of Alabama, so Senator Harry Byrd persuaded him to join a special committee to draft a more tactful, factual statement. This committee was composed of Strom Thurmond of South Carolina, Richard Russell of Georgia, John Stennis of Mississippi, Fulbright, and Daniel—the latter two representing those who preferred a more moderate document.[54] Remembered Fulbright, "Daniel and I insisted that we would oppose the decision only by legitimate constitutional means, that we would go along with nothing extra-legal—no force or anything of that kind." [55] Before long the committee produced a sixth and final draft of the document known as the Southern Manifesto.[56] The measure no longer accused the Court of acting illegally or glorified disobedience, yet it still expressed strong dissatisfaction with the Warren decision. According to the Manifesto, the Court had not followed the principles of the

Constitution, but instead had "substituted naked power for established law." It accused the judges of exceeding their judicial powers, asserting they had "substituted their personal political and social ideas for the established law of the land," and concluded that southerners should slow down judicial usurpation of power and use "all lawful means to bring a reversal of this decision which is contrary to the Constitution." [57]

The document received the signature of every southern senator except Lyndon Johnson, who was not asked to sign because of his role as majority leader. "Neither Price Daniel nor I, nor probably a few others as well, was for the final manifesto, but we didn't want to desert the other senators, either," recalled Fulbright. "We hated very much to stand out against our colleagues from the South. There was a sense that we were the poor part of the country, that we had historic reasons to band together against northerners who were again imposing on us. Much of that has changed now, but it was a palpable pressure in those days." [58] The Manifesto, never officially sanctioned by Congress, was presented as a resolution. But its backers did not put much muscle behind it. "It was primarily for public consumption in the South, and it probably confirmed the opinions of many that the Supreme Court had ignored the Constitution," observed one historian. "It gave constituents hope that means would somehow be found either to circumvent or reverse the Court's ruling." [59] The Southern Manifesto's introduction in Congress would mark a high point in the sectional strife over race relations during the period.

Many Texans criticized Daniel for signing the document, claiming that it was undemocratic and an open invitation for mob violence. In response, he emphasized his strong opposition to any use of federal force to implement the decree and reiterated his belief that Texans of all colors and creeds were "entitled to justice and protection of the law." [60] As in the McCarthy controversy, the Manifesto revealed Daniel's ability to find, when necessary, suitable compromises. The adjustments in language and the toning down of fiery rhetoric allowed him to continue to express concern about the Court's opinion without appearing to be a southern firebrand. If the tidelands battle had branded him rigid and unyielding, these two issues—the Manifesto and McCarthy—revealed his willingness to find common ground.

Early in 1955 Daniel received a grand jury resolution from Federal Judge Joe Ingraham of Galveston which set him on another long and winding crusade. It revealed the wide extent of illegal drug trafficking in South Texas and urged him to take action that would strengthen federal agencies. Adding to his concerns, Charles F. Herring, U.S. attorney for the Western District of Texas, mailed Daniel's Washington office alarming statistics concerning drug sales and usage. This news came at the same time reports were filtering through Congress that Communist China was flooding the Far East with narcotics to weaken several allies of the United States.[61]

Daniel expressed concern on Capitol Hill, and on March 28 Senate colleagues selected him to head a special investigative subcommittee to direct a nationwide narcotics probe. Vowing to keep expenses at $30,000, much less than the Senate was willing to appropriate, he was determined to produce feasible, specific recommendations for new federal legislation. Beginning in June his committee conducted a two-week series of intensive hearings, quizzing over 100 individuals and producing 2,000 pages of testimony. Witnesses in Washington and Philadelphia charged that Communist China had actively sought to addict American soldiers in Asia. A young woman claimed her addiction to marijuana, opium, and heroin had led to prostitution and thievery, and two federal prosecutors testified in favor of legislation to permit wiretapping in narcotics cases. In August, Daniel journeyed overseas with a few other senators to represent the United States at the Atoms for Peace Conference in Switzerland. While there he studied drug problems in Italy, France, and England. Upon returning home, he continued his extensive narcotics probe along the eastern seaboard.[62]

The ongoing hearings quickly thrust Daniel back into the national spotlight. As the subcommittee traveled from city to city, he held televised press conferences, outlining his daily itinerary and latest findings. The hearings made him a well-known political personality, as hordes of news correspondents and photographers from across the country regularly reported on his often off-center, colorful witnesses.[63]

In the course of the investigation Daniel learned of massive Mexican involvement in the narcotics trade. In an October committee session at the Driskill Hotel in Austin, Col. Homer Garrison, head of the Department of Public Safety, informed him that over 90 percent of all marijuana and heroin in Texas had originated from south of the Rio Grande. As a result of this and other narcotics leaks, he contended, the state ranked sixth in the country in illicit drug traffic. By mid-October, after further probes in San Antonio and Houston, Daniel learned that the largest shipment of illegal cocaine ever to enter the United States had passed through Houston in false-bottom suitcases en route to New York City before being seized by federal agents. Throughout November he traveled to Los Angeles, San Francisco, Chicago, and Cleveland to question several underworld figures about the easy accessibility of narcotics. One witness claimed that he could leave the room and return in twenty minutes with an impressive load of heroin. Wherever the senator traveled, the stories he heard from young and old alike were strikingly similar.[64]

On November 26, in the midst of the investigation, Daniel returned to Washington and received word that his mother was seriously ill back in Liberty. He caught the next flight home, where he sat with family members by her bedside. He had arrived just in time, for Nannie Daniel would not make it through the night. In a December 8 letter to a friend in Austin, the senator best expressed his feelings: "Although I shall miss her greatly, it was God's will, and I pray that He will make me more worthy of her life and love."[65]

The Daniel hearings concluded in December and were regarded as the most extensive congressional probe of narcotics traffic in history. Over a seven-month period the subcommittee had collected more than 8,000 pages of testimony from 357 witnesses across the United States and abroad. And Daniel had done this, as promised, by spending only $30,000, which was $20,000 less than the Senate had appropriated.[66]

When the second session of the 84th Congress convened in January 1956, Daniel gave Senate colleagues an account of the subcommittee's results and recommendations. Illegal narcotics trafficking was a business worth $500 million annually, he reported, and was responsible for one-quarter of all reported crimes in the United States. Even more alarming was the number of drug addicts pumping a steady flow of money into the pockets of these narcotics smugglers. According to the subcommittee, there were over 60,000 drug addicts in the United States, thirteen percent of whom were under the age of twenty-one. To curtail such activities, the subcommittee advocated a global crusade against narcotics with a special emphasis on Communist China. Furthermore, the sale of heroin was to be outlawed and the number of narcotics agents increased immediately by 100. The subcommittee concluded that punishment was lax in too many instances and that current federal laws were ineffective in stopping drug peddlers.[67]

Daniel felt the death penalty should be an option in extreme cases, such as the one in which a man started forty high school students on heroin in San Antonio. "Heroin smugglers and peddlers are selling murder, robbery and rape, and should be dealt with accordingly," he said in a Senate speech. "Their offense is human destruction as surely as that of the murderer. In truth and in fact, it is 'murder on the installment plan,' leading not only to the final loss of one life but to others who acquire this contagious infection through association with the original victim."[68] He also recommended that wiretapping be permitted in narcotics cases under sealed orders from a court. "Big time traffickers are seldom caught and convicted because they avoid all direct contact with the peddlers and ultimate buyers," he contended. "Their operations are almost wholly limited to the telephone. Federal agents are not permitted to intercept their communications or to use such evidence in court. As a consequence, the United States government is unwittingly giving narcotics violators, especially the larger racketeers and wholesalers, a great advantage over federal law enforcement officers in their effort to stamp out illicit narcotics traffic."[69]

Daniel formally introduced a bill on April 30 which he claimed targeted much of the narcotics corruption uncovered during the investigation.[70] He urged its passage on the Senate floor, stressing the need for the death penalty in certain cases, as well as the admissibility of wiretap evidence against big dealers. Senator Morse argued that the use of wiretap data would violate basic constitutional rights and managed to build a strong consensus for his position. Willing to compromise rather than jeopardize the entire bill, Daniel dropped this section altogether. Within a few days the modified legislation unanimously passed the Senate, serving at that time as the most stringent narcotics regulations in United States history. But maybe even more important, this measure, upon becoming law, would establish expanded treatment facilities and drug education programs.[71]

It was during his Senate tenure that most Texans got their first taste of Price Daniel's strict moral code. Wrote Paul F. Healy of the

Saturday Evening Post: "More and more, Daniel has become the prototype of a strait-laced Baptist. A former teacher of Bible classes, he packs his Bible when he goes out of town and reads a short passage every night. Today he does not smoke, drink or swear. He chews on small cigars which people are always trying to light for him. His strongest expletive is 'Golly-darn!'"[72] Along with Senator Frank Carlson, a Kansas Republican, Daniel led a successful campaign to provide a nondenominational prayer room in the nation's Capitol, where members of Congress, while making tough and timely decisions, could be alone with their thoughts and prayers. "There are times when the prayer room seems to be the only place on Capitol Hill where a member of Congress can find solitude," Congressman Jake Pickle would later write.[73]

Daniel's relationship with Lyndon Johnson blossomed during their years together in the Senate. They managed to put their political differences aside on many occasions and solidified a friendship that, despite experiencing many turns in the years ahead, would last until Johnson's death. Daniel was not intimidated by the power and influence of his senior colleague. When he had a difference of opinion on an issue, he would let his view be known. One day in particular, after Johnson had gone into a tirade on the Senate floor, Daniel wrote him a blistering note: "I was embarrassed by the way you acted today." Although Johnson instructed his secretary to bury the note as deep as she could in the files,[74] it was this forthrightness that he admired in Daniel. The junior senator was not about to be a puppet in the hands of the powerful majority leader, and thus earned the lasting respect of Johnson.

Daniel continued to treasure time with his family and often went out of his way to eat three meals a day at home. Once when notified that one of his children was running a mild fever, he quickly excused himself from business at the Capitol and hurried home. When church let out on Sunday afternoons, it was not uncommon for the Daniels to load up picnic baskets in the family car and head off for a scenic drive. And one winter morning, when Price, Jr., was on an overnight Boy Scout trip, Daniel substituted for him on his paper route before reporting to the Senate chamber. He was extremely conscious of the fact that his political career placed a burden on his four children. Each semester they were transplanted from schools in Austin to schools in Washington,

D.C. Therefore, the Daniels tried in every way to accommodate their children. Their Liberty ranch, Holly Ridge, remained a frequent vacation destination for fishing, hunting, cookouts, and horseback riding. In fact, so popular was Holly Ridge with the children, it eventually evolved into the family's primary residence.[75]

In the 1956 session of Congress a hot debate reemerged concerning the process of electing a president and vice president. For some time a number of prominent senators, including the likes of Henry Cabot Lodge, had pushed for changes in the electoral college but had failed to make much progress. Daniel became the leading spokesman for a proposal to abolish it and, instead, divide the electoral votes in each state to match the candidates' percentages of the popular vote. Under this proposition, if a candidate were to win three-quarters of Texas' popular vote, instead of automatically pocketing all of the state's electoral votes, he or she would win only 75 percent. Electoral college reform was necessary, Daniel argued, because under the present system it was possible for a presidential candidate receiving a majority of the nationwide popular vote not to get the majority of the electoral votes. (Such had been the case in 1888, when Benjamin Harrison actually received fewer votes than Grover Cleveland but received an electoral college victory with 233 votes to Cleveland's 168.)[76] Public opinion was on Daniel's side. It was widely believed that Texas and the South were throwing away millions of votes each election. Once a majority vote was reached, many argued, all of the Democratic surplus votes were wasted. Under Daniel's plan, a vote in Texas would count as much as one in New York.[77]

An editorial appeared in the *Austin-American Statesman* on March 11 entitled, "DANIEL ELECTORAL PLAN HAS TOP SENATE CHANCE." It predicted that "support for reforming the electoral college system can be expected" if proponents could simply get together on the proper method.[78] Over the next few days Daniel realized this would be an arduous task. Expecting rough waters ahead, Daniel and company looked for allies. They found support from another group which preferred allowing state legislators to give one electoral vote to the leading presidential candidate in each congressional district, with the candidate who captured the whole state pocketing the two remaining electoral votes. Leading this charge was South Dakota Republican Senator Karl Mundt. Realizing that one group had little hope without support from the other, Daniel and Mundt compromised by combining the two proposals into one heavy package and delivering the results to the Senate as a proposed constitutional amendment.[79]

In a news conference afterward, Daniel contended that the amendment would most likely increase voting in the South since both parties would have a chance to influence the electoral vote. Mundt concurred, adding that it would "no longer be necessary to play up to the big metropolitan states" in picking presidential candidates. "Previously it was always asked, 'Who can carry New York City?'" he quipped. "Under the amendment the question would be, 'Who can carry the nation?'"[80]

Despite the proposed amendment's complexity, the Daniel-Mundt coalition managed to muster a broad range of support. Southern Democrats were told the proposal would increase their influence in the party, northern Democrats that they would have permanent control of the White House, Republicans that they would gain strength in the South, and so on. And within a few months a large bipartisan group of senators joined Daniel and Mundt in co-sponsoring the measure, which appeared to ensure the two-thirds vote necessary for an amendment.[81]

Many liberals had serious doubts about the Daniel-Mundt package, however, believing it would damage the balance of the political system by eliminating the "winner-take-all" component of the electoral college. But they were even more fearful of the Mundt provisions because of the high number of congressional districts which they believed were gerrymandered. Taking the lead for this group was John F. Kennedy, who, for the first time, was beginning to emerge as an effective legislator. The Massachusetts senator was influenced by a letter he received from Arthur Holcombe, his former American government professor at Harvard, who wrote: "Under present conditions the preponderant influence of the big close states on the executive branch of the government checks the disproportionate influence of the small and often more one-sidedly partisan states in the Senate."[82]

The odds were heavily stacked against Kennedy's plans to stop the Daniel-Mundt measure. He would have to battle not only a bipartisan coalition but also widespread endorsements by the media. Kennedy researched the issue extensively, took advantage of every opportunity to speak on the Senate floor, and debated convincingly anyone who opposed him. Other than some help from a couple of colleagues who were able to provide him with statistics showing the great extent of congressional district gerrymandering, Kennedy was on his own. He relied on wit and a strong grasp of American history to respond effectively to attacks from all directions. He referred to the Daniel-Mundt package as nothing more than a "shotgun wedding" and scoffed at the "hybrid monstrosity" which had come about as a result. He also insisted the bill was a detriment to all groups it was proposing to help, from the northern and southern Democrats to the conservative and liberal Republicans.[83]

On the floor, Daniel agreed with Kennedy that a direct vote for president and vice president was not the answer, but suggested that "we should get as close to it as we possibly can." Kennedy quickly responded: "The reason why the senator may also be against direct elections is that it would place tremendous influence, a disproportionate influence, in the major, pivotal states. So the senator wants to go just far enough to deprive the states of their rightful influence, but not to go so far in the other direction as to give them what they truly deserve."[84]

"Not a single argument," Kennedy pleaded, "has been put forth for adoption of this radical change which is demanded by no state, which has been discredited in the past and which promises only doubt and danger for the future.... I know of no other step which could be taken to disrupt more thoroughly and more dangerously the American constitutional system." In the end, Kennedy's tactics proved remarkably successful.[85] Fifty-four senators originally signed the amendment, but several withdrew their support as the debate progressed on the floor. The final vote was forty-eight to thirty-seven, far short of the necessary two-thirds.[86]

Discouraged that the "compromise" revision of his proposal failed to muster enough support, Daniel agreed to send it back to the Judiciary Committee for further study. But throughout the remainder of his years as a public servant, he would never regret this battle. The day would come, he contended, when Congress would adopt such an amendment making electoral votes reflect popular totals. Many senators insisted that Daniel's original plan might have succeeded had he not compromised with Mundt.[87]

Back in Texas, Governor Shivers' third term in office was being severely scarred by statewide dissatisfaction with many of his programs as well as allegations of corruption. Farmers and ranchers, comprising a large block of the electorate, were fed up with Shivers' handling of the great drought that had begun plaguing the Southwest as far back as 1951. The governor, they insisted, had failed to establish a state disaster fund or a comprehensive water program. Moreover, some existing programs were either wrapped excessively in red tape or had extremely tough eligibility requirements.[88] Also haunting Shivers were the insurance scandals of the 1950s. State regulations had been notoriously lax on the industry, causing insurance companies to sprout up in large numbers and, more often than not, go out of business. In fact, at one point Texas was home to 215 of the 793 legal reserve life insurance companies in the nation. In 1955, at the height of the problem, Lieutenant Governor Ben Ramsey had informed the state legislature that due in part to inadequate laws, eighty-six insurance companies had folded within the past decade.[89]

Daniel had been keeping a hawk's eye on political developments back home. With the exception of the tidelands controversy and a few other wars he had waged, he was not content in Washington. The daily routine of a senator was not to his liking. His energy was constantly devoured by having to labor over thousands of individual assistance requests from home, and he often complained of having to spend more time running errands and doing favors than studying important issues. Furthermore, he was growing homesick for Texas. As far as he was concerned, his mission in the United States Senate had been accomplished.[90]

Governor Shivers remained a powerful Texas icon. However, as evidenced by the fact that the Shivercrat coalition was rapidly losing supporters to liberal groups, the Democratic Party was crumbling around him. In fact, four Texas factions of Democrats had emerged—Brass-Collar Democrats, Liberal Loyalists, Shivercrats, and Wright Morrowcrats.[91] It had become apparent by 1956, when Shivers announced that he would not seek reelection, that whoever was going to lead the party would have to have the capability to weld a coalition of divergent elements. Many of the governor's enemies accused the Shivercrats of attempting to head off a liberal victory in the upcoming election by enticing Daniel, whom one writer called "their last relatively popular candidate," to leave the Senate and run for governor.[92] But Daniel, who was never that close to

Shivers and who even attempted to dissuade him from seeking re-election two years prior, did not need to be drafted. Nothing would have kept him from entering the fray.

On March 12, with two years remaining in his Senate term, Daniel all but announced his candidacy in a statewide radio broadcast. Declaring that before becoming an official candidate he wanted to hear directly from the people, he asked for 25,000 Texans to write him in favor of his candidacy within two weeks. Nine days later his mailbags were full of letters, easily surpassing the quota.[93] On March 25 he flew to Dallas and officially announced himself a candidate for governor of Texas.

At first Lyndon Johnson was not pleased by his colleague's decision. "He thought I was foolish," Daniel recalled. "He tried to talk me out of it. When he saw that I had my mind made up, he then was helpful in trying to plan ahead in ways that would be helpful to me. The main thing he wanted to be sure of was that we would work as a team, if I was elected governor, on water development in Texas and on Democratic Party machinery, such as the State Democratic Executive Committee—that I would work with him on seeing that his enemies didn't get on that committee and take over the party in Texas. He proposed that we work together there." [94] Shivers later recalled a conversation with Johnson at the LBJ Ranch concerning Daniel's decision to return to Texas and run for governor. "Bentsen was threatening to run for governor then and several others," noted Shivers. "But Lyndon told me himself that he thought Daniel was the only one who could actually beat Yarborough." [95]

Daniel's decision was almost unprecedented. In fact, Sam Houston was the only other Texan who had come home from the Senate to run for governor. As George E. Reedy wrote in *The U.S. Senate,* "Texas, at that time, had a long tradition of separating its politicians between those interested in state office and those who sought seats in the House and the Senate. Generally speaking, there was an unwritten truce between the two groups that they would leave each other alone. There were a few exceptions in which a politician on one track would cross the line and run for another office—such as Price Daniel." [96] Upon announcing his decision, Daniel turned heads in Washington by claiming that he would "rather be governor of Texas than president of the United States." [97]

CHAPTER 11

The Race of '56

Price Daniel was pitted against a variety of characters in the 1956 Democratic primary. There was Pappy O'Daniel, known for traveling across the state with a red firetruck and his hillbilly band; J. Evetts Haley, a noted right-wing Texas historian; Reuben Senterfitt, a former Texas House Speaker; and J.J. Holmes, a racial integrationist.[1] But the senator's most serious challenge would come from Ralph Yarborough, the state's foremost liberal politician. Yarborough, who had already run for governor twice and lost both times, had never really quit campaigning since his last defeat two years earlier.[2] He had been badly beaten by Shivers in 1952 and lost again in a runoff election in 1954.[3] Yarborough was banking on success in 1956, for he had the support of organized labor groups and most other liberal Democrats. The July 28 primary was expected to be close.[4]

Positions were quickly defined. Daniel kicked off his active campaign for governor in Harris County, the state's most populous county, by asking "true moderates and conservatives" to work together in a fight against left-wing radicals. "Let's forget differences of opinion and join together in this fight to keep out radicals who want to take over the governor's office," he pleaded. "The big issue

of this campaign is whether the government of Texas shall be controlled by the people of Texas or by the left-wing radicals."[5]
Yarborough quickly responded to Daniel's call for moderation, la-
beling himself the only candidate for governor of Texas who supported Speaker Sam Rayburn's and Senator Lyndon Johnson's program of moderation in the May conventions. "I'm for moderation,
and I'm moderate about everything except corruption in government. I do not intend to be moderate toward corruption in state office when I'm sworn in next January."[6]

Daniel's Harris County rally had been a tremendous success,
with Daniel enlisting well over 700 campaign workers. He rounded
out the week with similar engagements in El Paso, Lubbock,
Plainview, Amarillo, Wichita Falls, and Fort Worth. At each stop he
continued to blast "left-wing radicals" for disregarding Lyndon
Johnson's plan for moderation a few weeks earlier at the State
Democratic Convention in Dallas. "I am going to fight that crowd
with all my strength," he promised. "I am going to make this the
most vigorous campaign of my career to bring the truth to the people of Texas. Their attack will center on me because I am the chief
obstacle to their plot to usurp the power of the governor's office
with the purpose of chaining the government and Democratic Party
of Texas to the forces of radicalism."[7]

Daniel appointed longtime friend Joe Greenhill of Austin as his
state campaign manager and named his brother, Bill, chairman of a
"speakers bureau." And since all successful campaigns are won in
the trenches, Daniel called for 25,000 volunteers to knock on doors
and distribute literature.[8] It is unknown exactly how many workers
he enlisted, but he built a huge organization, driven by county managers and coordinated from Austin. Along with an abundance of
campaign folders, car window and bumper stickers, and mats for
local newspaper advertisements, these managers were given copies
of Daniel's personal correspondence lists containing the names of
friends and supporters in their respective areas. Consistent with
Daniel's political philosophy, each manager was responsible for the
mechanics of the campaign in his or her county.[9]

Although the managers called their own shots, Daniel expected
them to maintain the positive tone of his campaign. One letter to
the county managers asserted that "the people of Texas are tired of
the bitterness, hatred, and name calling that have characterized

some of our recent campaigns. I have no intention of dealing in personalities no matter how much mud slinging and name calling may be done by the opposition. Texas needs clean politics as much as it needs clean government, and I intend to keep my part of the campaign on a high level... worthy of the dignity which should go with the office of the governor of Texas." [10]

According to an early statewide survey released on April 13, Daniel was on top with support from 41 percent of those polled. Yarborough followed with 21 percent; O'Daniel, 18 percent; and undecided, 11 percent. [11] These results prompted a glowing endorsement of Daniel in an Austin newspaper, claiming there was "substantial evidence that the middle-ground area of citizenship is fed up with the excesses of both sides (liberal and conservative)." According to the editorial, Texans were "fortunate this year in having in the governor's race a man who represents the moderate, middle-ground sentiment, ideas and ideals. He is a man who can appeal to all by the devotion to principle, integrity and good government." Continued the endorsement: "That man is Price Daniel," who "would be a governor of all the people, united on a common ground of sound principle and constructive service to Texas." [12]

During the election Yarborough charged Daniel and Allan Shivers with responsibility for certain irregularities of the Veterans Land Board. Composed of Bascom Giles (commissioner of the General Land Office), Shivers, and then-Attorney General Daniel, the board directed a $100-million program by which the state purchased land for resale to veterans. Shivers and Daniel customarily sent aides to sit in for them at the board meetings. Giles, on the other hand, stayed on top of all board activities and soon found himself involved in an illegal "block deal" scheme. Friends of his would buy a ranch, cut it into small tracts, jack up the price, and find veterans to buy the tracts from the Veterans Land Board. They sold the tracts to the state for quick cash and pocketed huge profits. [13] Yarborough publicized reports of fraud and irregularities, which resulted in investigations by grand juries and Senate and House committees. The charges did little to damage Daniel, but instead sent Giles, who had just been elected to his ninth term, to the penitentiary for six years on charges of misrepresentation and perjury. [14]

O'Daniel also tried to link Senator Daniel to the Veterans Land Board scandal, but his popularity had plummeted to the degree that such attacks fell on deaf ears. In fact, only 1,500 people attended the announcement of O'Daniel's candidacy in Waco, compared to 8,000 who had turned out in the same town in 1938. But nothing took the air out of O'Daniel's sails more than a Houston multi-millionaire by the name of Hugh Roy Cullen. Cullen had been a strong financial backer of O'Daniel and exerted great influence in the business community; however, it soon became evident that Cullen's allegiance to O'Daniel was purely pragmatic and had little to do with issues or principle. Cullen attempted but failed to persuade Daniel to stay in the Senate, and then switched his allegiance to the senator. It was a fatal blow to O'Daniel's campaign. The only candidate now breathing down Daniel's neck was Ralph Yarborough.[15]

Yarborough, who formally launched his campaign on June 1, made the elimination of political corruption a top priority. "Tonight, we meet together in our final campaign to lift the reputation of the Lone Star from the dust where it was flung by greedy men," he declared. "We will raise it high again, to the hallowed place where our forefathers lifted it."[16] As the campaign progressed, Yarborough attempted to link Daniel with the corruption that he insisted was pervasive in Texas politics. A vote for Daniel, he declared, was an endorsement of the continuation of everything that was unethical and corrupt in government. Subtly, Yarborough even sought to slight Daniel's World War II military record. "I entered the Armed Services, as he did," reflected Yarborough in a campaign speech. "I served overseas, as he did. (But) I served overseas before the fighting ended."[17]

Yarborough made "party disloyalty" the center of daily attacks, referring to Daniel's defection to the GOP and Eisenhower in 1952. He proudly hailed himself as "the only true Democrat" in the race, citing his unbroken record of support for Democratic nominees in all brackets. In turn, Daniel found himself having to prove his loyalty to the Democratic Party. He tried to deflect Yarborough's charges by insisting that party regularity was not as much of an issue as he had expected, adding that those who disagreed at least understood his position. Cleverly, he explained his support of Eisenhower in terms of what was best for the children of Texas. "It came down to a question of the Democratic candidate or the school children of Texas," he would say. He vowed to work hard for the Democratic Party in the future, but confessed that if a Democratic presidential nominee were once again to oppose Texas on a serious question, he would be forced to weigh his options. "I'm not trying to leave an escape route," he contended. "What I'm trying to get over to you is that I want to support the Democratic candidate, but at the same time I don't want to tie my hands if an issue comes up that seriously affects the state."[18]

Yarborough, while campaigning hard, encountered some setbacks. For instance, his racial stand failed to attract urban liberals. He had spoken out against "forced" integration and thus forfeited an endorsement by the NAACP. He tried to make headway by stressing proposals for soil and water conservation, old-age pensions, and increased funding for schools, teachers, and public health. However, he hurt his cause by referring to Daniel as "junior," underscoring the fact that he was Texas' junior senator, as well as calling his own backers who decided to support Daniel "turncoats."[19]

Daniel focused on a number of issues. He appealed to the farm vote by accusing the Congress of Industrial Organizations (CIO) of attempting to take over Texas farms and ranches and pointed out that, from 1952 to 1955, the national net farm income had declined 28 percent. He expressed support for new farm legislation which required the selling of cotton on the world market at competitive prices and, at the same time, would prevent further reduction in acreage allotments. In addition, he called for lobby restrictions, school improvements, narcotics control, old-age pensions, and water conservation.[20]

Daniel also received valuable support from his Senate colleague Lyndon Johnson, the Texas press, as well as big oil and corporate interest groups. The latter sent thousand-dollar campaign contributions via persons such as Texas Eastern Transmission vice president Charles I. Francis, Rex Baker of Humble Oil Company, E.B. Germany, Lamar Fleming, and corporate attorney Leon Jaworski.[21] In fact, Daniel racked up nearly $370,000 in donations, well over twice as much as Yarborough and O'Daniel combined.[22]

Despite the lingering drought, Daniel turned a few heads by insisting that Texas did not have a true water shortage. "What we lack," he contended, "is a way to save some of that 85 percent of our potential water supply which runs off into the Gulf of Mexico." He reminded Texans that he and Lyndon Johnson had sponsored the bill allocating additional funds for ten new projects that came within federal navigation and flood control programs. And, as could be expected, he contended that the overall development of the state's water resources should be managed at the state level: "There is hardly a place in Texas that isn't suffering from water shortages. We must develop every river and every stream in Texas and engage in a vast dam program if Texas is to continue to prosper. My convictions are very strong on the subject. The state has the responsibility to take the lead." [23]

Support from the Texas press was an important asset to Daniel, although an earlier *Fort Worth Star-Telegram* editorial seemed to endorse Jimmy Phillips, a conservative state senator who had hinted of gubernatorial aspirations. Daniel asked his friend Raymond Buck to look into why the article had been written, and the wealthy insurance executive soon returned with good news. The newspaper did not support Phillips, but wanted Daniel to remain in the Senate because his replacement might be less satisfactory. And indeed, the *Star-Telegram* did eventually endorse Daniel. Likewise, William P. Hobby, editor of the *Houston Post*, had initially pledged Phillips his support but quickly changed in favor of Daniel. Even the *Lubbock Avalanche-Journal* had praised Phillips but supported Daniel once he announced his candidacy. The Lubbock daily feared Phillips would split the conservative vote, thereby enhancing Yarborough's chances. For his part, Phillips backed out of the race upon learning that Daniel had received the support of the oil industry. [24]

In late June, Daniel was outraged by a statement attributed to Yarborough and printed in a Fort Worth newspaper. While campaigning in Memphis and Iowa Park, Yarborough supposedly called Daniel the "crown prince of Governor Allan Shivers and Shivers' Republican Executive Committee," all of whom he contended were attempting to seize the upcoming September convention to throw out presidential electors. "If that is tossed to me, it is a wild and irresponsible charge, without foundation," Daniel countered. "I'll not be a party to doing that or in any other way disenfranchising anyone. And I will certainly fight to see that those presidential electors duly and legally named may be placed on the ballot." He also made it clear that the party machinery debate was not his top priority. "I intend to concentrate on the governor's race and, while I'm winning that, the precinct convention will take care of itself. I will say, however, that my friends should attend the precinct conventions, because the

September state convention is normally set up to form a platform for the new governor."[25] The precinct conventions, held the same day as the primary elections, determined who had a say at subsequent county and state conventions and thus, in effect, who would control the upcoming September 11 governor's convention.

A harsh editorial in the *Kountze News* applauded Yarborough's "crown prince" attack. Under a heading entitled "P. Daniel Too Much Like A. Shivers To Merit Governorship," the writer began: "Every day even the Republican daily papers get fuller and fuller of the incompetency of the state government and this is as good a time as any to single out one Price Daniel and say that if you are going to elect him governor of Texas in 1956 you will have more of what you've got now. Because he's the dear, dear friend of the boys who have been running Texas into the mud and slime for the past ten years." The editorial went on to say that Texas was in need of a governor who was not supported by the same daily press, the same lobbyists, the same big money which it claimed had kept former Lieutenant Governor John Ben Shepperd, Allan Shivers, Ottis Lock, Ben Ramsey, and "all the other incompetent tools of their masters" in office. Calling Daniel the "white hope for the Shivercrats," the paper tagged the two men "political brothers under the skin—and their skin is thick."[26]

"Price gets more like Allan every day," Yarborough echoed on the campaign trail. "And much as he wishes they would, Texans will not forget this."[27] There were indeed striking parallels between Daniel's campaign and those of Shivers. Having shared the same opponent, Daniel hired some of the same advertising people Shivers had used, and as a result, the Shivers and Daniel campaigns were similarly organized and conducted.[28]

Yarborough's charges were not the only rough feather in Daniel's cap. Daniel's campaign managers were growing concerned by reports of splits in his conservative support. A few weeks prior, he had appeared a cinch to lead the field in the first primary. However, increased voter attention to dark-horse conservative candidates J. Evetts Haley and Reuben Senterfitt began to eat into his strength. In addition, Yarborough was enlarging the strong liberal voting bloc he had monopolized in previous races. One Daniel aide reasoned, "Every vote that will go to Haley and Senterfitt will amount to a vote for Yarborough."[29] Divisions among conservatives almost guaranteed a runoff, as well as giving Yarborough a good chance of leading the first primary.

As each crucial day of campaigning passed, more and more damaging attacks were leveled against Daniel. W. Lee O'Daniel continued his Daniel bashing in Austin by telling a rowdy crowd of 3,000 that "the people of Texas are not going to put one member of the Veterans Land Board in prison and send another to the governor's office." In a similar rally in Lockhart, he guaranteed Daniel's demise: "He's not sure of himself. He's not even sure he's going to be elected. He's hanging onto his job in Washington and drawing pay for it, but I can tell him one thing: he's not going to be elected governor." [30]

Because of Daniel's commitment to a clean campaign, he avoided responding in kind. Actually, it was unnecessary for him to comment, because the media was quick to defend him. Kenneth Towery, a Pulitzer Prize winner for his role in uncovering the scandals of the Veterans Land Board, wrote: "Probably realizing that his promises sound a little far-fetched, O'Daniel has now undertaken the task of attempting to tie Senator Price Daniel to the sordid land scandals. Here again, O'Daniel will fall flat. Price Daniel is as clean as a hound's tooth." [31]

As the Democratic primary grew near, the dark-horse candidates had little choice but to make desperate stabs at the front-runner. In early July, Senterfitt and Haley received heavy statewide newspaper coverage by calling Daniel a "proven failure" and asking him to resign from both the Senate and the governor's race. Senterfitt tagged him a "wish-wash little junior" and said that "by his own admission he can't make up his mind whether to stay in Texas with his fast-sinking campaign for governor or rush belatedly to Washington where legislation he should have attended to is sinking." Haley echoed Senterfitt's charges at a rally in Midland, but shifted the focus to Daniel's strong ties with the oil industry. He scoffed at the powerful lobby, saying that it continues to "bet on Price to come in with a political gusher when he is actually digging them a dry hole." [32]

In the face of these "shotgun" attacks Daniel confidently predicted victory. He accused the other candidates of driving away their own support by running cheap and degrading campaigns. "This election is going to prove that a clean campaigner can win in

Texas," he told a statewide group of newsmen. "I have campaigned solely upon my own record and platform without calling the name of an opponent or making any personal attacks upon them." [33] But Daniel had more concrete reasons to be optimistic, having the most solid and effective campaign in the field. Organized from top to bottom like a fine-tuned machine, his campaign did not miss a single opportunity to get a vote. Huge billboards were placed at strategic locations along highways, flashy bumper stickers and buttons were dispersed by the thousands, and surrogate speakers were lined up for every small group and function that the candidate could not attend himself. Especially impressive, even a "Price Daniel for Governor" kids' club was organized, complete with membership cards. Hundreds of children sent in for free campaign kits that gave detailed instructions on how to help elect Price Daniel governor. [34]

The campaign of 1956 was historic in that for the first time a healthy percentage of the electorate was able to get a bird's-eye view of the candidates without leaving home. The advent of television has since been credited with the downfall of giant political rallies in Texas, for no longer were mass numbers of voters willing to leave the comfort of their homes to go outside in the blistering sun and rally on the courthouse steps. Although coverage was sparse by today's standards, Daniel benefited the most in the 1956 campaign from television. "Daniel's introduction on statewide television by Fess Parker, 'the Davy Crockett of Hollywood,' was apparently successful enough to draw the fire of one of his opponents, who accused him of becoming a theatrical producer," opined the *Austin-American* in late July. [35] In fact, television advertising proved to be Daniel's most costly campaign expenditure. [36]

Shortly before the primary, twenty-seven newspaper editors and publishers were asked to sum up the governor's race in their respective regions. Sam Wood, a political writer for the *Austin-American Statesman*, said that Daniel and Yarborough were in a "neck-and-neck race" for first place: "In some sections a good many moderates, some of whom supported Yarborough in 1954, have given their support to Daniel as a result of the Lyndon Johnson-Allan Shivers fight for precinct control. Generally, though, according to the reports, Yarborough has held his former support. On the same basis there were reports that Yarborough is losing some support in East Texas ... because of the backing he is receiving from labor leaders."

The assessment also revealed that Haley had gained ground, O'Daniel was beginning to steal votes from Daniel and Yarborough, Daniel was not receiving as many votes from the old Shivers machine as expected, Houston was a "toss up," Yarborough was ahead in northeast Texas, and West Texas was "close."[37]

On election eve, Daniel campaigned in Houston, Galveston, Port Arthur, Beaumont, and Liberty. He told a hometown crowd that the leadership of Texas would fall either to the people or to outside pressure groups and special interests.[38] Many in the audience had helped him in his early legislative races. Most, if not all, had kept track of their hometown celebrity through newspaper clippings and television accounts. It was most fitting, therefore, that he finished the campaign in Liberty.

Continued pressure from Yarborough and other candidates notwithstanding, Daniel breezed through the initial vote tally. He carried the three most populous counties with nearly 629,000 votes, followed distantly by Yarborough, with about 463,400. O'Daniel, winning most of the rural old folks and the segregationist bloc, carried sixty-six counties with 347,750 votes, while Haley obtained nearly 88,800. Although the front runner, Daniel had failed to get an overall majority, which forced him into a runoff with Yarborough.[39] He had won a strong majority of the white upper-class vote, but his racial policy and ties to big business cost him the support of African Americans and laborers.

The second primary proved to be even more heated. Daniel received a crucial endorsement from Shivers, and Yarborough one from O'Daniel. Despite numerous ideological differences, Yarborough had told a group of O'Daniel's constituents in Georgetown that he desired an opportunity to carry out O'Daniel's plans. O'Daniel had originally intended to run as an independent in the November general election and figured that Yarborough would be an easier opponent to beat than Daniel.[40] Vengeful and not particularly fond of Daniel or his ardent supporter, Lyndon Johnson, O'Daniel changed his mind and tightened the race by asking his backers from the first primary to shift their support to Yarborough.[41]

Both candidates eventually pushed the limits of decency in the runoff by trying to link the other with political liabilities. Yarborough tried hard to associate Daniel with George Parr, the notorious "Duke of Duval (County)" who became known for delivering scandalously lopsided votes in five South Texas counties.[42] Daniel denied even knowing Parr, but Yarborough nonetheless called Parr Daniel's "bosom friend" and credited the Parr machine for his opponent's victories in previous races for attorney general and senator.[43] In fact, Yarborough blamed his lopsided defeat in the first primary on "every pistol-packing border boss in South Texas" who "openly endorsed my opponent and packed the votes in for him in Duval and other similar border domains."[44] Conveniently, Yarborough failed to mention that Parr had carried Duval County for him in his unsuccessful gubernatorial races against Allan Shivers in 1952 and 1954. Daniel, also playing this game, tried to link Yarborough to Walter Reuther of the CIO. His supporters circulated a photograph of Reuther giving a check to NAACP officials. Daniel's backers, who failed to mention that the photograph had been taken in Detroit and had no relation to the Texas elections, were attempting to smear Yarborough by linking him to both the CIO and NAACP. According to historian George Green, "Daniel knew that the CIO had merged with the more conservative AFL but managed to overlook it in his campaign rhetoric."[45] And Daniel also knew that the NAACP opposed and even denounced Yarborough, yet proclaimed to supporters and the media that the organization was behind him.[46]

Yarborough, now referring to his opponent as "the little man who wants to hold all the high offices," accused Daniel and Governor Shivers of having held a secret "swapping session" in the Governor's Mansion. "All my opponent's false charges against me cannot wipe out his midnight deal with Allan Shivers to swap the Senate seat for the governor's chair."[47] To crowds in Dublin, Comanche, De Leon, Eastland, Cisco, and Abilene, Yarborough described Daniel's campaign tactics as "smokescreening for as cheap and dirty politics as was ever practiced in Texas."[48]

Daniel's most effective campaign weapon proved to be support from the press. There was little Yarborough could do to stop the avalanche of statewide newspaper endorsements of Daniel, not to mention the dwindling of his own campaign funds.[49] Daniel knew that because Yarborough was still behind in the polls, things were bound to get even dirtier. During an August 20 speech in Dallas, he warned: "This last week of the campaign will bring on a smear attack against me the likes of which Texans have never seen. My opponent has accused me of responsibility for just about everything that's gone wrong in this country for the past ten years." [50]

In the closing days of the campaign, both candidates courted O'Daniel's constituency. They also made it a point to travel to towns in which they had received a poor showing in the first primary. Daniel campaigned in Galveston and Orange counties, while Yarborough brushed through Rockwall, Hunt, Collin, Denton, and Dallas counties, all of which had gone for Daniel in the first primary. [51]

When the polls closed, it was Daniel who squeaked out a victory, obtaining 698,001 votes to Yarborough's 694,830. He dominated South Texas, while Yarborough was more successful in the state's northern counties. [52] Daniel had obviously been hurt by public reaction to the Veterans Land Board scandals. Some conservatives explained the close race by pointing to such returns as the Tarrant County African American box, which favored Yarborough 1,036 to 26. Allegedly, many of the names had been inserted in alphabetical order. [53] Daniel's critics insisted that his victory margin, fewer than 3,200 votes, was due to "the Parr majority," which traditionally carried as many as 3,600 votes. [54] However, Yarborough was victorious in Jim Wells County, one of the five counties believed to be controlled by the Parr Machine. [55]

The frustrated Yarborough felt cheated. He had now lost three gubernatorial campaigns, two by narrow margins. "The big job done on me came on the run-off vote on August 25," he snapped. "That night the Texas Election Bureau gave Daniel a slight lead, but they reported that thirty thousand votes were still to be counted, and almost all were in counties favoring me. At midnight I learned that Daniel's men were seen at the airport leaving with briefcases for all parts of Texas to fix the vote. Instead of the expected thirty thousand votes, only five thousand were sent in during the next two weeks, and the fictitious certified totals sent to Shivers' Democratic Executive Committee gave Daniel a thirty-five-hundred-vote margin. There was nothing I could do about this stolen election." [56]

In the days immediately following the election Yarborough told the media that "many sizable errors" had been found in the returns, and he expected more to be uncovered. [57] A number of irregularities were reported, and a grand jury in Tarrant County went into special session to address specific allegations of fraud. [58] Yarborough supporters even claimed to have discovered hundreds of marked but uncounted ballots in trash heaps near polling places in several parts of the state.[59] In the end, however, Yarborough's charges were never substantiated. And, when presented with the opportunity, he chose not to push the issue any further. "I do not intend to file a contest in the governor's race," he said in a prepared statement a week after the election. "While I know that this will be a disappointment to the many who have furnished me with evidence of illegal voting in Webb, Duval and other counties and are urging a contest, the involved and expensive contest procedures with resulting delay make such a course too impractical to pursue." [60]

Yarborough later won the Senate seat vacated by Daniel and held it for two full terms. During that time he became highly respected on the national scene, contributing to passage of the GI bill, establishment of the Padre Island National Seashore and the Big Thicket Biological Preserve, and enactment of some major pieces of the Great Society's social advances.[61]

Daniel's victory, rather than ending controversy, set the stage for the September State Democratic Convention in Fort Worth. Actually, the die had been cast months earlier at the May convention, when Lyndon Johnson, determined to contest Shivers' control of the delegation to the presidential convention, decided to join forces with liberals in order to defeat him. Since this was a presidential election year, Johnson and Rayburn did not want Shivers, who refused to pledge support to the Democratic presidential nominee, to chair the state delegation to the national convention and exercise traditional control of the Democratic machinery. Nor did they want the labor-liberals, who had gained support as a result of the Shivers scandals, to win control. Rayburn, determined to "give Mr. Shivers a good licking" [62] and to assimilate the liberals, announced that Johnson would be Texas' favorite son for president and would also serve as chairman of the delegation to the national convention. Shivers was furious since he had planned once again to head the Texas convention forces.[63] He traversed the state denouncing Johnson and Rayburn as "ultra liberals" who were in the pocket of "radical" special interest groups such as the CIO, NAACP, and the Americans for Democratic Action. So outraged was Shivers, in fact, that he compared Rayburn to one of Texas history's arch villains, Mexican dictator Santa Anna.[64]

Daniel, happy to stay out of the fight, remained in Washington while Johnson and Rayburn traveled to Texas to make what, with the exception of one notable incident, proved to be a successful fight.[65] Johnson had wanted to elect ultraconservative Beryl Ann Bentsen as the national committeewoman, but the labor-liberals preferred Frankie Randolph, a wealthy Houston liberal who had almost personally rebuilt the Democratic organization in massive Harris County. Neither Rayburn nor Johnson could sell the liberals on Bentsen, so he withdrew and Randolph was elected in a runaway.[66]

"After seeing that they couldn't lead this group who had helped them win control, then Johnson came over to me in the Senate to tell me all about it, that they went with the wrong people to beat old Shivers," recalled Daniel. "They went with the wrong crowd. He told me about the disrespectful way they had treated Mr. Rayburn and him and wanted to know if I would work with him in trying to have a Democratic Party that we could keep and a Democratic Committee that would be friendly to him—one that wouldn't have his enemies on it, one that would be willing to work with him. I said 'Yes, I would be willing to do that.'"[67] Consequently, Johnson advised Daniel's managers not to issue an invitation to Frankie Randolph for the September convention, even though she was the highest-ranking woman official in the state party.[68] Other than the defeat of Bentsen as committeewoman, Johnson got everything he wanted at the May convention. Shivers, on the other hand, had suffered a grave defeat and later admitted that as a supporter of Eisenhower he had "no business" trying to control the Democratic proceeding.[69]

Tensions from the May convention culminated at the September state convention in Fort Worth. This time, however, Daniel could no longer enjoy the luxury of watching from the sidelines. As governor-elect he would be forced to take center stage. As expected, party factions were deep and rancorous. The liberals, most vocally represented by Ralph Yarborough, demanded a loyalty oath of all Democratic nominees so that the party bolting of 1952 would not be repeated. Arguing that the conservatives were not honoring liberal delegates duly elected in senatorial district caucuses, they were prepared to challenge a number of county delegations. The conservatives, still called Shivercrats, wanted nothing to do with a party loyalty oath and claimed the real intention of the liberals was to steal the convention by whatever means necessary, to oust Daniel, and to certify Yarborough as the party's nominee.[70]

Meanwhile, Daniel was trying to steer a moderate course somewhere between the two. He firmly opposed a loyalty oath but planned to support Adlai Stevenson. Denying he was working against the Democratic presidential ticket, he told Yarborough to end "misrepresentation and personal vilification against me."[71] Daniel knew the stakes were high. Without control of the convention, he would not be able to shape the makeup of the new State Democratic Executive Committee or even the platform on which he would run. The convention's primary purpose was to set up party machinery for the next two years. If he and his supporters were to lose control, chances of a second term for Daniel would be slim.[72]

As the convention neared, rival factions began arriving in Fort Worth to prepare for battle. In anticipation of turmoil, local officials erected a chain-link fence topped with barbed wire around the Fort Worth auditorium.[73] The liberals, contesting seven counties' delegations and threatening nine more, established headquarters at the Hilton Hotel, while the conservatives, still claiming that Yarborough's supporters hoped to steal the convention and declare him the nominee, settled in at the Hotel Texas. These factions were well aware that, in order to shape the sixty-five-member Executive Committee and control the party machinery for the next two years, they would need to secure 945 votes at the convention (the amount required to win a majority of the 1,888 total).[74]

Rumors circulated about an agreement that Daniel and Lyndon Johnson had reached on how to avoid a bitter fight. Fundamental to the deal was a strong convention endorsement of the national ticket, along with a new State Democratic Executive Committee that contained both liberal-loyalists and Daniel supporters, the latter being a majority. And there would be no loyalty oath. Each delegate would follow his or her own conscience.[75] "Johnson, Rayburn, Daniel and Shivers apparently agreed to steal the convention from the labor-liberal faction if there was no other way to win it," asserted one observer. "There was no other way."[76]

Daniel arrived in town on Sunday night, September 9, and immediately huddled with Lyndon Johnson, John Connally, and Sam Rayburn, who was determined to hold the party behind Stevenson. Rayburn emerged from the meeting claiming that senatorial districts should be allowed to name their own members of the Executive Committee and that these members should publicly support state and national party nominees. Daniel had already indicated that he would not endorse a public loyalty pledge, but would support these district caucuses if they named members from his backers. He was confident his supporters would be able to organize the convention. Johnson, meanwhile, was trying to find some middle ground. He, too, did not like party oaths, but contended that senatorial caucuses should be able to select Executive Committee members and that these persons should endorse Democratic candidates. However, Daniel inserted a major qualification: The committee should not contain members who were trying to destroy the program he had been advocating. It should, in his opinion, consist of "people interested in the Democratic Party as well as in supporting Price Daniel." [77]

As the Tuesday opening neared, tension and accusations mounted. Referring to the Palo Pinto County Sheriff's Posse that would provide door guards, Jim Sewell, a county judge from Corsicana and staunch liberal, charged state Democratic Chairman George Sandlin not only of setting up a concentration camp "guarded by storm troopers" but also of exercising "dictatorial control" in selecting a meeting hall that seated fewer than 3,000 persons and would exclude qualified, legal delegates. And all the while Yarborough called on Daniel to pledge support to the national ticket, while Daniel told him to "evidence more faith in his fellow man." [78]

All day Monday and late into the night hearings were held at the Hotel Texas to determine which delegates would be seated. More than 500 participants and spectators filled the meeting space and spilled outside. In seventeen contests the liberals were challenging 497 seats. If successful, this would give them a majority in what was being billed as the closest state convention in modern history. Pivotal was the Harris County delegation, the state's largest, with 270 votes. Its outcome was likely to determine the fate of the convention. [79]

When Yarborough arrived, he went straight to work. At a liberal rally he called on all Democrats who had voted with the Republicans in 1952 to pledge loyalty to the party. As the night wore on, he spoke to at least four caucuses, confident they were choosing a good portion of delegates committed to him. Far into the night the outcome was still too close to call. And even when

Daniel was nominated for governor that evening, the Executive Committee, after officially certifying him as the nominee, worked into the wee hours to determine contests that would decide who controlled the convention.[80]

Daniel awoke Tuesday morning to a Fort Worth newspaper headline declaring "Daniel's Chances to Control Convention Appear Shaky." [81] Indeed they did. Accompanied by Jean and his brother and sister, he arrived at the convention site (Will Rogers Auditorium) and waited in a tower office as speeches and debates rang through the auditorium below. The convention was so spirited that at one point, amid rumors that liberals were going to seize the rostrum, a man in the balcony watched closely with his pistol drawn.[82] After a twelve-hour struggle, boosted by the lobbying efforts of Johnson and Rayburn and the decision to allow Harris County's conservatives to cast the county's 270 votes for themselves, Daniel eventually won control of the convention with a 1,006–869 vote and a two-to-one majority on the Executive Committee. He had also survived a last-ditch effort by liberals to substitute their delegates for those seated by the outgoing Executive Committee. In addition, he received almost everything he wanted in the platform, including the call for a statewide crime commission and lobby control bill, as well as a plank supporting the right of local school districts to control their own affairs. "I could not have won the convention without the support of Lyndon Johnson and Sam Rayburn," he conceded. "Our relationship had to remain extremely close to keep control of the party." [83] Johnson, having settled the score with the revolt-minded liberals, would describe his backstage maneuvering at the convention as a "lesson in political integrity." [84]

His victory sealed, Daniel entered the auditorium and made his way to the podium accompanied by Lyndon Johnson. Liberal catcalls greeted Johnson as he underscored his commitment to support Democrats from the courthouse to the White House. The response to Daniel was even more raucous. Unable to speak over the jeers that filled the hall, he announced that he could wait as long as they could. "I stayed up there at the mike for five or ten minutes and took it and let them yell themselves out," he recalled. "It seemed like an eternity. I had a very short speech to give, but I gave it." [85] In fact, the situation became so contentious that the sergeant-at-arms and several Sheriff's Posse members pushed their way into the crowd and hauled two men out who had gotten into a shoving match. Despite loud outbreaks during his twenty-minute speech, Daniel pressed on, thanking delegates for their support and announcing that he would resign his Senate seat when a special nominating primary could be held.[86]

Daniel felt that a show of support for the national Democratic ticket was necessary. While still opposing a loyalty oath, he assured delegates that he would be "laboring for the Democratic Party in both the state and nation." Accordingly, his floor managers did not object when the convention adopted a resolution endorsing Stevenson and Kefauver.[87] In the coming days Daniel assured voters that his endorsement was contingent upon Stevenson supporting the Texas tidelands position, but that he had no reason to expect a problem.[88]

As one Texas historian later observed: "It was a tribute to the political abilities of these three men (Daniel, Johnson, and Rayburn) to withstand attacks from the left and right, win control of the Texas Democratic party, and prevent a major split for the first time in a presidential election year since 1940. Daniel's hope that his candidacy would help bring harmony to Texas politics was realized."[89] Learning from this tense experience, Daniel worked in the next two years as governor to establish a better union between the executive office and party officials, encouraging the Democratic headquarters in Austin to help educate party workers and better handle party affairs.[90]

Meanwhile, Texas Republicans had gathered in Corpus Christi and nominated William R. Bryant of Sherman for governor. Bryant, who already had been defeated once by Daniel in the 1948 race for attorney general, told supporters that things would be different this time around. "Wait and see!" he declared in his acceptance speech. But Bryant's campaign never got off the ground. In fact, the Republican Party made only a half-hearted effort. And, since O'Daniel had failed to get his name on the ballot as a third-party candidate, forcing his supporters to write his name on the ballot, Daniel was a shoo-in. On November 6, when the ballots were tabulated, he had accumulated a whopping 1,350,736 votes. Bryant trailed with 261,283, while O'Daniel placed a distant third with 110,234 write-in ballots. Although Eisenhower carried the state by a large margin, Bryant, the other major Republican on the ballot, did not carry a single Texas county.[91]

Daniel celebrated his victory at home in Liberty. He announced that he would return to Austin on December 3 to make preparations for the inauguration and to hold conferences with legislators regarding his legislative program. Daniel knew that many lawmakers were intensely loyal to Shivers, with whom he had clashed over the last couple of months, and so he felt it necessary to hold meetings day and night with every member of the state legislature who cared to discuss the problems of the state with him. He used this opportunity to swap ideas, while at the same time checking the legislative pulse and gauging the level of support for future proposals.[92]

Meanwhile, Jean Daniel focused her energy on the myriad details accompanying the move from Washington back to Texas. In addition to packing and shipping the family's belongings, she arranged for the children's school transfers—first from Washington to Liberty, then from Liberty to Austin. Price, Jr., would attend Austin High School, Jean would go to University Junior High, and Houston and John would be enrolled in Pease Elementary.[93]

The Eisenhower landslide over Stevenson did not alter the composition of the Senate, with forty-nine Democrats and forty-seven Republicans remaining intact. However, Senator Johnson felt compelled to take action ensuring his majority leadership. Since Daniel had two years remaining on his Senate term, it was Johnson's strategy to have him resign his seat on Capitol Hill the same day he was sworn in as governor. This would allow Daniel to name his successor.[94] The problem was that Daniel had promised Texas voters throughout the campaign that they, not he or anyone else, would have the opportunity to select his replacement. "After I am nominated governor," he had pledged on August 8, 1956, "I will resign from the Senate at such time that the voters will have the freest possible choice in naming my successor. That is my guarantee."[95]

Shivers, however, foiled Johnson's plan by demanding that Daniel resign, thereby permitting him, as governor, to select a temporary replacement who would serve until the general election the following year. This worried Johnson because Shivers had strongly supported the Republican presidential nominee, and the party affiliation of Shivers' selection would determine the balance of power in the Senate. Thus, Shivers had the power to reduce Johnson from majority to minority leader if he so desired.[96] Shivers contended that Daniel's January 15 resignation was timed to let him control both offices. He would resign as senator, Shivers charged, become governor, then immediately name his successor to the pivotal Senate seat. Daniel countered by saying he had submitted his resignation in such a way that Shivers could have called the special election for November 6, general election day, but had failed to do so. Either Shivers would have to act quickly or leave the decision for Daniel to make. Fearing that Shivers would pick a Republican and alter the power in the Senate, Daniel hoped the decision would be his.

It soon became apparent to Daniel that Shivers was not going to call a special election. In a last-ditch effort, he wrote to Shivers urging him to reconsider: "You and I were falsely accused of having made agreements concerning appointment of a successor. I continually branded this as a falsehood and stated that I would time my resignation so there would be ample opportunity for an election rather than an appointment by me or by anyone else. That was the purpose of my resignation and it can be carried out even now if you will reconsider." [97] But in his return letter, Shivers contended that the law prohibited the governor from calling elections to fill vacancies until they actually occurred. And, in Daniel's case, he argued that no actual vacancy would exist until January 15. [98]

Shivers released this letter to the press the same day he put it in the mail to Daniel. This further aggravated Daniel. "Since Governor Shivers took 47 days to answer my letter of resignation," he quipped in a statement on November 13, "I shall take at least a few hours before making a full reply." In his response, Daniel said he did not understand Shivers' motive unless it was to help the Republicans organize the Senate. "Although Governor Shivers is as wrong as he can be on the law," Daniel stated, "if he had advised me of his opinion in time for me to change my resignation in order that the election might be held by January 3 under the statute he prefers, I would have done so gladly. But for some strange reason he has delayed his proposal until it is now too late under his statute (requiring 60 days) for an election to be called until after Congress meets January 3." [99]

On November 21 Daniel wrote to Shivers and told him how common it had been for senators to resign from the Senate as he had done. And, in some cases where objections had been raised similar to those of Shivers, the Senate had overruled them every time and approved the calling of elections. "In all frankness," Daniel added, "I must say that I do not know of any action on your part to avoid the controversy. From the beginning, it appeared to me that you disagreed with my advocacy of an election." [100] Three days later Daniel wrote Sam Rayburn and told him he was glad Rayburn had not publicly entered the controversy "because nothing would suit (Shivers) better than to try to make the conservatives think that this was all part of a deal with you and Lyndon. Thus far I think I can hold my own with him even among the conservatives, and I know that the loyal Democrats are supporting my position." [101]

Since Shivers did not accept his resignation and call a special election, Daniel reluctantly returned to Washington in early January and helped organize the Senate, but he refused to accept any salary. "I drew the checks but the government wouldn't let you give the checks back," he recalled. "I had to finally end up endorsing those checks over to first one church and then another... About $2,000 each. They said there was no way of paying it back into the treasury or having those checks canceled. Said it would mess up their books." [102]

Much to Daniel's dismay, Shivers had waited literally until the final hours of his administration to determine who would fill Daniel's vacated seat. Meanwhile, the governor-elect spent his last evening as a low-profile citizen at a dinner hosted by the Senate Ladies, then returned home to put finishing touches on his inaugural address slated for noon the following day. His work, however, was constantly interrupted by a barrage of telephone calls from the Shivers camp. "Almost continually Governor Shivers was trying to persuade me to make the appointment to the Senate or to say that that's who I would have appointed," Daniel later recalled. As the clock neared midnight, still without word on Shivers' decision, Daniel retired to bed without knowing if it would be his choice to select someone who would determine the balance of the Senate. [103]

Eisenhower, aware of the magnitude of Shivers' decision, had made a trip to Texas to inquire of the governor's choice. Recalled Shivers, "Eisenhower said, 'Well, I'm sure you're going to get a lot of pressure to appoint a Republican with the situation like it is.'" But the stern Texan would not give into the president's lobbying. "Well, I don't think I can do that," he replied. On the morning of the inauguration, Shivers appointed Dallas reactionary Democrat William A. Blakely, chief stockholder in Braniff Airways and a self-made ranch and real estate millionaire. [104] In fact, the governor later stated that he never had given much thought to appointing a Republican. [105]

Lyndon Johnson was delighted to get a phone call from Shivers informing him of the good news. "Shivers is tough," the majority leader told reporters afterward. "He'll grab the flag and take his folks somewhere. I like that in a leader." [106]

Thus, a new era in Texas politics was dawning. The torch was to be passed from the conservative forces of Allan Shivers to a new coalition of moderate Democrats led by Price Daniel.

CHAPTER 12

A Dream
Come True

ormer Texas governor Joseph Draper Sayers once said that a
Texas governor has only two happy days—"the day he is inau-
gurated and the day he retires."[1] Price Daniel's goal, however,
was to put as much distance between his two "happy days" as possible.

"Price Daniel did not pick for himself a bed of roses when he
chose to leave what, in all probability, could have been a lifetime job
in the U.S. Senate to run for governor," editorialized the *San
Antonio Express* on the morning of his inauguration. "He inherits a
myriad of problems in a growing state of widely-divergent economic, political and cultural interests and a general disposition toward balkiness at new taxation measures."[2] Indeed, Texas was experiencing significant change. Since the 1940s, migration from countryside to cities had rapidly accelerated until, by 1950, more than
half of all Texans were metropolitan. The state now claimed almost
eight million citizens. Moreover, some powerful economic interests
were emerging that would influence the coming years. Texans were
also beginning to debate polarizing issues that were previously con-

fined to the national stage. And, as one Texas historian observed, "there are very few issues that have created controversy nationally that have not filtered down to Texas, where the intensity of the conflict is sometimes even greater than that generated nationally." [3] Daniel was well aware that he would encounter many of these divergent issues—that he would govern over a transformational period in Texas history.

To help him face these challenges, Daniel chose to add a spiritual emphasis to the beginning of his administration. He asked Reverend Billy Graham to preside over what would become the first Governor's Prayer Breakfast of its kind on the morning of January 15, 1957. As a prelude to Daniel's inauguration, Graham addressed an audience of 500 in the Maximilian Room of the Driskill Hotel. "I know of no more Christian statesman in the world today than Price Daniel," said the charismatic evangelist from North Carolina. [4] Moments earlier Daniel had made his last speech as governor-elect. "I do believe that God guides the destinies of nations as well as of individuals, and I will acknowledge and solicit the aid of God in my administration," he pledged. [5]

Hours later, biting cold weather forced inaugural ceremonies to be moved to the House chamber inside the Texas Capitol. Daniel, together with Lieutenant Governor Ben Ramsey and their families, stayed outdoors only long enough to ride in the front of a ceremonial parade and then witness the procession of military units, bands, sheriff posses, and the like pass in front of the reviewing stand at the head of Congress Avenue. Shortly thereafter the Texas Tech band played in the visitors gallery of the Capitol, awaiting the grand entrance of the governor-elect. At 11:55 A.M. artillery on the Capitol grounds nearly shattered windows when a nineteen-gun salute signaled the entrance of Daniel, Ramsey, and retiring governor Allan Shivers. [6]

After listening to a short inaugural address from Ramsey, who had now set a record for his length of service in that office (four terms), Daniel stepped forward. Placing his hand on a small, brown Bible provided by the Texas Supreme Court and dating back to 1840, he took the oath from Chief Justice John E. Hickman. The move indoors made the ceremony even more meaningful for Daniel, for he now stood in the same hall where he had served as a young legislator from Liberty and at the same rostrum from which he had presided as House Speaker. His inaugural speech began by calling attention to the last sentence of the oath he had just taken: "So help me God. With this supplication I have sealed my solemn pledge to you," he said, as loudspeakers carried his voice to a throng in the corridors who could not gain entrance. "With this same prayer for divine guidance, I accept the sacred trust which has been bestowed upon me." [7]

The indoor festivities proceeded smoothly, with only one noticeable glitch: The crowd had pressed so close together that the student officers could not lower their sabers. "When last seen the two bright blades were slowly moving toward the Capitol entrance where there would be room enough to sheath them," wrote one newspaper reporter. [8] After the ceremony, Daniel made his way to the governor's offices—offices which only a few minutes before had been occupied by Shivers staff members. But now they were gone, and a new era in Texas government had begun. [9]

That afternoon the Daniels hosted 100 relatives and close friends for a hot lunch at the Governor's Mansion. The meal was prepared and left by the outgoing Shivers family in keeping with a time-honored custom. [10] Shivers, already en route to New York, had been visibly distant from Daniel throughout the day. The outgoing governor had skipped the morning prayer breakfast, had no plans to attend the evening reception at the Capitol rotunda or any of the four inaugural balls, and even seemed gloomy during a perfunctory handshake with Daniel on the Speaker's rostrum. As one reporter observed, "There was an obvious lack of cordiality." [11]

Daniel knew that his strained relationship with Shivers was extremely detrimental from a political standpoint. Having presided over Texas politics for eight years, Shivers' influence, exerted through his appointees, could easily extend well into a second Daniel term. Furthermore, many members of the legislature were intensely loyal to him. Even Allen Duckworth of the *Dallas Morning News* predicted that the incoming governor was "likely to run into coolness in the legislature on the part of some of the Shivers people." [12] Because the Texas Constitution concentrates strength in the lawmaking body, Daniel would be successful only to the degree that he could work with and through the legislature to shape policy. Therefore, he had conducted conferences day and night with every member of the legislature—swapping ideas and checking the pulsebeat of the political scene in Austin. These meetings would later prove highly worthwhile in his attempts to smooth any hostilities left over in the Shivers aftermath.

At the same time Daniel was being sworn in as the governor of Texas, President Eisenhower was finishing a tour of the drought-plagued state. The dramatic juxtaposition of those much-publicized events underlined the prime challenge facing Daniel's administration: the development of a bold and sweeping state water-resources program. "Texas stands at the crossroads of accelerating progress or economic stagnation, and the way we take depends more on the adequacy of solutions sought for this state's number one problem—water—than on anything else," one newspaper proclaimed.[13]

In confronting this and numerous other crucial matters, Daniel chose one of his predecessors, former governor Beauford Jester, as a model for his administration. At the time of Jester's inauguration ten years earlier, Texas had been in bad need of repair. The depression had many vital institutions such as schools, prisons, and mental health hospitals in shambles. But because the state had supplied virtually the entire Allied cause with oil, considerable revenue had been raised and Texas had a surplus in the state treasury. Jester's task was to wade through the seemingly endless stream of demands on the state's resources. The governor laid out a full plate of broad-ranging proposals, and his progressive effort to use these funds to repair everything he felt was broken in Texas made a great impression upon Daniel.[14] Now, ten years later, he still felt that there was a lot left to be done.

In his first message to the legislature on January 17, Daniel called for a vast array of sweeping legislation. Unlike some past governors who had been elected on the basis of one or two issues, the new governor had a plan in mind for just about everything. He laid out specific proposals for a water conservation program, with special provisions to bring relief to drought-stricken farmers and ranchers; the establishment of an eleven-member state law enforcement commission to investigate corruption in government affairs; stricter regulations for insurance, loan, securities, and investment companies; an equitable lobby registration law; tougher narcotics laws; expansion of the highway patrol as part of a statewide safety campaign; drivers' license laws; an accelerated highway-building program; increased payments for old-age assistance; continued improvement of the state hospital and prison systems; higher pay for schoolteachers and state help in assisting local school districts in their building programs; growth and conservation of Texas' recreational resources; and the list went on.[15] Daniel spent fifty minutes delivering the 6,000-word speech, which covered some twenty-five major topics. "It was the most meticulously done speech on state government I have ever heard," Representative Barefoot Sanders of Dallas remarked afterwards. "It was ambitious, forward-looking, and bold."[16] And Representative Howard Green of Fort Worth told reporters afterward that he anticipated "one of the finest administrations of the present era."[17]

Even though the message was well received by the legislature, many questioned Daniel's ability to pay for such programs while keeping his goal of no new substantial taxes. "I want to see how he's going to raise the money," mumbled Representative Robert Hughes of Dallas as he exited the chamber.[18] But if the day should come when new or higher taxes were inevitable, Daniel reminded the legislature in his closing remarks that the purpose of state government was not to prevent new taxes, but to "fully meet the needs of state government and completely exercise the responsibilities which are necessary to preserve the rights of our state and our people."[19] Calling this a "hint," the *San Antonio Express* warned its readers to get ready for a tax fight: "He has promised to try to get more money for school teachers and state employees, among his other proposals. If his budget goes beyond anticipated revenues, the 'honeymoon' may be near an end because there is considerable sentiment in the legislature in favor of avoiding a new tax this session."[20] Most of the state's media, however, lured to Daniel's optimistic blueprint, gave the new governor the benefit of the doubt. "Governor Daniel may not get from the legislature all that he asked," reasoned the *Federationist,* "but the program he has mapped out would go a long way toward bringing Texas out of the dark ages and into being as a modern, progressive state."[21]

Daniel was aiming high. "He totally overwhelmed the legislature with the number of things he was recommending," recalled George Christian. "It was a full plate, and he would eventually call for everything that he recommended."[22] To assist him in reaching these objectives, Daniel put together a capable staff, one willing to commit enormous amounts of time and energy. He promoted Christian to administrative assistant in charge of press relations and Jake Jacobsen to executive administrative assistant, and he held over three members of the Shivers staff: Jess Erwin, William McGill, and Jimmy Banks. Longtime assistant Emma Ward was placed in charge of internal administration, and Daniel's sister, Ellen, volunteered her services as executive secretary.

Daniel had one last battle to wage with the outgoing Shivers administration. Five days before leaving office, Governor Shivers submitted six names to the Senate for confirmation: three to the Board of Regents of the University of Texas and three to the Board of Directors of Texas A&M College. Daniel strongly objected, citing a 1933 opinion of the Texas attorney general which declared it was the privilege of the entering governor, not the exiting one, to make such appointments. "All outgoing Governors had respected the right and privilege of incoming Governors to make the appointments except outgoing Governor Pat M. Neff, whose appointments in 1925 were rejected by the Senate," Daniel contended. To allow the appointments to stand would not only establish an undesirable precedent, he explained, but also would leave him with no representation on either board during his two-year term since Shivers had appointed the remaining board members.[23]

On February 19 Daniel formally asked for the Senate's consent to his withdrawal of the names submitted by Shivers. Responding to newspaper articles that accused him of trying to get rid of a Republican nominee, he went out of his way to emphasize that his action was not aimed at any one of the appointees. Instead, he said other factors needed to be taken into consideration, such as geographical distribution of the board members (it troubled him that two of the six members were from Dallas). He also thought it would be appropriate for one of the appointees to reside in Austin. Meanwhile, George Christian had telephoned Jim Chambers of the *Dallas Times Herald* regarding one appointment. Chambers told him that "this thing is getting pretty hot in Dallas and most people consider it an affront to Dallas after the way the county went for Daniel." Chambers assured Christian, however, that the paper would not editorialize on the matter for the time being.[24] Finally, on February 25, the Senate unanimously consented to the governor's request. The next day Daniel sent the legislature a message: "I attempted to make it clear that I was concerned with the principle and policy involved rather than with any person or political objection to the nominees." [25] Then, in typical Daniel fashion, he resubmitted for confirmation the names of all of the original appointees. More importantly, he urged the legislature to define more clearly the dates for the beginning and ending of the terms of board members in order to prevent the problem from recurring.

On March 25 Daniel fulfilled a campaign promise by making his first periodic report to Texans concerning "state affairs and the program of progress." As he had preached throughout his campaign, he believed that citizens could govern themselves best when they had access to accurate and complete information. Sensing that Texans were growing tired of hearing about scandals in the halls of government, the new governor effectively used reform as the theme of his first report: "I wish it were possible for me to report to you that all is well in your state government, but that I cannot do. All will never be well in this or any other government unless we expose and punish the few who have violated their public trust, and restore public confidence in the great majority who have been faithful in the discharge of their duties." Of the 40,000 state officials and employees, said Daniel, the integrity of less than one percent was in question. "Nothing is more dangerous or unfair," he added, "than to indict an entire government because of the actions of a few." And he reminded the electorate of his progressive program to combat corruption—a lobby registration law, a code of conduct for state officials, a law requiring the registration of all persons who represent others before a state agency, insurance reform, and the establishment of a state law enforcement commission.[26]

Legislative investigations revealed that a number of lawmakers had received retainers or other fees from various concerns, particularly from the U.S. Trust and Guaranty Company. This helped explain why loopholes in the insurance code had existed for so long. And when the state's newspapers began printing stories on these investigations, the public could more fully appreciate Daniel's statements of the previous year advocating a crusade for clean government in Texas. The legislature killed his proposed bill to require the registration of persons representing others before state agencies, but overwhelmingly passed a code of ethics for legislators and other public employees designed to prevent a conflict between private and public interests. It did not, however, prohibit members from accepting retainer fees from private concerns.

Daniel sent the legislature a special message urging emergency consideration of his proposed law enforcement commission to investigate official misconduct. Since proposing its creation, he said he had "come to feel even more strongly that legislation of this nature is vital to the welfare of our state." [27] On the very same day, 102 House members co-signed with R.H. Cory of Victoria a bill to create the commission. It was promptly referred to the committee on criminal jurisprudence which favorably reported it, but no additional action was taken. Likewise, Ray Roberts of McKinney introduced the bill in the Senate, where it was referred to the committee on state affairs but never reported out.

Ironically, these actions coincided with the resignation of Representative James E. Cox of Conroe, who was indicted for consenting to accept a bribe of $5,000 for a favorable vote on a bill to regulate naturopaths. Speaker Waggoner Carr appointed a special nine-member House investigating committee, but many legislators, especially the East Texas group, which was not represented on the special committee, felt the investigation should be conducted by the regular House committee on representation before the legislature.

This incident brought considerable attention to the scope of Daniel's proposed law enforcement commission. Representative Cory insisted the commission was not proposed as a "super-grand jury," since it would not have the authority to indict. But Representative John Crosthwait of Dallas best summed up the arguments of the commission's critics when he stated: "I don't believe in turning the investigations over to anyone who is not responsible to the people." [28] Because there was no precedent and everyone had widely differing views on what the commission should do, Daniel learned quickly that it would be difficult to get such a proposal through the legislature. He realized that legislators were hesitant to pass laws which would directly affect themselves, but he refused to give up.

"He really changed the political atmosphere in Austin," recalled former representative Zeke Zbranek. "In my first term under Governor Shivers, the special interest lobby was able to stop all efforts to pass any progressive legislation. The best we could do was try to stop their worst legislation. But under Governor Daniel, the people had an ally. We actually passed legislation to improve public schools and universities." [29] To get the ball rolling in the state legislature, the strategy of the Daniel administration was to change floor leaders as the issues under discussion changed. Thus, when public education became the hot topic, Senator A. M. Aikin, Jr., took control of the floor debate. And when it was time to sponsor tax measures in the House, in stepped Representative George Hinson. In addition, Daniel assigned both his executive and administrative assistants, George Christian and John Goldsum, to legislative relations. [30] Under this plan, when a crucial vote was to be cast, the governor would have able men in position to help rally support for his measures.

Daniel worked to improve communications between lawmakers and the governor. He distributed information sheets to individual legislators, providing each with detailed summaries of measures being discussed. When trying to push his escheat bill, whereby the state would take over personal property for which there was no lawful owner, Daniel personally financed and distributed a brochure listing ten reasons for the bill's adoption. The brochure also contained a thinly veiled threat, telling legislators he hoped a special called session would not be necessary to get the measure adopted. [31] Little did they know then how serious the governor's threat would prove to be.

Daniel worked quickly to tame the insurance industry, which he felt had gotten far out of hand during the Shivers administration. Actually, the insurance business had long been a serious problem in Texas. During the 1880s, Attorney General James Hogg had succeeded in expelling companies from the state which were not only poorly financed but also guilty of taking money from the public under false pretenses. The Robertson Insurance Law of 1907, sponsored by Hogg's former law partner, James H. Robertson, caused many out-of-state insurance companies to leave Texas in protest of the requirement that they reinvest 75 percent of premiums in Texas. Consequently, there was a huge increase in the number of Texas-chartered insurance companies, most of which prospered. In 1954, 1,202 of the 1,875 insurance companies operating in Texas were chartered. However, the lack of adequate restrictions on the sale of stock in these companies provided many opportunities for promoters and "fly-by-night" operators. As a result, while a vast majority of Texas insurance companies remained in sound financial condition, eighty-six of them collapsed between 1945 and 1955 alone. Daniel commended the 54th Texas Legislature for the reforms it had enacted, passing twenty-two new laws regulating insurance and raising the minimum capital requirement for insurance companies. However, he said that action had not come in time to prevent the failure of several major businesses, such as the United Services Trust and Guaranty Company, in which some 128,000 investors had an interest, and the giant ICT Corporation, which controlled seventy-four insurance and security companies.

But even more important, Daniel believed that the administration of these laws, passed under Governor Shivers' watch, was flawed. For instance, the Insurance Code enacted in 1955 directed the Board of Insurance Commissioners to act and conduct business as a single board, rather than to operate in separate capacities as commissioners of life, fire, and casualty insurance. But, Daniel told the legislature, this directive had not been followed: "It is freely admitted and well known that the commissioners continued to operate their own divisions with separate mailing rooms, machine accounting, agent licensing, supply rooms, reproduction facilities, and other services. The three commissioners still maintain offices on separate floors. For the next biennium each commissioner submitted his individual budget request, signed only by him, for his own division." Therefore, Daniel concluded that there had not been sufficient exchange of information to provide each commissioner with a knowledge of the activities of all three divisions, and so he recommended that there be an executive director to coordinate the divisions and allow the board to function as a unit. The appropriate time for this reorganization, he said, was before new commissioners became accustomed to the old way of doing business. "We must select the highest type of individuals as members so as to raise the prestige and respect of the Insurance Commission," he declared. He likewise recommended the creation of a State Board of Insurance to replace the Board of Insurance Commissioners, proposing that the members be selected by the governor and that the agency be directed by a commissioner of insurance appointed by the board.[32]

The current Board of Insurance Commissioners consisted of Morris Brownlee, Mark Wentz, and Chairman John Osorio. A bitter argument soon developed between Daniel and Osorio, who had been appointed by Shivers to fill a vacancy on January 1, 1957, just days before Daniel took office. In a letter to Osorio, Representative Jerry Sadler posed a series of questions which were worded in such a way as to imply that Daniel's desire to reorganize the board was a result of the disagreement with Osorio.[33] In a response given to the press, Osorio promptly informed Sadler that the governor's sole aim in reorganization was to gain control of the board. According to Osorio, Daniel had offered him a job if he would support the governor's plan. He further charged that Daniel had tried to block his confirmation in the Senate after a Daniel aid had promised that the governor would do so.[34] In response, Daniel simply referred to his campaign platform in which he had advocated reorganization of the Board of Insurance Commissioners. "From the moment John Osorio's appointment was announced," Daniel added, "I believe I said that it was a great mistake to place a man at the head of the insurance department who had been so closely associated personally and politically with the past chairman."[35]

The reorganization bill was introduced in the Senate on February 11 by William Fly of Victoria. It was killed in committee, but a substitute measure was reported favorably and passed by the Senate one month later. The bill was then sent to the House, where some amendments were made to the Senate version. The principal difference between them was whether the board should be part-time or full-time. The joint committee reached a compromise by which the board would serve full-time the first year and part-time thereafter. On May 23, the last day of the session, the committee's report was eventually adopted by both houses. Daniel appointed a new board, which in turn selected William Harrison as commissioner of insurance.

Daniel's first address to the new board expressed hope that the members would "promptly rid the industry of its few remaining 'rotten apples' and that your strict enforcement of the law, without fear or favor, will soon bring about the full and complete protection intended by law for the people, policyholders and industry."[36] Texans were overwhelmed by his quick progress. In addition to naming an entirely new insurance commission, the governor helped push through sixteen brand new insurance laws and brought about an audit of the state's insurance companies, which resulted in more than a hundred of them being denied permits to resume business.[37]

Daniel was also behind the creation of the State Securities

Board, which assumed functions formerly preformed by the Board of Insurance Commissioners and the Secretary of State's Office. The new board was given the responsibility of regulating the sale of securities to the public, as well as the testing and licensing of security dealers and agents. The governor called the act creating the board "one of the most outstanding measures in history for the protection of the public against fraud and swindling." [38]

In addition, working to cure farmers' drought problems which had haunted the Shivers administration, Daniel secured a water plan—the first of its kind in Texas. [39] He proposed two bond amendments, one creating the Texas Water Development Board, the other a water planning agency. The first would allow the issuance of $200 million in bonds to create the Texas Water Development Fund, administered by the Texas Water Development Board for the purpose of assisting local governmental units in constructing water conservation projects. The second would allow $100 million to be used for the purchasing of storage space for water behind federal dams.

The first piece of Daniel's water plan moved ahead smoothly. There was little opposition to the House joint resolution submitting the amendment for aid to local projects. It was introduced on January 21 and passed the House four weeks later. The Senate made some alterations to the bill before passing it, but the differences were smoothed over in a joint committee. The House accepted the report on April 23, and the Senate agreed to it on May 21. An enabling act creating the Development Board also passed without difficulty. The amendment, submitted to the voters on November 5, 1957, was overwhelmingly approved and became codified as Article III, Section 49c of the Constitution. By December the Texas Water Development Board was in operation.

Daniel was discouraged, however, by the legislature's unenthusiastic response to the other half of his water program. A conference committee was appointed to settle the differences between House and Senate versions of the water storage proposal, but the clock ran out on the session before anything could be done. In the end, the seven-year drought, which had bankrupted many of the state's farmers and ranchers, ended when torrential rains and floods hit Texas in the last half of 1957. [40]

During Daniel's tenure, the state's position on segregation would slowly begin to change. Much had already transpired in this

Daniel at the age of four.

Nannie Partlow Daniel.

*Daniel (left)
with sister Ellen
and brother Bill.*

Young Price Daniel, dressed as Uncle Sam, poses with his father, who served as postmaster at Dayton, Texas.

The Daniels at their Fort Worth home in September 1923.

*Daniel at Central High School
in Fort Worth.*

Price Daniel with his father, M.P. Daniel.

Daniel, a nattily dressed country lawyer.

Freshman Representative Daniel (right) with deskmate Judge Jack Langdon.

Price and Jean with their first child,
Marion Price Daniel, Jr.

As Speaker of the House in 1943, Daniel presided over a sparse Texas legislature as many of the members were overseas fighting in the war.

Private Daniel, U.S. Army, June 1943.

The Daniel family in Liberty: Price, Jean, Price, Jr., Jean, Houston, and John.

Holly Ridge Ranch.

Cartoonists made the most of the tidelands controversy. This cartoon, from the Tyler Mornin[g] Telegraph, *depicts the heated conflict between Daniel and Lieutenant Governor Allan Shivers.*

With maps in hand, a confident Daniel boards a train for Washington to argue the tide-lands case before the U.S. Supreme Court.

The Daniel family takes a break on the Senate campaign trail.

Senator Lyndon Johnson (middle) watches as Vice President Barkley administers the oath of offic to the new junior senator from Texas.

Senators Spessard Holland, Robert Taft, Lyndon Johnson, and Daniel (left to right) congratulate each other for the tidelands victory in May 1953, after a twenty-seven-day filibuster.

President Dwight Eisenhower presents Daniel a pen used to sign the act restoring submerged lands to the state. As a result, Texas won title to over four million acres in the Gulf of Mexico.

Price and Jean look over a stack of letters urging the senator to return to Texas and run for govern

Candidate Daniel seldom missed an opportunity to court votes.

Daniel being sworn in as governor of Texas in January 1957.

Governor Price Daniel.

Price and Jean dance at their first Inaugural Ball.

he governor stands outside the U.S. Supreme Court Building in 1959 after again presenting Texas'
:im to ownership of the oil-rich tidelands.

*The Daniel family stands on the steps of the Texas Governor's Mansion: Price, Jean, Price, Jr., Jea[n]
Houston, and John.*

Jean Houston Baldwin Daniel.

Under their mother's portrait, Governors Price and Bill Daniel listen to election returns. When Bill (right) was governor of Guam, they were the first brothers to be members of the National Governors' Conference.

Daniel, president of the International Christian Leadership, has a word with John Kennedy at th *1962 Presidential Prayer Breakfast. Billy Graham (left) shared the speakers' podium with Dani* *and Kennedy.*

As assistant to the president for federal-state relations, Daniel was President Johnson's liaison wit *the governors of the states and territories. Here he is at the Cabinet table with the president an* *Governor Cal Rampton of Utah. During the same period, 1967–68, he also served as director of th* *Office of Emergency Preparedness, a member of the National Security Council, and the NATC* *Advisory Council.*

Jean lends Price a helping hand at his Texas Supreme Court induction.

Daniel with fellow Supreme Court justices in 1971: (seated) Justice Ruel Walker, Chief Justice Robert W. Calvert, Justice Joe Greenhill; (standing) Justices James G. Denton, Thomas M. Reavley, Zollie Steakley, Jack Pope, Sears McGee, and Daniel.

...aniel swore in his son, Price Daniel, Jr., in January 1973 as Speaker of the Texas House of ...presentatives.

Daniel relaxes at his Liberty ranch.

arena since he helped draft the Southern Manifesto in the Senate. After the Supreme Court's monumental *Brown vs. Topeka Board of Education (Brown I)* ruling in 1954, declaring the separate-but-equal doctrine unconstitutional in public schools, the Court returned the case to the docket for further argument on implementation of the decision. Attorneys general from all of the states affected by the decision were then invited to submit a brief and to present oral arguments. Texas Attorney General John Ben Shepperd accepted the invitation and, on April 13, 1955, told the Court that "any attempt to effect immediate or too-sudden mixture of white and colored pupils, especially if made by an authority outside the individual school district, would be rash, imprudent, and unrealistic."[41] Indeed, in the spring of that year, a poll showed that 45 percent of Texans favored resisting integration, while 35 percent would accept gradual integration, and only 14 percent would accept immediate integration.[42]

On May 31 the Supreme Court released an opinion, which became known as *Brown II*, acknowledging that local school districts, not the courts, would bear most of the responsibility of desegregation. "School authorities have the primary responsibility for educating, assessing, and solving these problems... [and] to admit to public schools on a racially nondiscriminatory basis with all deliberate speed the parties to these cases." The words "with all deliberate speed" were something of a victory for segregationists, who seized the opportunity to stall and delay the integration process as long as possible.[43]

By the time of Daniel's election as governor, more Texans were opposed to integration than they were in 1954 or 1955.[44] Texans increasingly debated such issues as school integration, states' rights, and the encroachment of federal government into state and local responsibilities. Many whites were disgruntled in 1956 when blacks brought a successful lawsuit to desegregate all public parks in Texas.[45] Race relations reached a new level of tension in early 1957, when a Texas court issued a permanent injunction against the NAACP, restraining the organization from collecting contributions and filing lawsuits.[46] These issues, compounded by the Civil Rights Act of 1957, forced a reluctant Daniel to make some tough decisions regarding the pending integration of Texas schools.

Governor Shivers had left office confident that his segregationist policies would be implemented by Daniel. But the newly elected governor confronted the mounting furor over civil rights with no more bravery than most other southern politicians. Not wanting the controversy of the southern resistance movement to cloud his first days in office, Daniel pushed nearly a dozen segregation proposals—each of which was meant to circumvent the Supreme Court's mandates in *Brown I* and *Brown II*—to the end of the 120-day session.[47] He had begun agonizing over the whole question of racial equality and segregation. But he was walking a fine line—his conscience on one side, and his role as governor of a strongly pro-segregation state on the other. For the first time in his career, he was uncomfortable, even somewhat embarrassed with his position on a great moral issue.

"Taken in an absolute sense, Texas' attitude toward race has not been a cause for Texas pride," wrote historian Joe B. Frantz. "On the other hand, Texas observed *de jure* integration with a reasonably good attitude, and followed the same deliberate *de facto* segregation path that practically everyone else trod. When the time came for Houston schools to integrate, the city fathers asked Governor Daniel to assist them with troops, not so much to open up white schools to blacks as to keep blacks away to 'avoid trouble.' Governor Daniel wisely told Houston that the school board had its orders and that keeping blacks out of Houston white schools was not part of the governor's prerogative. Houston integrated with relatively little incident."[48]

Still, Daniel faced criticism from civil rights advocates such as Joseph Martin Dawson, a fellow Southern Baptist who in a 1958 issue of *Christianity Today* voiced agitation at the governor for not pursuing a more enlightened racial policy.[49] But race was still one of the few issues where Daniel tried to hold middle ground, which was essential for many politicians in the 1950s—especially the governor of a southern state. As it was, those on each extreme of the racial debate viewed Daniel's policies as being closely aligned with the enemy. But those who rode the fence on segregation, which constituted the majority of Texans in the late 1950s, understood Daniel's position. Public officials in other states also on the periphery of the Deep South, including Florida, North Carolina, Arkansas and Tennessee, were also supporting local-option arrangements.[50]

"Before 1960 no southern governors were yet willing to take

pro-civil rights stands openly," explained one historian. "The major reason some governors soft-pedaled the racial issue was economic. They knew that racial disturbances brought undesirable publicity that could adversely affect the decisions of corporation executives who were considering locating industries in southern states." [51] Daniel was no exception, but in his mind more was at stake than economics. Having already hit the integration issue head-on as attorney general with his involvement in the monumental Sweatt case, and with years to reflect on the issue, he came to realize that integration was not only inevitable but also favorable. And because some state universities had desegregated prior to the Brown decision, he could no longer argue that Texas was uniquely qualified to preserve a tradition of complete segregation in public education. Believing, however, that rapid, forced integration would be rash and imprudent, he contended that the process should be implemented at the chosen pace of specific school districts across the state—each of which would encounter different levels of resistance. [52] This position prevented Daniel from having to impede the integration movement publicly, but, at the same time, it allowed him to avoid responsibility for its growth.

Nine of the eleven segregation bills that were finally submitted to the Texas House in 1957 passed, but only two won Senate approval and ultimately the governor's signature. One required the continuance of a dual school system until abolished by an election in the local school district, while the other authorized districts to place pupils in facilities "so as to assure the best practical educational curriculum and environment for the individual pupils consistent with the paramount function of the state's police power to assure social order, good will and the public welfare." [53] This law stipulated that no students could be forced to attend an integrated school against their will. Although in line with public sentiment in Texas, both laws were essentially counter to the school integration decisions made by the Supreme Court. [54]

Daniel was not particularly proud of the new legislation but knew that he could not oppose it and still survive politically. "With his wide experience as attorney general, Daniel surely recognized the invalidity of the acts, for he made no real effort to enforce them during his years as governor," noted one political historian. "Indeed, Texans could consider themselves fortunate that some of the more radical proposals passed in other Southern states were never enacted in Texas. No doubt, Daniel's own refusal to promote the issue and pressure from anti-segregationist church groups throughout the state were mainly responsible for limiting the scope of Texas segregation legislation." [55]

In addition to all these matters, back in Washington the tidelands issue had resurfaced. U.S. Attorney General Brownell was still pushing for radical change in the tidelands legislation Daniel had pushed through the Senate. Daniel had been warned by Lyndon Johnson that Brownell was going to file suit against Texas after the 1956 elections but did not worry after outgoing Governor Shivers announced he had obtained the attorney general's assurance that no such suit was planned. However, in October of 1957 Daniel received word that Brownell was indeed planning to file suit against Texas, claiming that the state's historic boundary of three leagues was invalid and also that the Submerged Lands Act of 1953 restored its title to a distance of only three miles from shore. Surprised, Daniel immediately sent the president a telegram which said, "During our last visit on this subject it was my impression that the Justice and State Departments would acknowledge the original boundary of three leagues." [56] Eisenhower responded in a November 7 letter to Daniel, stating his continued support of Texas' position but stressing that it was important for the Supreme Court to decide if the congressional action did, in fact, accomplish its purpose of restoring state ownership. [57] The same day Eisenhower wrote this letter, Brownell, on his last day as attorney general, filed a pleading with the Supreme Court which essentially sought to take away two-thirds of the lands granted to Texas by the Submerged Lands Act.

Eisenhower's apparent lack of influence over the attorney general bewildered Daniel. "Several times the President had to use strong language with Brownell, saying, 'You do not sue Texas,'" the governor recalled. "Finally, just to show you how even a President loses control of situations, Brownell finally persuaded him that he must file this suit. So the President says, 'All right, but in your brief you make it clear that I don't think you're right and quote what I said when I ran for president.' The funny thing about it is that I wrote those quotes back there on those speeches." [58]

Knowing he had to act, on November 20 Daniel addressed the

legislature concerning what he called an "impossible suit" in the Supreme Court attempting to repudiate Texas' three-league boundary in the Gulf of Mexico. He implied that something was wrong when the attorney general would file a lawsuit directly contrary to a policy fixed by the president. "It makes us wonder who is running the administration in Washington," he said. "We have heard for years that Attorney General Brownell has had a lot to do with it, and I for one am glad that he is gone." [59] He then recommended that legislators pass a resolution requesting the president to direct the attorney general to recognize the three-league claim filed in the Supreme Court briefs. Many considered this speech to be one of Daniel's best since becoming governor.

Daniel's resolution passed the House unanimously the following day and, despite Dorsey B. Hardeman's opposition, it also passed the Senate with relative ease. Hardeman had been critical of Daniel for some time. He told his colleagues that, as senator, Daniel had been "lulled into a sense of false security by the siren song and sinister front of Brownell, while the school children of Texas received the 'stab-in-the-back' of vagueness and garbled phraseology." [60] There would be no conflict, he insisted, had Daniel made sure that the 1953 act of Congress expressly stated Texas' entitlement to three leagues. Daniel, not one to let charges go unanswered, responded the very next day. "Senator Hardeman is the first Texan I have heard of who questions or denies the clear intent and effect of the law as restoring to Texas its full three leagues," he countered.[61] Previously, Hardeman had accused Daniel of wasting thousands of dollars belonging to the Texas Teachers Association in an attempt to save the tidelands. This same association quickly dismissed Hardeman's accusations and presented the governor with its first Distinguished Service Award "in recognition of outstanding service in retaining the tidelands for Texas and in contributing to the improvement of public education." [62]

The legislature appropriated special funds for Texas Attorney General Will Wilson to fight the case. Wilson, acknowledging Daniel's expertise on the matter, asked him to assist in both writing the brief and arguing it before the Supreme Court. So once again Daniel focused his attention and energy on the Texas tidelands, spending many late nights working in his office at the east end of the mansion's upstairs hallway. In fact, one night, while preparing the brief, he dictated until sunrise the next morning.[63] He was confident that Texas would prevail, but surely felt some apprehension about going back before the Supreme Court. After all, in his two previous appearances, he had come away empty-handed.

Again, Daniel traveled to Washington and made his case, but this time the Court ruled in favor of Texas by affirming the state's historic boundary at three leagues from shore as provided by the Congress of the Republic of Texas in 1836.[64] "That was quite an experience to argue the case and get a Supreme Court victory for a change," he admitted.[65] Finally, the tidelands crusade, which over the years had helped push Daniel up the political ladder, was a closed chapter in his political career.

Until his death in 1961, Sam Rayburn, still somewhat bitter about his failed compromise plan, contended that Texas would have fared better under his proposal. Allan Shivers agreed. "I saw nothing wrong with it then, and do not now," Shivers said in an interview two decades later. "We were not able to do that [effect a compromise] because immediately Daniel and some members of the legislature began to accuse me of trying to give away Texas' claim, and that this was a patriotic thing and they didn't care whether we never got a nickel out of it." [66]

But Daniel countered these attacks in later years by reminding his colleagues that no definite compromise was ever presented on behalf of the federal government, "and the only one ever talked about was the splitting of revenues that the next Congress could have changed... they could have taken the whole thing away from us." He also contended that under the proposed compromise, the Department of Interior would have controlled the state's beaches and all swimming off them. "People couldn't get it in their heads that there was more than oil involved in this fight—there are coasts involved, there are beaches involved, and the use of that for recreation—so I never would have supported it." [67]

In the end, it is hard to question the results of Daniel's uncompromising stance. As of August 1983 alone, the Texas Public School Fund was reported to have received $1.5 billion from oil leases and royalties on the tidelands money that otherwise would have been deposited into the federal treasury.[68]

Long before the Supreme Court rendered this welcome verdict, Daniel and his family were already adjusting to life at the Governor's

Mansion. Governor Shivers had partitioned off an office area in the upstairs hallway of the executive residence which Daniel continued to use so that he could spend more time with his family. Daniel also hosted many state functions at the mansion, ones which other governors might have opted to have elsewhere. But for him, it was important to be a gracious host, to let those around him be welcome into his inner sanctum. He made it a point to have every state legislator over to the mansion for lunch at least once in order to lobby certain bills. In fact, it was not uncommon for him to bring twenty legislators in at once. His schedule was always flexible enough to give friends, legislators, and concerned citizens a piece of his time.

Perhaps Daniel's most unforgettable gathering at the mansion was a reception he and his family hosted for a relative from Liberty. Daniel was walking down the large spiral stairway when a woman approached. He took a step forward and extended his hand. All of a sudden a giant, twenty-four-pound piece of plaster fell from the ceiling and landed where he had just been standing. While greeting guests in the Blue Room, Jean heard the crash and screams from the hall. After making sure no one was injured, she had the Texas Rangers rope off the area, and the party continued.[69] When workers came to replace the plaster, it was discovered that that the foundation underlying the central part of the mansion was in such desperate need of reinforcement that the entire staircase was sagging. Had the plaster hit Daniel on the head, it likely would have ended his term rather abruptly.

As a result, the Governor's Mansion would benefit from improvements and repairs during his administration. The hallways, stairways, and master bedroom were completely refinished. In the restoration process, the central stairway, foundation, and walls were shored and braced with steel beams. The outer walls were repainted and the screens removed from the upper story of the front gallery so as to restore the original outer appearance. In 1962 the Board of Control would install an adequate central heating and cooling system and make extensive repairs to the utility system, basement, and foundations.[70]

In advancing his agenda, Daniel did not hesitate to continue some earlier initiatives that had proven successful. For instance, Governor Shivers had put together a citizens' group in 1953 designed to research public schoolteacher salaries in the state and, to a lesser extent, other unrelated problems which might arise. Daniel not only continued the study commission but expanded it into several groups that would tackle such relevant issues as law enforcement, education, water, taxation, the aged, oil imports, as well as a revision of the Constitution.[71] By such means the governor could keep a constant watch on the specifics of a variety of issues and also monitor public opinion. These groups, which served throughout his administration, proved to be responsible for the reorganization of what is now called the Texas Water Commission, as well as recommendations which led to an increase in Texas teachers' minimum salary.[72]

Daniel pressed hard to achieve his goals. Aware that many states were receiving large returns from advertising, such as the attraction of new industries and increased tourist trade, Daniel pushed through a constitutional amendment to allow state funds "for the purpose of developing information about the historical, natural, agricultural, industrial, educational, marketing, recreational and living resources of Texas."[73] He also fulfilled his promise of enhanced assistance to senior citizens with a constitutional amendment that increased state participation in pensions by five dollars monthly. Other legislation aided needy children, the blind, and the permanently disabled. Recalling all this, Representative Zeke Zbranek said, "I think he was the best governor the people had in this century. I rank him with Jim Hogg and Sam Houston as one of the 'Big Three' in our history as a state. I guess that's why I always called him 'governor' instead of 'judge' as he was more popularly addressed in his later years."[74]

Shortly after Daniel became governor, he received word that many of the state's archives had been moved from the Highway Department building across from the Capitol to a Quonset hut at Camp Hubbard. The department needed to clear space for a new computer and was forced to find another home for the documents. Furious that such historical records had ended up in a metal hut, the governor made a special trip to the site, where he found original treaties and maps, as well as the records he had used as attorney general in the tidelands case. It was a bitter cold morning when he examined the documents, yet the papers were stored so close to a gas heater that they were hot to the touch and obviously highly susceptible to fire. He could not believe these irreplaceable documents were being handled so carelessly. His dissatisfaction with their storage conditions sparked a crusade to build the archives a permanent home.[75]

"He was a very smart man," said former State Library director Dorman Winfrey. "Money was tight back then. What he had to do was work out an arrangement with Colonel Homer Garrison [then director of the Department of Public Safety] to use fees from the Motor Vehicle Inspection fund to build the library. That didn't require any taxation. No one would fight something like that." [76] Daniel reported what he had seen to the 55th Legislature, and funding was designated for a new archives building before the session adjourned.

He knew exactly what he wanted for this facility and enjoyed planning every detail. "Daniel practically designed the building," recalled Winfrey, referring to the governor's constant supervision before, during, and after the building's construction. In 1964 two artists were commissioned to create a forty-five-foot historical mural in the front lobby. Daniel, who by that time had been out of office for a year, flew from the Democratic National Convention to Austin to inspect the final product. "When he saw the mural, he got upset," remembered Winfrey. "He said the artist must have thought Texas was as dry as New Mexico." Daniel wanted changes made, such as the addition of more water and greenery. He also spotted other mistakes, such as the improper way a horse was tied and the odd fashion in which smoke was coming from a locomotive. "He got Miss Golden's typewriter [the library receptionist], sat down under the mural and wrote about two pages of corrections that had to be made," said Winfrey. "This man's knowledge of Texas history was unbelievable." [77] Every correction Daniel requested was made.

While her husband kept a rigorous schedule of gubernatorial duties, Jean worked equally hard at home to maintain a "normal" environment for the four children. Whenever possible, she preferred that state entertaining be done at breakfast and noon so that no one would expect liquor to be served. Her goal was to keep evenings free for the family to spend time together. On Saturdays she encouraged the children to invite friends over to the mansion for hamburgers, and on Sundays, following worship services at the First Baptist Church, she assembled the family to discuss what had happened to each over the course of the week. [78]

Jean's contributions, however, went far beyond those of motherhood. She became instrumental in the state's effort to preserve the mansion and the history of its former inhabitants. Undertaking what soon became known as "Jean's Project," she collected a personal memento from each of the former Texas governors who had occupied the mansion. She got the idea after noticing that Marialice Shivers had collected several items from earlier governors' terms and had displayed them in the breakfront in the Blue Room. She began to contact the descendants of the former governors and, by 1962, completed the project. At an open house honoring those who had helped her assemble the collection, she expressed hope that the "reminders of the people who helped make Texas history might inspire present and future generations." [79] The Daniels donated an antique silver almond dish and a large silver tray to the collection, as well as rock crystal dresser pieces that had belonged to Margaret Houston. [80]

In addition, Jean conducted research to identify each piece of furniture as well as accessories which had been in the state rooms of the mansion. She made public appeals and wrote letters in order to acquire old photographs or clippings that might identify where each piece had originated. Her work resulted in the production of a 104-page inventory of mansion furnishings, listing the location, description, and historical information about each item. Daniel was thrilled that his wife had taken interest in one of his greatest passions—Texas history. [81]

One Texas historian, describing Price Daniel as not merely a knowledgeable student of the state's rich heritage but also a genuine product of a traditional Texas upbringing, said that "of all the recent Texas governors, [Daniel] was the most Texan. And you could tell he was Texan in the way he talked—not so much from his accent, but from his laid-back approach to things." [82] Indeed, he was the quintessential Texan. When not drafting legislation in Austin, he was tending cattle on his ranch in Liberty. His Stetson hat and pointed-toe boots were customary not only while playing cowboy at Holly Ridge but also at semi-casual state functions, where they blended with his more polished attire.

Former New York governor Alfred E. Smith once observed that a chief executive's energy is so consumed with trivial details of a clerical or subordinate nature that little time is left for more important functions of the office. [83] Daniel was no exception. Much of his time was spent dealing with form letters and filling out routine papers. But he loved detail. Much like his father, he insisted that every document bearing his name had to meet his rigid specifications. One aide in particular actually claimed to have seen the governor editing a daily newspaper. In a collective effort to increase his overall productivity, staffers quickly learned to keep all "non-essential" documents out of his sight. One Saturday afternoon, *Dallas Morning News* reporter Allen Duckworth entered the governor's office with an article he had just written for the newspaper. "I thought you would like to see this, Governor," he said, handing the paper to Daniel. After glancing over the page, Daniel grabbed a pencil and started to make a correction. "My God!" Duckworth exclaimed, jerking the paper out of his hands, "I bet you would edit a menu!" [84]

Daniel's habit of editing did not stop with newspapers. He seldom read a book without scribbling dozens of notations and corrections in the margins. In his copy of *Making the Most of Your Life,* a 1932 classic by John J.B. Morgan and Ewing T. Webb, he strongly disagreed with the authors' assertion that "ambition is based on discontent. A man can never desire anything unless he is dissatisfied with what he has." Along the bottom of the page he wrote in pencil: "Be content but not satisfied. Writer fails to distinguish between discontent and dissatisfaction." [85] In his 1954 copy of *Sam Houston: The Great Designer,* where author Llerena Friend wrote that Andrew Jackson planned to employ United States troops to aid the Texas Revolution by claiming the Neches and not the Sabine River as the western boundary of the United States, Daniel scribbled: "True, he did this briefly." [86] Even Dale Carnegie was subject to Daniel's editing. When Carnegie asserted in his bestselling book *How To Win Friends and Influence People* that people are only interested in themselves, Daniel wrote: "No—wrong." [87]

Though Daniel was meticulous about language, his tobacco habits fell somewhat short of this description. As a bachelor he had smoked cigars but promised Jean that after their wedding day he would never light another one. He was true to his word. Rather than smoking the cigars, he often kept an unlit one in his mouth, chewing on the end, then rolling the wet tobacco in his fingers and stashing small balls in desk drawers, shirt pockets, even pant cuffs. Wherever he went, he was usually accompanied by numerous tobacco balls. [88]

Daniel practically worked his staff to death. With the exception of church, he even put them to work on weekends. "His habits were not that of a tyrant, but were sometimes oppressive because you had to adjust to whatever he was doing," recalls George Christian, who later said that working with Daniel provided good training for his years under Lyndon Johnson. "They were a lot similar in that respect. They had so much on their minds, so much that they wanted to do—so much that if you worked for them, you worked all of the time. So it wasn't a great shock to me when I went to Washington for the second time to work for Lyndon Johnson because I had already been through all of that with Price." During his six years with the governor, Christian remembers only one vacation—his honeymoon. But perhaps the staff's least favorite task was having to drive to Daniel's ranch in Liberty. The governor would perpetually forget something and ask a staffer to make the four-hour drive from Austin. "I only had to do it a couple times," remembers Christian. "I would leave after dark. I remember driving through Montgomery County in the pitch dark, dodging cows in the middle of the road. It was my biggest horror. It was hot and steamy, and I thought it was the most God-awful country. But he loved it." [89]

Some staffers joked that Daniel was the only governor in Texas history who kept the schedule of a night watchman. Official state business was commonly performed at 2:00 A.M. in the master bedroom of the Governor's Mansion. He would parade back and forth across the room in his pajamas, gripping an unlit cigar as he dictated letters to exhausted staffers. For some reason, Daniel was at his best at night. In the wee hours his creative juices flowed freely. But while he sometimes slept late, his staffers, still dragging from having stayed up most of the night and not having that luxury, often had to face the state press corps early. Even when Daniel himself was scheduled to be at a morning press conference, it was not uncommon for him to arrive thirty minutes late. "He baffled the press," remembered Christian. "He left the impression to the press that he was not tending to his duty. But nobody tended to his duty any better than he did. He was on top of everything all of the time. But he could have adjusted his work habits and projected a slightly different image than he did." [90]

In that respect, Daniel was a total contrast to his predecessor. Governor Shivers projected an image of being totally in charge. He had his allies and enemies, and there was a clear line between the two. On the other hand, Daniel smudged that line considerably by cooperating and working with some of the more liberal members of the legislature who had been Shivers' bitter foes. His philosophy was simple: If your ally in the legislature is against you, then you have to go find another ally. As a result, there were seldom any good-guy, bad-guy showdowns, making it difficult to define the governor clearly. In turn, however, Daniel built a strong base of support among various factions of the Democratic Party, which was crucial if many of his sweeping reforms were to have a chance.

Daniel was personally on hand May 23, 1957, as the legislative clock ran out on the first regular session of his administration. His allies had made a final effort to pass a measure increasing water storage space but failed in the House by twenty-one votes. Still, the session proved to be an overwhelming success for Daniel. Under his leadership, the legislature passed laws that appropriated nearly $400 million more than the previous budget over the next two fiscal years. Public schools received an additional $125 million in funding, and teachers' annual base pay increased by $399. New agencies were created, such as the Texas Council on Migrant Labor, the Texas Youth Council, and an adult parole division in the Board of Pardons and Paroles.[91] But despite the fact that nearly all of his proposals were enacted, Daniel still was not satisfied. Lawmakers had stalled three of his pet projects: the law enforcement commission, the water storage space amendment, and lobbyist registration reform. Considering the emphasis the governor had placed on these unfinished bills, many began to wonder if speculation was true that there would be a special session.

They did not have to wonder long. Ten days after the regular session adjourned, Daniel made a second televised report to the people. He praised the legislature, which had passed forty-seven of his fifty-one major recommendations, but said that time had run out before the second part of the water program and several "clean government" measures could be passed. Therefore, he would indeed call a special session in October in hopes of enacting a strict lobby registration act, a law requiring registration of persons who represent others before state agencies, and a state law enforcement commission. He justified calling the special session by explaining how crucial he thought it was that these registration acts be on the law books before the 56th Texas Legislature convened.[92] It also did not hurt his cause that, while he was making this speech, devastating flash floods were taking heavy tolls on property throughout the state. Texans agreed that drastic measures needed to be taken soon.

However, the *Dallas News* reported on an organized movement to call off the special session.[93] A memorandum sent to a select group of people throughout the state urged them to write Daniel in protest, proclaimed that the governor should be satisfied with many victories in the regular session, and asserted that his prestige could be jeopardized by calling the special session. House Speaker Waggoner Carr jumped on the bandwagon, citing the high cost of such action and the possibility of new taxes being enacted. Likewise, a prominent business firm began trying to create opposition to the special session by stirring up a tax scare, prompting Daniel to pledge publicly on August 24 that he would not submit a tax measure. "If I thought a tax bill was necessary," he said, "I would submit it." Promising to hold expenses to $225,000, he claimed: "The cost of the session is 'peanuts' compared to the good name of the state. The cost is not going to be anything compared with the millions of dollars we are losing through unfavorable national publicity."[94] On September 10 he officially announced at a Democratic rally in Huntsville that the special session would meet on October 14 and address lobby control, water development, law enforcement, and the registration of those who represent others before state agencies.[95] Opinion surveys affirmed his assertions that the public was behind him all the way.

Daniel would learn to use the special session to his advantage like no governor before, so much so that some accused him of abusing his power. In his six years as chief executive he would call eight special sessions. His final one, in January 1962, was so resented that talk circulated of adjourning within the first hour of the meeting. Such threats notwithstanding, he once again emerged from the session with many of the measures he had sought.[96] Some legislators resented him for being too involved in their daily activities. There was talk that he was too domineering, that he left nothing to chance. Even his allies would concede that he frequently pushed too far in competing with the legislature for dominance. But both sides welcomed the unusual luxury of being able to walk into the governor's office and argue their positions with him alone. They knew he did not rely on anyone else to back him up or to take the heat for mistaken calculation. What they saw was what they got.

Daniel's first special session convened in Austin on October 14 as planned. He thanked legislators for taking part and subtly reminded them that his personal convictions were more important to him than political posturing. "I did not seek this office to maintain the status quo or to surrender the rights and responsibilities of my state through timidity or inaction. That is why I have called this session." [97] Once again Daniel was aided by the timeliness of certain outside events that coincided with his issues. The bribery trial of Representative James E. Cox was in progress in Austin when the legislators assembled. In addition, several indictments were still pending from the insurance scandals, and the Dallas trial of promoter Ben Jack Cage was imminent. News coverage of these events prompted Texans to demand legislative action on lobby reform at a time when elections were just around the corner.

One measure in particular faced a problematic outcome. The lobby reform bill, which had been extremely controversial in both the House and Senate, was thrown into a conference committee just three days before adjournment of the session. "The strategy of the opposition was to delay us until the final hours so that the governor and his supporters would accept a meaningless measure that would satisfy the lobby," recalled Zeke Zbranek. "They had miscalculated the dedication of the governor." At 5:00 P.M. on the last day, after all other matters on the agenda of the special session had been dealt with, Zbranek and Senator Crawford Martin presented a proposal they had worked out with Daniel. One objecting senator, who argued that crooks will be crooks regardless of what is written in the law books, told the pair that he wanted a two-hour recess to "caucus with his conscience." [98] In other words, he needed time to report the proposal to lobby leaders downtown. "With a smile and no acrimony whatsoever in his voice," remembered Zbranek, "the governor told this senator: 'You may tell your conscience that the bill will have to make the lobbyists register and report their expenses under penal sanctions or I'm going to call a special session every thirty days until we get it.'" Approximately fifteen minutes before midnight, the new law was intact. [99]

In the end, Daniel succeeded in passing all four of the measures he had sought. The lobby bill, although not as strong as he recommended, represented the first legislative action on the subject in twenty-seven years. The water program was the first of its kind in

Texas history. But one other issue remained. When Arkansas governor Orval E. Faubus announced that he was sending the state militia to stop integration of Little Rock's Central High School, a group of eight representatives urged Daniel to call a special session to consider segregation issues. He obliged and, immediately following the first one, called for another. He then sought and secured an antitroop bill, which allowed schools adequate measures to secure law and order, and the second special session was swiftly adjourned.

Daniel had gambled and won. Had his special session flopped, it would have marred his otherwise successful first term. Most important was the fact that he had managed to finance his major objectives without any substantial fights over a proposed sales tax. However, as the *San Antonio Express* had predicted two years earlier, he was slowly heading toward a huge clash with the legislature over new possible sources of revenue. The more his programs succeeded, the closer the state moved to a financial crunch. So far, he had held off sales-tax advocates with a convincing media campaign aimed at the fears of middle-class consumers.

With his first term quickly coming to an end, Daniel soon found himself back on the campaign trail. The liberal faction of the Democratic Party had not cooled off since the 1956 convention and, in the meantime, had formed an organization called Democrats of Texas, otherwise known as DOT. The group had two ambitious goals: to make a good showing in the upcoming 1958 primaries, and to seize the party's convention. To the organization's dismay, however, DOT found the electorate unresponsive not only to its cause but also to that of the conservatives.[100] Accordingly, Daniel's moderate stance helped him breeze by liberal challenger Henry Gonzalez on his way to reelection.[101] Gonzalez, the NAACP's Man of the Year, had galvanized the DOT delegates with his call for liberal activism. But with little organization and no state headquarters, he would succumb to the governor's organization and statewide popularity.[102] "Daniel had an unusual ability to demonstrate to the average voter his complete honesty," recalled Waggoner Carr, former attorney general and Speaker of the House during Daniel's administration. "He made them feel he was their governor. He never tried to exaggerate himself. He was a man of the streets."[103]

All that now stood between Daniel and a second term was the party's 1958 convention. Sam Rayburn told Ralph Yarborough that if he and Daniel were going to fight out the 1956 gubernatorial nomination again he "did not have much stomach" to attend the convention.[104] Likewise, he wrote to Daniel that he was "not interested in personalities" and trusted that the Daniel-Yarborough conflict "will not be fought out at San Antonio... Who are temporary and permanent chairmen is a matter about which nobody has consulted with me, and I assume they won't, but anyone who is a Democrat will be satisfactory to me."[105]

Daniel had hoped for a better reception in San Antonio than he had received two years earlier in Fort Worth, but failed to get his wish. Moderate voting trends in a strong majority of precinct conventions around the state had handed him control of most county conventions, as well as the September state convention, and his selection of temporary chairmen was approved. But he ran into trouble when he chose to veto the selection of two liberal nominees for seats on the State Executive Committee.[106] This move caused nothing short of an explosion on the convention floor. A *San Antonio Express* reporter described the spectacle: "A thousand outraged members of liberal delegations milled around the auditorium for forty-five minutes shouting, chanting, and walloping the floor with placard poles after they were refused a roll call vote on replacement of the nominees."[107] Daniel was even concerned about the safety of his family at the wild proceedings. Despite the furor, he eventually managed to escape with undisputed control of the party.

Daniel began his second term on January 20, 1959, and quickly worked himself back into his normal, hectic schedule. "The governor's job is a day and night job," he once declared. "I usually get up at seven in the morning and start answering the telephone and looking over the mail. I have interviews and meetings all day, and then in the evening at the mansion... I take calls and messages until late at night. It's a big state, so many people. It is true that the job is a full time proposition... but the people are considerate and my assistants handle many problems."[108] Most of his correspondence was of the usual but necessary inconsequential sort expected of public officials. He made a valiant attempt to respond personally to as many letters as possible, but received enough requests for autographs to require a pre-printed reply card. One of those cards, sent to a young autograph collector, ended up in the mailbox of the governor's future son-in-law.[109]

In some ways Daniel set a spartan tone. "He didn't have a private airplane, or an entourage, like some politicians," recalled George Christian. "He traveled by himself. He knew where every state dollar was going. He had a small staff. He rode them closely. When we worked for him, we felt that we had to do as he did. He set a moral standard in the governor's office that everyone stood by. He didn't like hanky-panky; he didn't like a lot of swearing around the office." [110]

But despite the image he projected, even Daniel liked to have a drink now and then. At a social event, when he would instruct a staffer to go and get him a "Coke," it was understood that he wanted a little rum added to the drink. Christian remembered the day the governor finally decided he could trust him to retrieve a Coke. "He was keeping me pristine," laughed Christian. "He didn't want me to know that he needed a little rum now and then. But when I returned with his Coke, he was very pleased." [111] Daniel also enjoyed evenings out on the town, eating good food and listening to music. Once, after a meeting of the State Democratic Executive Committee in El Paso, he and Jean decided to go across the border to Juarez with Bob and Hazel Haynsworth and assistant Jake Pickle. Haynsworth knew of a room in Juarez with good music and called ahead to get assurance from the manager that the governor of Texas would receive no special publicity. After all, the last thing "teetotaler" Daniel wanted was to be spotted or, even worse, photographed, in a Mexican bar. Arriving at the establishment, the group was seated at a big table up near the band. "Everything went fine for a few minutes," said Pickle. "Then the band, which had been playing lively Mexican melodies, suddenly stopped, then executed a drum-roll flourish. The governor and I looked at each other and thought, 'Uh oh.' He sank lower in his seat." [112]

The worst was yet to come. Grabbing the microphone, the bandleader announced, "We are proud to have with us tonight the governor of the State of Texas, the honorable Price Daniel!" A giant spotlight swept across the room and stopped at Daniel's table. The governor sat still with his head down. The announcer repeated the proclamation, this time in Spanish. But again, Daniel sank lower in his chair. Becoming agitated, the bandleader made one last desperate attempt: "Please! Will the governor of Texas stand and be recognized?" Jean whispered to Pickle, "Jake, for goodness sake, will you do it?" The governor also prodded him. "Jake, I bet you've always wanted to be governor—here's your chance." To thunderous applause and a rendition of "The Eyes of Texas," Pickle stood up and waved to the crowd. "I must admit," said Pickle, "I got a great reception." [113]

Back in Austin, as expected, the sales-tax debate quickly resurfaced. This time it was going to take more than television commercials to make it go away. Texas was struggling with various forms of taxation, and money was not being generated in sufficient amounts to accomplish what a majority of citizens wanted. When the legislature convened in January 1959, it faced a deficit of $90 million in the state general revenue fund due primarily to plummeting proceeds from the oil production tax. The state's economy had been undermined by the development of huge oil fields in the Middle East and the resulting drop in prices for domestic fuel. Texas had been producing nearly 40 percent of all the oil in the United States, but foreign oil priced at a dollar-per-barrel soon flooded the state. The deficit left lawmakers with no choice but to raise taxes before they could make final appropriations for the 1959-61 budget. They agreed on a record $2.4 billion budget but had trouble agreeing on how to raise the money. To Daniel's dismay, more and more lawmakers began favoring a general sales tax. [114]

Daniel had, for the time being, successfully portrayed himself as the protector of the average citizen against "unfair" sales taxes. "I've got my fighting clothes on," he told reporters. [115] Under his plan, businesses would carry more of the load. The gas industry in particular was taking resources that could never be replaced and should bear a heavier burden, he reasoned. These business interests, insisting that they could not stand more taxes themselves, began splitting from the governor to join some of the forces in public education agitating for a broad-based tax. Daniel managed to drift from these big-business interests without getting into a political bed with the labor-liberal crowd, which applauded his program but thought it did not go far enough.

The governor was banking on public sentiment, not the big wheels, to help put over his program. Thus far into his administration he had succeeded. Wrote Allen Duckworth of the *Dallas Morning News:* "A sober political truth is beginning to buzz in the brains of his enemies: Price has built up a powerful political gang—the people." [116] The 56th Legislature eventually recoiled from enacting the largest tax bill in the history of the state, and three special sessions were called before the impasse was resolved by increasing individual taxes on cigarettes, automobiles, radio and television sets, and levying new taxes on hotels, boats, air conditioners, and other items.[117] Although a majority of Texans applauded Daniel for protecting their pocketbooks, his defiance would exact a huge political price: a tarnished relationship with Speaker Waggoner Carr, Lieutenant Governor Ben Ramsey, and several key senators. "It was a tough time for Price," recalled George Christian. "Those were some horrendous fights."[118]

Daniel was a master at keeping his political foes in check. When gas industry leaders accused him of being their enemy, he simply reminded them of his fights against oil imports, for retention of the depletion allowance, and for state ownership of the tidelands. Considering all he had done for them, he reasoned, the least they could do was pay a little more taxes. When pressed by a reporter about whether he would eventually seek a third term, he said that if the gas industry tried to "pull the wool over the eyes of Texans" about the tax situation, he would most certainly run. "Good gosh," responded one of the governor's critics in the House. "Let's pass the bills—quick!"[119]

Daniel had polished his image of being somewhat of a political maverick. He seemed to be oblivious to praise or criticism from business, labor, farm organizations, or any minority groups on any issue. Instead, he preferred to go his own way, adhering to his strictly personal point of view. Perhaps this explains why he never established any permanent political alliances. Those groups which opposed him on one issue would likely be his biggest supporters on the next. Some even kidded him, claiming that every political group in the state had been both his ardent supporter and his bitter critic. "All in all, I find it refreshing to see a politician who will take the time to analyze differences within the industry, instead of brushing us off with the statement that he can't do anything about our problems," said one gasoline company official. "Price Daniel is something unique on the political scene in this respect because he will examine the basis for such differences, and then unhesitatingly take the side he thinks is right."[120]

Seldom swayed by special interest groups or party platforms, Daniel avoided being "labeled" as this or that type of politician. On some matters, such as local self-government and states' rights, liberals considered him ultra-conservative. Yet on other issues, such as his fight against a general sales tax, conservatives would insist he was a liberal. Even his closest friends could not bank on his support. Always confident that he could muster support for his pet projects, Daniel was seldom worried about alienating key constituencies or being politically correct. He tried not to let the spotlight of political office separate him from his own ideals. Those ideals, in turn, affected his decision-making as governor.

Daniel used much of his time and energy in late 1959 helping Lyndon Johnson campaign for the Democratic presidential nomination against Massachusetts senator John F. Kennedy. He had made close friends of most governors while attending the governors' conferences around the country, and did not hesitate to call them in an attempt to drum up support for his former Senate colleague. One such call was to Governor Ross Barnett of Mississippi, in which Barnett told Daniel he just wished that Johnson would come out in support of segregation. "People are hungry for our message," Barnett told Daniel. "Why just last night, I addressed a very large crowd and they gave me a standing ovation."

"Where did you make that speech, Governor?" Daniel asked.

Barnett hesitated, then replied, "Birmingham, Alabama."[121]

CHAPTER 13

A Penny for Price

As co-chairmen of the Texas delegation at the Democratic National Convention in 1960, Price Daniel and Sam Rayburn were sitting side-by-side as the state of Wyoming cast the final vote to nominate John Kennedy for president. Rayburn picked up a nearby telephone and instructed Daniel to stand in between him and the media, making sure his conversation would not be overheard. He then proceeded to call Lyndon Johnson. "Now, Lyndon," Rayburn said, "they may be calling you and asking you to get on the ticket. The answer is no! Do you hear me? The answer is no!" [1]

Daniel and Rayburn rode together back to the Los Angeles hotel where they were staying in adjoining suites. That evening a group arrived at the hotel, including Congressman Hale Boggs of New Orleans, to try to talk Rayburn into agreeing to put Johnson on the ticket. "Only later would I learn that Jack Kennedy had been told by Johnson that he would first have to get Rayburn's approval before he would consider joining the ticket," Daniel would recall. "This group of visitors may have been sent by Kennedy to talk Rayburn into letting Johnson run." [2] Regardless, by the time the group left Rayburn's suite, the Speaker was convinced that it was in the best interest of the Democratic Party for Johnson to help Kennedy out in the South.

Daniel walked down the hallway to Johnson's suite and was instructed by Johnson to make sure that the entire Texas delegation would be present at the caucus the following morning. He was also informed that Johnson had indeed been offered the vice presidency by Kennedy, and that he was going to accept it. Johnson said that Bobby Kennedy was strongly opposed to his nomination and had suggested instead that he take the chairmanship of the Democratic National Committee. According to Johnson, he and Rayburn told Bobby to "go to hell," that "it will be the vice presidency or nothing." [3]

Daniel sat in the room with Johnson waiting to hear whether Kennedy was still extending his offer. Senator Bob Kerr, a brash ally of Johnson, soon entered the suite and approached Johnson with his hand in the shape of a pistol. "I am going to shoot you Lyndon if it's true what I've heard about you," he said, "that you are going to accept the vice presidential nomination." Johnson instructed Kerr to talk it over with his aide Bobby Baker, and the two men disappeared into the bathroom. By the time they came out, Kerr was convinced that Johnson should indeed be on the ticket for three reasons: He felt that Kennedy, a Catholic, could not win without Johnson, especially in Kerr's home state of Oklahoma; if they lost in 1960, Johnson would be in a good position to run again in 1964; and, Johnson would only be a proverbial heartbeat away from the presidency. [4]

Suddenly, there was a knock at the door. It was the chairman of the Arkansas delegation, who asked Daniel to step out into the hall. Arkansas Governor Orval Faubus had instructed him to vote the same as Daniel throughout the convention, and the chairman told Daniel that he wanted to cast Arkansas' vice presidential vote for him. Daniel thanked him for the consideration, but told him that if he could wait just a short while there would be someone he could vote for in earnest. Around 2:00 that afternoon, Kennedy called Johnson and officially asked him to be his running mate. [5] Johnson accepted.

Daniel had campaigned hard for his old Senate colleague, having even worked with the legislature to move the state primaries up a couple of months so that Johnson could get his Senate reelection behind him before the Democratic National Convention convened in the summer. [6] In fact, it was he and Rayburn who had formed the Johnson-for-President Committee and made plans to open a campaign state headquarters in Austin. [7] "We had sold ourselves trying to elect

Johnson," conceded Daniel. "We preached that Kennedy could not win. We had gotten so far along that line and we were really believing it."[8] But Daniel quickly shifted focus and backed the Kennedy-Johnson ticket, even playing host to the duo in Austin as they passed through on a campaign trip. On the night of their visit, Kennedy, plagued with a bad back, roamed through the mansion in search of a bed with the hardest mattress. After a detailed inspection, he found the governor's bed most adequate. And, of course, Daniel obliged.[9]

Kennedy and Johnson, however, were not the only ones in the midst of a campaign. The governor's second term was quickly winding down, and in his usual style he worked tirelessly to recapture his post. In his 1960 reelection campaign, Daniel delivered well over a hundred formal speeches and aired just as many radio and television spots promoting safety, extending holiday greetings, discussing concerns for different study groups, and the like.[10] His opponent, conservative Jack Cox, campaigned on passing a sales tax. Cox stole much of the business support that Daniel had enjoyed in the past, and, even more impressive, one of his principal supporters was former Texas governor Allan Shivers. However, the help of Shivers and the active support of Citizens for a Sales Tax were to no avail. Cox was soundly defeated.[11] On May 7, 1960, Daniel was the proud recipient of the largest vote ever given a Texas candidate for governor in a primary election.[12]

In this campaign, unlike previous Texas gubernatorial races, specific references to segregation issues had been rare. Gradually moving toward the center of the Texas political spectrum, Daniel was the first "borderline nonsegregationist" gubernatorial candidate in the South to defeat a segregationist opponent. Even so, Daniel's critics on civil rights contended that his reclassification was due far more to his avoidance of segregationist oratory than to any overt support for racial change. But this campaign marked the beginning of the end of segregationist rhetoric in Texas politics. In fact, just two years later, the *Texas Observer* would declare that "racism is dead in statewide Texas politics." Major candidates, including Daniel, would now be able to solicit black support openly.[13]

When the 1960 State Democratic Convention rolled around, Daniel warned the delegates it would be a harmonious gathering of Texas Democrats if he had to see to it personally. He was fully aware that the national ticket would need a strong coalition of support from Texas to fight off the Nixon challenge, and leaders of both parties agreed that the close race could ultimately be decided by the state's twenty-four electoral votes. So when two electors insisted that the Kennedy-Johnson ticket would not receive their support if the party carried Texas, the governor recommended they quit. One of the men complied, but the other refused and was ejected from the convention. Another distraction took place when a woman rose to her feet and made public her dissatisfaction with Lyndon Johnson, then pleaded: "If we want to get this country back, it will be by the people, not by yellow-dog Democrats!" [14]

The media had been expecting the liberals and conservatives to do battle over the state Democratic platform and were not disappointed. The liberals approved of the national platform and had come to Dallas with all intentions of giving it their endorsement. The conservatives wanted no such thing. [15] Neither side would be completely satisfied in the end, for Daniel had plans of his own. The governor took center stage and ironed out a semi-conservative states' rights platform that repudiated the national one on many counts. Among other things, it supported the Texas right-to-work-law, as well as the oil depletion allowance, and condemned sit-ins. [16] And before either slate of opponents had a chance to voice opposition, Daniel struck his gavel to adjourn the gathering and quickly escaped the furious assembly through the nearest exit. [17]

The governor never made specific mention of the national platform or the Kennedy-Johnson ticket at the convention, and thus, while pushing a state platform, managed to remain devoted to the Democratic presidential duo. [18] In effect, he gave his patron Johnson a more desirable states' rights platform on which to campaign, as opposed to a "New Frontier" stand, which would support increased federal activity. [19]

Despite the few aforementioned outbreaks, the 1960 convention had proven itself to be the most harmonious of Daniel's incumbency. Actually, it was the first such gathering in which the governor had not felt compelled to oust anyone from the State Democratic Executive Committee. [20]

In November the Kennedy-Johnson ticket managed to carry Texas by the narrow margin of 24,019 votes. The Lone Star State was not the deciding factor in the election, as some had predicted, but its Democratic margin of victory closely mirrored the national outcome. Overall, Kennedy defeated Nixon by approximately 214,000 votes. In the meantime, Daniel, as Shivers before him, appointed William Blakely to the United States Senate, this time to fill Johnson's vacated seat.[21]

Daniel's power was now stronger than at any other time in his career. In addition to his gubernatorial duties, he chaired the Southern Governors' Conference and the Interstate Oil Compact Commission. He received primary credit for reversing the long-standing free-trade philosophy of southern states by getting the Southern Governors' Conference to go on record for more effective protection of hard-hit domestic industries, notably oil. And, as chairman of the Interstate Oil Compact, he was successful in helping restore to Texas and other prorating states some portion of the markets lost because of purchaser discrimination.

One droll occurrence in particular during Daniel's third term concerned then-Lieutenant Governor Ben Ramsey. Daniel viewed the role of lieutenant governor as somewhat of an extension of the legislative branch, and thus never called on Ramsey to serve in any administrative capacity. He once wrote: "When the governor is preparing to leave the state, he or his staff then tries to acquaint the lieutenant governor with any pressing matters, but even then the lieutenant governor does very little in the way of carrying out the duties of the executive in our state. In fact, there is usually an understanding that he will not do anything involving policy matters." [22] Ramsey, however, apparently had different ideas about the responsibility of his post. When Daniel briefly exited the state in July 1961, a state senator had carefully planned to use the occasion to go before the Board of Pardons and Paroles for a convicted narcotics carrier. "I know Price would never approve a parole," the senator told a reporter, "so I tried to arrange for the board to recommend the parole while Price was out of state and Ben was acting governor." Although furious when notified upon returning that Ramsey had indeed allowed the prisoner to go out on parole, Daniel nonetheless spared the lieutenant governor the embarrassment of revoking his decision.[23]

One of the more laborious fights of Daniel's administration involved the enactment of a law protecting the property of lost owners and providing for enforcement of escheat to the state in the event no owners existed. An article of the Revised Civil Statutes carried forward the age-old principle of escheat to the state of any personal property for which there was no lawful owner. Prior to Daniel's administration, Texas had no law requiring the reporting of this type of property or advertising for lost owners, even though many states had followed the recommendations of the Council of State Governments, the American Bar Association, the National Conference of Governors, as well as the National Association of Attorneys General, and had adopted legislation of this nature. In 1959, and every session thereafter, Daniel recommended to the legislature that it enact an abandoned property law which would require the holders of personal property to advertise for owners or heirs whose whereabouts had been unknown for more than the seven-year statutory period after which death is presumed, and to report to the state when owners could not be located. But he had encountered stout opposition each time, led by the Texas Bankers Association.[24]

Finally, in 1961, the 57th Legislature passed Daniel's measures with respect to all persons and corporations except banks, prompting a Special House Committee to study the need for similar legislation that would apply to banking institutions. The committee eventually concluded: "We agree with Governor Price Daniel that this is an emergency matter requiring prompt attention at the Special Session called for January 3, 1962. Otherwise, with another year's delay, we estimate that 100,000 more dormant accounts and at least another $1,000,000 will be lost to owners and the state through the procedures of banks."[25]

Daniel waged this battle at no small political risk, for many of his conservative, business-oriented backers felt betrayed and predicted he would be significantly crippled. But he was not to be dissuaded, believing not only that he was doing the right thing but also that he would find support. In fact, many bankers, especially those who were not following the practice of absorbing or converting these dormant accounts, conceded in private that Daniel's measures were necessary. After three years of strong opposition, the Texas Bankers Association gave in. As a result, Article 3272b was enacted. It required preservation of dormant accounts of lost owners; prohibited conversion or charges against such accounts; required that names of owners be published if their whereabouts had been unknown for more than seven years; stipulated that if owners were not located within one year thereafter, their names, together with all amounts of less than $25.00, would be delivered to the state treasurer; and called for accounts in excess of $25.00 to be advertised until the owners were found or until the attorney general brought escheat proceedings.[26]

Reflecting on Daniel's personal style, George Christian remembered: "He was a hands-on person. He knew what he wanted to do and he sat down and did it. He was a journalist by background. He was an excellent writer—accurate—knew how to do all the things that have gone by the boards now. Well-read. Understood history. Certainly knew just about everything there was to know about Texas history, and used that greatly to his advantage." Christian recalled that "On major speeches, he wrote his own. He did a lot of his own letter writing. Anything you see that came out of his time in public service in writing, he either wrote it or he edited it or he approved it." [27]

With approximately 1,000 positions subject to gubernatorial appointment, this power of the governor of Texas is quite extensive. In fact, Daniel considered appointment-making his most difficult task as governor. In 1960 alone he appointed 275 members of various boards and commissions, 80 public weighers, 74 branch pilots, and 65 judges.[28] As for many other tasks, he delegated authority. Unlike several of his predecessors who preferred to deal with administration officials on an individual basis, Daniel was more inclined toward the use of his cabinet. He found cabinet meetings to be helpful on specific matters, but only included those department heads who had some part in the function under discussion.[29] "I like to be divested of powers that can be handled best by someone else, instead of gathering them under me," he once confessed.[30]

The sales tax skirmishes in Daniel's first two terms proved to be merely warm-ups for the battle to come. With Texas facing serious revenue shortfalls, pressure was mounting from Daniel's allies for him to support a tax increase. Many business interests split with him, as did a strong coalition of teachers and educators. Even some liberals in the legislature who had adamantly opposed the tax began to reconsider. Daniel, however, refused to budge. Having flirted with sin, gas, and single-shot taxes, he had experimented with everything under the sun to try and avoid the sales tax. "He was the last to concede that it was time to go to a sales tax," remembered Christian. "He had made so many statements against the sales tax that for him to turn around would be more than people could take. But, he had a tendency to take on a fight longer than he should have." [31]

Sensing the shifting tide of public sentiment, many of Daniel's closest advisers began suggesting that he reevaluate his sales tax resistance. With an election year rapidly approaching, they argued, the opposition could soon grow invincible. But despite the political consequences, he stubbornly held his ground, unwilling to reverse his position on an issue that had much defined his career as a public servant. "The trouble is that I started fighting it back there when it really would have been a hardship," Daniel recalled. "I started fighting it back in 1939, and at that time there was a different situation. I got locked in on it through campaign promises and pledges that I would continue to fight it." [32]

In a 1977 interview Daniel reflected on his desperate attempts to raise revenue without enacting a sales tax: "In the 1961 session we tried to raise the money through taxes on oil, on gas, especially the gas that was leaving our state. And corporate franchise taxes— I'd been for those being increased. I think nearly every session we increased the cigarette tax and some luxury taxes... we wanted to tax natural resources and those who could best afford to pay and try to keep the sales tax off as long as we could." It greatly concerned him that a state sales tax would place the greatest burden on the lower middle class. "I felt that a sales tax was almost like an income tax on everybody who spent all they made," he said. "If you spent all that you made, it was a pretty good bite out of the pocket of the people. It was not for those who saved, invested, and they weren't being taxed in the same proportion as those who spent all they made." [33]

Daniel was publicly criticized by Attorney General Will Wilson, who appeared before the House Committee on Taxation and Revenue in opposition to his tax proposals. While reprimanding Wilson for making these remarks, Daniel dismissed his tactics as an attempt to climb the political ladder. Wilson shot back, saying he had the duty to persuade the governor not to waste a half million dollars in a special session which he insisted would pass a general sales tax, regardless. [34] In an open letter to Daniel, he wrote: "Well, governor, if calling [the sales tax] the Will Wilson tax will ease your pain, I am quite content that it be so called. If by that device we can finance our schools and hospitals, I am willing to carry the political load which a governor should carry, and which under most governors, the attorney general would not have to assume. You took office with a comfortable surplus on hand, but under your administration the situation has steadily deteriorated until we are now eighty-odd million dollars in the red." [35]

Sensing that his political fortunes would be long tied to the outcome of this potentially explosive issue, Daniel allowed the sales tax fight to consume him. He met with several committees of the legislature to present his views. Once, awakened near midnight by news that a conference committee had reached an impasse, he arose from bed, went to the Capitol, and worked until the wee hours of the morning.[36] When it finally became evident that lawmakers were determined to pass a sales tax measure at any cost, Daniel, aware that the Texas legislature had historically sustained gubernatorial vetoes 95 percent of the time,[37] issued an open threat by telling the press that he would veto any such legislation. The threat proved successful, for the session adjourned without passing a bill embodying a general sales tax.[38]

But Daniel kept fighting. He elicited an outstanding response from a radio broadcast that outlined his own sales tax position and invited citizens to express their opinions prior to his calling of a special session. He promptly received around 7,000 replies and was then able to tell lawmakers that a substantial number of citizens supported his views.[39] Eventually, however, after eight grueling months of debates and two special sessions, he became convinced that the powerful corporate lobbies' determination to push through the tax at any cost would prevail. When push came to shove, he actually sent his staff onto the House floor to lobby for passage of the sales tax, knowing it must be done or the doors of state government would have to be closed. In order to help the state avoid a financial crunch, he did not veto the levy, but at the same time he deprived the document of his signature.[40]

The levy, which became effective on September 1, 1961, was the first alteration in the state's tax structure in over twenty years. Regardless of his strong opposition to this measure, a large portion of the state electorate blamed Daniel. In fact, merchants frequently told their customers, "Let's have a penny for Price." [41] He had been placed in a no-win situation. Had he prevented the sales tax from being enacted, state government would have lacked sufficient revenue to function. On the other hand, having chosen to allow it to pass, albeit without his signature, he received heavy criticism. Actually, many of his opponents who vocally chided him for letting the sales tax pass had themselves openly endorsed it. They had seized an opportunity to pass a controversial measure that they favored, while at the same time shifting blame to the governor in the face of a reelection campaign. In the end, Daniel would come to accept the fact that a sales tax was essential for Texas. "I'm not going to ever say anything too good about the sales tax, but I certainly realize... after hindsight that it had to come," he would admit. "No way we could finance state government without it." [42]

Amid the sales tax bickering, Hurricane Carla struck the Texas coast on September 11, 1961, testing the state's disaster relief capabilities to the extreme. Fortunately, advance warnings had been issued from the U.S. Weather Bureau. In addition, Daniel had previously conducted a series of hurricane preparedness conferences in every major coastal city, outlining the duties of federal, state, and local emergency personnel. As a result, over half a million people were successfully evacuated from Texas coastal areas—the largest exodus of people in the history of the country. Had it not been for the evacuation and subsequent control of the area, it is estimated that more people would have perished than in the Galveston storm of 1900, when 6,000 people died. In all, only thirty-four lives were lost on the entire Texas coast, eight of whom perished at the hands of a tornado that followed Carla to Galveston. [43]

Since Texas shares a common boundary with Mexico and is home to millions of inhabitants of Mexican descent, Texas governors have often played a different role than chief executives from many other American states in having to promote better relations with a foreign country. Daniel occasionally entertained Mexican dignitaries in Austin, including President Lopez Mateos. He also adopted the practice of attending Laredo's annual Washington's birthday celebration, where he met prominent Mexican officials on the International Bridge to signify good relations between the two countries. [44]

Daniel was hoping that the political fortitude he exhibited in recent battles would ultimately win him favor with Texans in the upcoming election. Many predicted that it would, including Sam Rayburn. "I really think that this year in office has strengthened you with the people of Texas," he wrote in late 1961. "You showed willingness to fight for the things you wanted and I think you came out mighty well."[45] So despite myriad political hurdles, Daniel made the decision in 1962 to seek what no man had ever accomplished in Texas politics—a fourth term as governor. Little did he know then that he would ultimately fall victim to one of the best-organized and highly financed political campaigns in the state's history.[46] The same big business interests that had strongly supported him in the three previous elections were growing upset with him. Motivated in part by his opposition to the state sales tax, they began searching for new leadership. At the same time rumors were circulating around Austin that John Connally, then secretary of the navy, was receiving statewide encouragement for a gubernatorial bid.[47]

Connally had grown somewhat bored in Washington. He had proven himself by effectively managing the Department of the Navy, but his heart was elsewhere. Rejuvenated by success in the nation's capital, the lanky Texan decided to return home and run for office. A poll taken in June 1961 had shown Connally receiving only one percent of Texas voters' support for governor.[48] A similar poll the following year gave him only a four-percent approval rating.[49] But the candidate had many assets, one being friends in the right places. Dating back to his college days at the University of Texas, Connally had been building relationships with people who would go on to become social and political leaders across the state.[50] He knew their support was just a call away.

Having crossed paths in front of the Texas State Capitol one afternoon, Daniel and Connally engaged in a brief conversation that would ultimately lead to a new chapter in Texas history. Connally wanted an answer from Daniel, one way or the other, as to whether he would seek a fourth term as governor. At the time Daniel was in the middle of a legislative session and told him he had not yet decided. He candidly expressed his concerns to Connally that if he did not seek a fourth term, Will Wilson would stand a strong chance of being elected.[51] "But Price," Connally persisted, "I cannot afford to wait. I'm four percent in the polls, and I need to get up a statewide organization and start raising money." With Daniel refusing to commit himself one way or the other, Connally concluded: "Okay, then. I'm going to announce and run."[52]

It was rather unexpected that Connally would choose to run against Daniel, considering that he was one of the governor's biggest campaign contributors the previous election. In 1960 Connally, then a Fort Worth lawyer, donated $1,500 to Daniel's cause. Some suggest he was simply not expecting Daniel to seek a fourth term. "If Daniel had announced sooner, Connally might not have run," said George Christian, "but Connally didn't think Daniel was going to run." Daniel did not want to leave his post with constituents feeling he had wanted to escape defeat. "I'd rather be carried out of here feet first than be called a quitter," he told Christian, and thus another long campaign battle began.[53]

Connally launched his campaign at a huge barbecue on his ranch near Floresville in Wilson County. Well documented by television and radio news coverage, the "hometown" event was attended by approximately 10,000 people. In subsequent weeks a television series entitled "Coffee With Connally" was broadcast each morning between 7:00 and 8:00 in every section of the state, each program confined to one issue in the campaign.[54] Texans listened to Connally when he told them their state was losing hundreds of millions of dollars due to a second-rate system of higher education which had failed to attract scholars. Highly respected scholars, he argued, would in turn draw much needed federal grants and new industries to the state.[55] Striking an even harder blow to Daniel, he promised to seek a constitutional amendment that would limit Texas governors to either two terms of two years each or one four-year term. In the same breath, he tagged Daniel a "political czar" with close friends in most every office. "No governor should be awarded four terms," he told voters in a February 15 broadcast. Significantly, upon Connally's eventual election as governor, he not only failed to seek such an amendment, but also later urged passage of a measure increasing the governor's term from two to four years with no limits on the number of terms.[56]

Daniel's campaign strategists grew worried by Connally's increasing popularity. In a March 27 memorandum to George Christian, staffer Clyde Johnson wrote: "First, we must face the unpleasant fact that the picture has definitely changed since the governor's announcement—in Connally's favor. Of course, a reasonable uphill climb could be expected; but what we must try to avoid is a bandwagon peak for Connally on or about May 1. This Connally peak must be reached immediately, if not already. Secondly, the reports of Connally's growing strength—and these are coming—are accompanied by explanations that the governor has been in office long enough. We need to camouflage this with a good smoke screen—new thoughts, new ideas, a new Daniel 'image.' Thirdly, I believe with proper timing we can effectively abandon a defensive position and launch a vigorous counterattack to offset the 'early' Connally peak." [57]

The governor was famous for being put on the defensive, Johnson acknowledged, "but he is equally well known for his ability to come out of the corner punching—when necessary. April, especially the last two weeks, is the time to launch the attack, in my opinion. I'm convinced we've got to start fighting." [58] In retrospect, Daniel may have wished that he had started fighting harder at this point of the race. He was so confident of taking Connally to a runoff, however, that he opted to keep his big campaign weapons idle until that time came.

The Connally campaign caught momentum rapidly, much as had Daniel's first gubernatorial bid in 1956. Many of the state's 125 daily newspapers and 555 weeklies were behind the challenger, and large campaign contributions from the wealthy soon began financing his numerous appearances on costly television broadcasts. Even motorists had trouble escaping Connally's message, with hundreds of billboards featuring his face planted on roadsides throughout the state. [59] A large slice of his support came from the more conservative Shivers people, notably business groups alienated by Daniel's push for lobby control. It was Shivers' money that financed Connally's campaign, not Lyndon Johnson's. In fact, Connally inherited Johnson's supporters mainly because he was the one who had assembled much of the vice president's organization years earlier. Thus, many of Daniel's county campaign managers and others he had counted on in the past went to Connally. Some went by choice, while others, having predicted that Daniel would not seek a fourth term, had shifted to Connally in the best interest of their careers. [60]

There are conflicting opinions about Lyndon Johnson's role in Connally's decision to enter the race. On one hand, a story is told of Connally going on a hunting trip at the LBJ Ranch with some other political figures to discuss his candidacy. Johnson poked fun at Connally the entire weekend in front of his colleagues, calling him "Big Master John Connally," and chiding him for having (at that time) only four percent of Texas behind him. Upset by Johnson's harassment, Connally went home immediately following the hunt, not even staying for dinner.[61] "Lyndon did not want Connally to run," recalls George Christian. "In fact, Connally resented that Johnson was not stronger for him. On the other hand, Daniel probably thought that he was detecting some conspiracies, but Johnson was not mixed up in this. If he was, it was all peripheral."[62]

Others theorize that Johnson hand-picked Connally to challenge Daniel so that he would have more influence on calling the shots back in Texas. In the *Chicago Tribune,* reporter Robert Sherrill expanded on what he thought to be Johnson's motives: "It was at this point, with conservatives seeming to waver in their support of the time-honored one-party arrangement, that Connally was hustled to the front of the Texas political stage." He further wrote that "reporters who traveled with [Connally] in the 1962 campaign say he was furious with then Governor Price Daniel for 'letting the party get away from him.' Connally had been drafted from the job of Secretary of the Navy to come back to Texas and reunite the party for the conservative Democrats, re-recruiting the defectors to the Republican party. He did that job with great, if sometimes heavy-handed skill."[63]

Some Texas political observers believe Johnson's "unfavorable" attitude toward Connally's gubernatorial bid was merely a decoy. Johnson was a very close friend of Connally and certainly felt more allegiance to him than to Daniel. But his keen interest in the Texas gubernatorial race, they insist, went far beyond that. In 1960 Johnson barely escaped defeat from a relatively unknown political science professor by the name of John Tower. And the following year, when Johnson left the Senate to become vice president, Tower had captured the seat he vacated in a special election. Therefore, Tower's triumph, coupled with a growing revolt by the state's liberal faction, caused Johnson to fear losing his power base in Texas. He needed a fresh face, a strong Democratic conservative gubernatorial candidate in 1962. So while he publicly acted somewhat disinterested, Johnson, according to several seasoned observers, labored behind the scenes to promote Connally.[64] Will Wilson agreed: "John Connally's candidacy is a move by Lyndon Johnson to oust Price Daniel, oust me, oust Senator Ralph Yarborough and gain complete control of the state government."[65]

In the end, ironically, Connally used Johnson as a butt of campaign rhetoric. "Don't you come back and campaign for me,

Lyndon," Connally warned, noting that every time the vice president's name was mentioned along the campaign trail it received anything but a warm response. "When John Connally sits in that governor's chair, you're going to know who's governor of Texas," he assured supporters. "No man will occupy that chair with me or stand behind me." [66] Even Daniel tried to use the Johnson connection to Connally's detriment, distributing campaign signs saying, "Scratch *Lyndon's Boy John*."

It was not long before Daniel began feeling the heat not only from the carefully planned Connally campaign but also from other contenders, such as Attorney General Will Wilson and liberal Don Yarborough. Wilson went so far as to accuse the incumbent of making a huge profit on his Liberty land and mineral interests, while Yarborough was becoming increasingly popular in the polls.[67] Also on the ballot were distinguished West Texan Marshall Formby and Edwin A. Walker, a retired army general and right-wing extremist. In addition, the governor had to cope with being outspent by his contenders. While Daniel put just over $125,000 into his reelection, Yarborough dished out nearly twice as much, and Connally set a state record of $699,102.[68] Because much of his political apparatus had deserted to Connally, Daniel could not raise the necessary funds. In actuality, his organization and Connally's were virtually identical. "You can always tell who is the lead horse because all the rest are concentrating their fire on him," he told the *Washington Post*. "[In the end] people are more interested in the type of service than the length." [69]

Feeling the pressure, Daniel put his campaign in full gear. In a single day, he addressed morning coffees in Paris and Bonham and a meeting of the Denison Lions Club, appeared on television in the Sherman-Denison area, and then spoke to a crowd in Gainesville.[70] In each talk he tried desperately to distance himself from the recently passed sales tax. "There are people in the state who are still trying to blame the sales tax on me," he said, "when the truth is that I fought against it for 22 years and helped defeat it on several occasions. I finally had to let it become law over my objection and without my signature last year, because it was the only tax on which a majority of the legislature could agree in time to finance our schools, hospitals and other vital services." [71] Furthermore, he predicted that it would not be long before a new campaign was launched to increase the rate from two percent to three percent, or even higher, and to eliminate many of the items exempt under the present law. He promised to "vigorously oppose these efforts to increase the rate and to place such items as food and medicine under the tax."[72]

Daniel also implied that Connally, if elected, would be the one to push a sales tax increase. "It is worthy of note that many of the same lobbyists who worked the hardest for a general sales tax and against a pipeline tax during the sessions of the legislature last year are now to be found among the supporters of the candidate for governor who is doing the most boasting about the number of votes he is going to get in the primary Saturday. One of his top financial contributors is the chief lobbyist and chairman for the Citizens for a Sales Tax committee which engineered passage of the sales tax measure in 1961."[73] Try as he might, Daniel could never escape blame for the sales tax. Even more damaging, by having drifted from his political base to do what he believed was right, he had undercut himself politically.

In the end, Daniel could not survive the attacks from so many different directions. On May 5, 1962, he finished a distant third behind Connally and Yarborough,[74] who were thrown into a runoff. Connally eventually captured a narrow victory, 565,174 to 538,924.[75] Daniel had suffered only his second defeat since entering political life as a ripe youngster fresh out of Baylor. It would also be his last.

"I think that Price's downfall was not so much the sales tax, but rather the constant bickering and fighting over taxes," reflected George Christian. "He did not look like he was leading Texas out of the wilderness because of all of this scuffling with the legislature. The appearance of gridlock in state government undid Governor Daniel."[76]

Ronnie Dugger, editor of the liberal *Texas Observer* and longtime critic of Daniel, confessed in an editorial that he was among the many who lamented the eclipse of the governor: "Price Daniel's mortal fault as a politician was his Christian decency. He tried to run with the big money. They elected him to the U.S. Senate. As governor he advocated sane and reasonable programs for state progress. But when he insisted merely that business split the tab fifty-fifty with consumers, he ran, neck bowed, into a fact that somehow had escaped his notice: Big business controlled the state legislature and did not intend to go fifty-fifty with the people or Price Daniel, either. The collision broke his neck."[77] Indeed, holding true to his convictions, Daniel chose not to go into cahoots with either big money or the liberal-labor movement. Ultimately, he fell between them.

Daniel was shocked, not as much by the defeat as by the margin. Since he was so confident that he would be reelected, said insiders, he had "saved his big guns" until it was too late. For his part, Daniel offered no excuses. One day after the election a young reporter approached him in the lobby of Houston's Shamrock-Hilton Hotel and asked how he felt about his defeat. "Son," he replied, "I'm trying to be as gracious in defeat as I was in victory." [78] Indeed he was. The *Lubbock Avalanche-Journal* editorialized: "The conduct of Governor Price Daniel since his defeat at the Democratic primary polls last May has been such as to engender admiration from the Texas public: Not only in politics, but in all areas of human activity, as well.... When he leaves the Statehouse next January, there is one thing all fair-minded men must say of him, whether they liked him politically, or whether they didn't. That is: 'There goes a man.'" [79]

Months prior to the election Daniel had agreed to make a post-election speech in Dallas. At the time the event was scheduled, he expected to be preparing for an unprecedented fourth term as governor. "The whole family was very upset," Jean would later recall. "I reminded Price about the engagement in Dallas and fully expected him to cancel. But he insisted that, because he made the commitment, he would go." Overhearing the conversation was his daughter, Jean, who quickly spoke up: "Dad, if you go, I'm going with you." Daniel would later refer to this incident as one of his proudest moments as a father.[80]

Perhaps no one better chronicled the Dallas trip than Tom Wicker of *New York Times Magazine.* He recalled being at Love Field Airport in Dallas, where "a noisy knot of men and women surrounded a man who wore a white Texas hat, a black preacher's suit, and a shell-shocked expression." Wicker approached Daniel with a somber "Bad luck." Daniel responded, "Well, you know, the will of the people. Reckin' I'll go down to Austin for a few days. Think it all over." And when his flight was called, remembered Wicker, "his friends swarmed down upon him, clawing him with their genuine kindness, their transparent cheer. Price Daniel moved slowly across the tarmac, his white hat a degree more jauntily cocked than usual.

"A pretty girl skipped after him, caught his arm, walked beside him smiling—his daughter," wrote Wicker. "As I watched, she put her head for just a moment against his shoulder. He straightened perceptibly, adjusted his hat, and they went on toward the plane. I thought, with utter banality and complete sincerity, that there were some things damn well worth more than being governor of Texas. I thought that the human heart did not need so much to survive." [81]

In his final report to the legislature in 1963, Daniel gave a fourteen-point summary of accomplishments achieved during his six-year tenure. Some of the more dramatic progress of the Daniel administration, he believed, came in the field of conservation and development of the state's water resources. He and the legislature met the challenge not all at once but consistently during the regular and special sessions. Texas had 172 percent more water conservation storage completed or started than when he took office. Also on his watch, more progress was made in public education than in any previous period in Texas history. Enrollment in public schools increased from 1.7 million in 1956 to 2.2 million in 1962. To meet the needs of this enormous growth, the number of professional school personnel, teachers, and administrators was increased from 72,000 to more than 95,000 in the same period. Furthermore, the basic minimum salary for Texas teachers rose from $2,800 to over $4,000. [82]

Under Daniel's leadership, Texas had the most highway construction in its history. More than 7,900 miles of new interstate, U.S., state and farm-to-market roads were opened to traffic on the Texas Highway System. There was also more construction and expansion in the Department of Corrections than in any similar period in Texas history. The Texas Youth Council was created to administer the state's correctional facilities for delinquent children, as well as to provide programs of care, treatment, education, and training for their rehabilitation and reestablishment in society. Furthermore, Texas had become the second fastest-growing state in the nation and ranked at the top in monthly reports on location of new industries. [83]

Of the 151 major recommendations Daniel made to the legislature during his years as chief executive, 131 were enacted in whole or part. Practically all of the defeated proposals were in the field of taxation and law enforcement. The disagreements, though few in number, were so intense and extended that at times they obscured the more numerous and important points of agreement and cooperation between the governor and the legislature. There was agreement on a total of 1,976 legislative enactments to which Daniel affixed his signature; twenty-two were allowed to become law without his signature, and only forty-two measures were vetoed.[84] "In the final analysis, Price got everything done that he wanted to do," recalls Christian. "There was very little left undone when he walked out of there after six years." [85]

On the Daniels' last night in the Governor's Mansion, Reverend Billy Graham slept down the hall in Sam Houston's old bed. Ironically, Houston had occupied the house exactly one hundred years prior. Daniel gazed off the second-floor balcony that evening as the sun slowly set on his dream. He had accomplished what he had set out to do in life and was content with what he had achieved.

More importantly, Daniel had never lost touch with who he was. A college professor named Ron Roberts liked to tell his government classes a story about his first meeting with Price Daniel. Elected to the Texas legislature as a young man out of Hillsboro, Roberts found himself thrown head-first into the Austin political scene, still unsure of exactly what he was supposed to do. One day, while passing by the governor's office in the Capitol, he noticed that the door to the front office was wide open. Curious, he stepped inside only to find the door to the inner office also open. Sure enough, Price Daniel was sitting behind his desk and, noticing the young man, beckoned him to come in and have a seat. Roberts eagerly accepted the invitation and was stunned to see the governor push his work aside and take time out to answer all his questions. At the close of their conversation, Daniel urged the young legislator to come back whenever he felt the need. Sure enough, Roberts would make many more trips to Daniel's office, each time taking away more ideas or advice. When Roberts returned for the following session, he decided to visit the office and welcome the new governor to Austin. This time, however, the door was closed. The secretary told Roberts that the governor was busy and that he would have to make an appointment.[86]

History sometimes moves in mysterious ways. On November 22, 1963, Daniel received word of President Kennedy's assassination in Dallas. Had Daniel won the unprecedented fourth term he had sought, it would have been he, not Governor Connally, sitting in front of Kennedy in the presidential motorcade, the victim of a sniper's bullet.

CHAPTER 14

Lyndon's Request

Daniel remained good friends with John Connally after the election. In fact, the newly elected governor spoke at a fundraiser in Austin to help eliminate his old friend's campaign debt. At the end of the elegant affair, Daniel took the podium and cupped his hand against his ear. "Well," he said, trying to find humor in the situation, "I thought that I had heard those trumpets telling me to run for another term." The audience burst into laughter. Then, to Daniel's surprise, the master of ceremonies presented him with a set of keys to a brand new Lincoln. The car was purchased with funds left over after his campaign debts had been paid in full.[1]

"That was probably the first decent car he ever had," said George Christian, who frequently poked fun at the car Daniel drove while in the Senate—an old Pontiac with a wire wrapped around the front bumper to keep it from dragging the ground. "He didn't pay much attention to stuff like that. We decided to get him a car because we knew it was something that he really needed."[2]

In the upcoming months Connally urged Daniel to stay involved in Texas government. "You have too much experience, Price," he would insist. "You need to come back in and serve in some capacity." Connally asked him if he would be interested in a court appointment, or something along that line. Daniel kindly declined, stating his desire to get back into private life and resume his law practice. After further prodding, however, he did express to the governor his love for Texas history and his possible interest if a position on the State Library and Archives Commission opened. Before long he was appointed and became an active member of the commission.[3]

Meanwhile, Daniel resumed his law practice and set up shop on the eighth floor of the Brown Building in downtown Austin. Attorney Jim Keahey, who occupied office space next door, recalled: "The sign on my door read, 'James K. Keahey, Attorney at Law.' The sign on his said, 'Price Daniel, Lawyer.' If I hadn't been broke, I would have had the sign painter return and change my sign. Between our two offices was Governor Daniel's law library. It had an entrance from my office as well as his, and he generously let me treat it as ours. It was there I discovered that Governor Daniel was a scholar/politician—the only man I have ever known combining these qualities. He loved books, history and research."[4]

Keahey was actually brought in on a few of Daniel's cases. He recalled the time he and Daniel represented Dow Chemical Company and met with a few of the company's big guns from Michigan. The meeting was held at Maxim's, one of Houston's upscale restaurants, and the discussion concerned whether Dow could take water from one watershed to another to supply its chemical plant in Brazoria County. Upon learning of Daniel's presence, the restaurant's owner pushed aside the waiter and began taking the orders himself. "Dow's general counsel spoke up forcefully," Keahey recalled, "asking for a dry Martini and describing in some detail how it should be made. Others in his retinue followed suit. Sounded good to me; I asked for the same." Then, it was Daniel's turn. The owner raised his eyebrows at the former governor in great anticipation of his order.

"Do you have any buttermilk?" Daniel asked.

The owner looked stunned, but managed to nod his head.

"And can we order now? I'm sort of hungry."[5]

The owner snapped his fingers and an underling supplied him with a flourish of menus. "He distributed them as though dispensing rare gifts. The Dow corps studied them diligently. Then the general counsel ordered in French. Nods of agreement from his colleagues and a 'Sounds good' from me."

It was once again Daniel's turn to order. He flipped the menu over, then back over again. Finally, he looked up and asked, "Do you have anything that's not greasy?" The owner looked puzzled. "An underling took over," recalled Keahey. "The Michigan sophisticates looked puzzled. I smiled a big smile. I think the corners of Daniel's mouth curved upward a bit." [6]

Daniel filled what little spare time he had left over from his law practice and the Archives Commission lending a hand to many causes he felt worthwhile. He became active with the Campus Crusade for Christ, as well as working to fulfill his lifelong dream of making the Trinity River navigable all the way to Dallas. [7] He also served as attorney for the Alabama Coushatta tribe for an annual fee of one dollar. He knew well the story of the tribe's reservation, located north of Liberty, and how Sam Houston had helped secure the beautiful property in gratitude for the Alabama and Coushattas' role in the Texas Revolution. Daniel considered the chief, Fulton Batisse, a good friend and was allowed to sit in on tribal council meetings. When Daniel refused to take more money for legal services, Chief Batisse sent a number of the tribe's boys to Holly Ridge Ranch to plant dogwood trees as gifts.

In May 1965 Daniel was named "Baylor Lawyer of the Year" by his alma mater. In a congratulatory note, President Johnson wrote of his former Senate colleague: "Few men have contributed as much as Price Daniel to Baylor University, to the state of Texas and to this nation. None has been more dedicated, none more sincere and none has served with greater integrity and honesty in every area of civic, church, legal and political service." [8]

During this period Johnson had been trying to entice Daniel to come to Washington and serve in his administration in some capacity. Daniel, however, was in no hurry to return to the tiring demands of public service which he had known all too well his entire adult life. Nor were he and Jean eager to move back to Washington. Daniel had declined Johnson's offer to serve on a special committee in 1964, citing a "personal and professional commitment" which made it "impossible to devote time necessary for service." [9] The following year he turned down the position of comptroller general, citing "family and other commitments" that would make it "impossible... to move to Washington." [10]

In time, the president's determination to get Daniel back to

Washington only intensified. In 1967, needing a consultant in the field of federal-state relations, Johnson would no longer take "no" for an answer. He had started a tradition of placing former popular governors in the post for obvious reasons. When it came down to crucial matters where the president needed the states' cooperation, Johnson reasoned, the governors would feel more comfortable working with someone who had been in similar situations. Thus, his two previous appointments to the post were former governors Buford Ellington of Tennessee and Farris Bryant of Florida. Johnson believed Daniel had all the necessary qualifications and considered him the lone candidate for the position.

Under Johnson's plan, Daniel would also direct the Office of Emergency Preparedness (OEP). In this capacity he would be in charge of handling national disasters, such as hurricanes, tornadoes, earthquakes, and fires. In addition, it would be his responsibility to supervise and direct the stockpiling of strategic materials in case of war. Although enticed by the offer, Daniel still expressed to Johnson his lack of interest in the job.[11]

In February 1967 the Daniels traveled to Washington to attend the Presidential Prayer Breakfast. They were White House guests of the Johnsons for two nights, during which time the president continued to exhort Daniel to join his administration. "I need you, Price," he pleaded over and over with a sharp and direct tone.[12] "Your President needs you. Your country needs you. You cannot say 'No!'" he demanded, standing almost toe-to-toe with Daniel, displaying the legendary Johnson persuasiveness.[13]

Daniel soon gave in to the pressure and, on October 10, 1967, his fifty-seventh birthday, following a succinct confirmation hearing, he was sworn into office. The Daniels chose to live in the Watergate Hotel because of its proximity to the White House. Daniel's office, just a few blocks away, was located in the Executive Office Building adjoining the White House,[14] the same building that housed Union forces during the Civil War. In addition, Daniel's new position also made him a member of the National Security Council.

One notable, highly publicized incident involving Daniel occurred during his tenure under Johnson. It happened at a National Governors' Conference aboard the USS *Independence* in October 1967. As the vessel sailed from New York to the Virgin Islands, the heated topic of

United States involvement in Vietnam was gaining steam. With Daniel participating in the nine-day floating conference, Johnson rested assured that a grand endorsement in favor of his Vietnam policy was imminent.[15] However, his plan would soon backfire.

One evening aboard the ship, the Daniels were having dinner with governors Ferris Bryant and Nelson Rockefeller and their wives. Toward the end of the meal, an Associated Press reporter scurried into the dining room, knelt beside Daniel and began to whisper in his ear. A moment later, Daniel rose to his feet and turned to Bryant. "Ferris, there has been an emergency," he said in a soft voice. "Governor and Mrs. Rockefeller, please go ahead and continue eating with our wives and we'll be right back." The two men hurriedly exited the dining room, never to return to the meal. "They did not tell us what it was," Jean would later recall, "but just got up from the table and left. I knew something bad had happened, because it was very unusual for Price to do that." [16]

Daniel had just learned that a telegram was sent to his attention earlier in the day from Marvin Watson, an assistant to President Johnson. The message listed several favors the White House had afforded certain Republican governors and advised Daniel how, while on this trip, to persuade them to support a resolution backing Johnson's policies in Vietnam. A politically partial cable operator aboard the ship received the message, and opted to deliver it to California governor Ronald Reagan instead of Daniel. After reading the message intended for Daniel, Reagan called for a hushed meeting of Republican governors aboard the ship to discuss what actions, if any, should be taken. At the caucus Governor George Romney of Michigan insisted that the telegram be reproduced and given to the press. As a result, Daniel was one of the last people to see the telegram, which the White House had intended for his eyes only.[17]

"It wasn't until dinner that I knew about any such telegram," he admitted. "As a matter of fact, the AP man simply said, 'What about this? There's no use denying it, it's copied all over the ship.'" As Daniel exited the dining room, he was instructed by the reporter that the press was demanding some sort of statement on the matter. He quickly read the photocopy of the telegram and made his way up to the ship's telephone room. "I called Marvin Watson and told him not to deny that he sent this message because I explained the circumstances to him. I told him that if he wanted to communicate with me anymore to please do it by telephone, but that it would be better not to have the communication."[18]

In the meantime, Jean and her dinner guests finished their meal and were growing more curious as to what "emergency" had drawn Daniel and Bryant from the table. "Finally, we decided to go up and see what had happened. We went up on board and everything was just wild. The press was after Price."[19] After hanging up with Watson, Daniel made his way to an impromptu press conference, which had quickly been thrown together by George Christian. The mood was tense until one reporter in the back asked Daniel if he had spoken with anyone in the White House. Daniel nodded his head and said that he had just hung up the phone with Marvin Watson.

"What did he say?" the reporter asked.

Daniel paused, then replied, "He said, 'Keep up the good work.'"

The room erupted with laughter.[20]

Governor Reagan also called a press conference in which he triumphantly waved the telegram in front of reporters and labeled it direct proof of Johnson's persistent attempts to muster support for his Vietnam policy. With election time rapidly approaching, Republicans tried to use the cable as a much-looked-for excuse to part with Johnson without having to contest publicly his war policy.[21] Reagan was beginning to appear somewhat less than honorable. But he did succeed in making it look as if Johnson was calling all of the signals for his Democratic friends on the ship and begging for support of his Vietnam efforts.

Despite Daniel's objections, he continued to receive a steady flow of telegrams from Washington while aboard the ship. He privately told Jean that he wished the White House would cease such actions, fearing the consequences of confidential information again ending up in the wrong hands. "At one point during the trip," Jean recalled, "Price came into our room with a couple of telegrams and told me to lock the door. He tore them up and flushed them down the commode."[22]

The intercepted telegram had made headlines in newspapers both in the Caribbean and back in the States. Most articles were critical of Reagan for opening someone else's mail and noted that the governor, rooming in a cabin just across the hall from Daniel, could have delivered the telegram personally to Daniel when he saw that it was mishandled. But eventually the stolen telegram became something of a joke between the two men. Some time after the incident, Daniel was aboard an airplane when Reagan climbed aboard. "I asked him if he had received any more telegrams for me," Daniel recalled. "No," Reagan replied as he passed down the aisle, "but when I do, I'm certainly going to deliver them to you!" [23]

At a White House dinner honoring all of the nation's governors on February 29, 1968, Johnson expressed gratitude to Daniel for joining his administration: "He served in practically every important post there is in government—state legislator, speaker, attorney general, governor, and United States senator. Now he sits in the Security Council with us. He was your colleague as governor for many years; he was my colleague as a senator for many years. He knows government, I think, at all ends—the local, state, and federal level. I know Price Daniel as the soul of honor.... I doubt there is a man in this room from any state in the union who can do more with the President—and with the Cabinet—than Price Daniel. I tell you that only so you will know that you have a good lawyer retained here in Washington for you. He is your advocate.... I am glad and gratified that Governor Daniel and his lovely wife have come here to try to bring us closer together and to serve our common interests." [24]

Upon Daniel's return to Washington, more than half a million U.S. soldiers were fighting in Vietnam where, since 1958, communist guerrillas from North Vietnam had been trying to overthrow the non-communist government of South Vietnam. Despite efforts of former presidents Eisenhower and Kennedy to supply the South Vietnamese with military supplies and advisers to help defend their freedom, the war had only escalated. In an effort to put an end to the conflict, Johnson had ordered bombing attacks on North Vietnam and a massive increase in U.S. troops to fight side-by-side with the South Vietnamese.[25] Now, as a member of the president's staff, Daniel witnessed firsthand the frustrations Johnson was experiencing in the latter half of his administration. Whenever called upon, Daniel would make a trip across the street and lend an ear or a bit of advice to his old friend. During one staff meeting a disgruntled Johnson slammed his fist down on the table and declared, "I don't have one man who will do what I tell him to do!" Amidst the silence of the stunned staff, Daniel leaned in and confidently replied: "You've got one." [26]

During Daniel's one-year tenure on the National Security

Council, primary topics of meetings included U.S. food aid, economic aspects of a Middle East settlement, China's and Russia's support of North Vietnam, a draft treaty on non-proliferation of nuclear weapons, prospects for East-West trade and economic development, problems with NATO, and the decision to halt bombing in North Vietnam. But because the war dominated most of the council's time and Daniel was assigned primarily to domestic policy, he was not an active participant in many of the meetings. As director of the Office of Emergency Preparedness he would occasionally make presentations, such as one on October 31, 1968, in which he summarized a report on the strategic importance of copper. "The only strategic material which causes us trouble on the Hill is copper," he told the council, using charts to illustrate his point. "We can sell the Congress if we have a conservative approach. We will be able to convince those interested congressmen that we are not cutting our stockpile objectives down merely in order to obtain funds from sales to help balance the budget." [27]

During this period Daniel's responsibilities were widespread. He oversaw the nation's disaster relief efforts when storms and floods ravaged property and lives. From Hawaii to the East Coast, when these tragedies occurred, he dispatched aides to assess damage and estimate the recovery effort required. When necessary, he asked the president to make official emergency declarations so that federal funds could be utilized. [28] And as Johnson's primary link to the states, he arranged briefings for the nation's governors on the war in Vietnam. [29]

Daniel stood behind the president's Vietnam policy. Although sympathizing with those who supported American troop withdrawal, he never publicly wavered from Johnson. He was no doubt encouraged, however, when on March 31, 1968, the president declared a partial halt to the bombing in an effort to illustrate America's intentions to negotiate peace. [30] At the same time, he was surprised by Johnson's announcement not to seek another term. Johnson later referred to this day, March 31, as one he "profoundly hoped would mark the beginning of the end of the war" and also as a day that marked "the beginning of the end of my career." [31] Consequently, this day also marked the beginning of the end of Daniel's career in Washington.

North Vietnam responded favorably to his March 31 address,

and in May negotiations began between American and North Vietnamese emissaries in Paris. But the peace talks dragged on through the summer and fall with no positive results because the North Vietnamese insisted that all bombing would have to cease before any legitimate agreement could be reached. Now, with only a few months remaining in office, the president found an opportunity to ease his conscience about widespread American bloodshed on foreign soil. On October 31 he entered the Cabinet room to meet with the National Security Council. Among those present were Daniel, General Wheeler (chairman of the Joint Chiefs of Staff), and CIA director Richard Helms. The war had taken its toll on Johnson. "I had awakened that day with a sore throat," he remembered. "By the time of the NSC meeting my throat was raw and my voice hoarse. The men around the table leaned forward to hear my words. Every person in that room knew we had reached a possible turning point, that the decision I had made was filled with both hope and danger." Johnson cleared his throat and began to speak: "We are ready to announce that we are going to stop bombing North Vietnam." The president's decision met such a quick and warm response of approval that he later quipped: "I had the feeling that I was perhaps the most doubtful man in the room." [32]

At 8:00 P.M. that evening an order was sent to the air force and navy to halt all aerial and naval bombardment of North Vietnam. Simultaneously, Johnson addressed the American people on national television. He discussed what had happened since the partial bombing halt in March and said that the countries "have reached the stage where productive talks can begin." Those talks, delayed for weeks by the reluctant South Vietnamese, would not materialize until just a couple of days before he left office.

"I regretted more than anyone could possibly know that I was leaving the White House without having achieved a just, an honorable, and a lasting peace in Vietnam," admitted Johnson. "But during those final days of transition, I felt that I was turning over to my successor a situation more promising and manageable than it had been for years." [33]

Although saddened by Johnson's decision not to seek another term, Daniel was ready to return home. Writing to Johnson in November that it had been a "real honor and pleasure" to serve the president, he offered to stay on and help with the transition process of the incoming administration. However, he added, "I am sure you understand my desire to get back to Texas," suggesting his lack of desire to stick around any longer than absolutely necessary.[34]

Daniel received praise for his work under Johnson, including a tribute from Governor John Connally. "Under President Johnson's leadership and your excellent direction of the Office of Emergency Planning, I feel these past few years have been the best federal-state relations which our national government and the states have enjoyed thus far in their quest for better government and better services for all of our people," wrote Connally. "You have done a tremendous job of interpreting the viewpoints and needs of the states and their governors to the President and we are deeply grateful for your leadership in this area of work."[35]

The Daniels remained in Washington only long enough to witness the departure of the outgoing president. Then, on the cold and windy afternoon of January 20, 1969, they boarded an airplane for the trip home to Texas. Two days later, Johnson sent Daniel the following note: "I am so thankful for your service as director of the OEP. As I said when you ran for governor in 1956, you are as capable as any man with whom I have ever worked. And I will always be grateful for your countless courtesies."[36]

CHAPTER 15

Boundaries and Courts

Upon returning to Texas, Daniel was about to be more involved with legal matters than he could have imagined. First came a request for his services that would lead to a battle which suited him well. The issue involved a long-standing boundary dispute between Texas and Louisiana. Texas contended its boundary was the middle of the Sabine River, whereas Louisiana argued it was the river's west bank. Origins of the controversy were old and complex, dating to the eighteenth century, when the area was the object of several transfers between France and Spain. Debated for years, the matter did not reach a head until the twentieth century, when oil revenues entered the picture.[1]

The stakes were high. At issue were rich oil deposits beneath some 250 miles of river, as well as Sabine Lake and Sabine Pass, involving millions of lease and royalty dollars. Also included was Pleasure Island, a seventeen-mile-long, highly developed strip of land considered part of Port Arthur and linked to the city by a $9.8 million bridge. Moreover, farther north, almost $70 million had been spent to build a dam and create Toledo Bend Reservoir, a popular destination for fishing and outdoor sports.[2]

Daniel had barely settled back in Liberty when Texas Attorney General Crawford Martin, aware of his experience and skill in this area of law, made him a "special" assistant attorney general and asked him to represent Texas and marshal the state's case. Daniel accepted the challenge with his usual zeal.[3] Working long days and far into the nights, he immersed himself in old treaties, correspondence, legislative and congressional acts, statehood agreements, leases, and maps. He even drove to the Sabine and photographed a state boundary sign perched above the middle of the river. Jean later laughingly recalled that, as driver, she let her husband off in the middle of the busy bridge and had to drive twenty miles to turn around and retrieve him. Meanwhile, Daniel was holding on to a two-foot railing that vibrated violently every time a car went over the bridge. "We could have lost him," recalled Jean.[4]

In the fall of 1969, Daniel officially filed Texas' suit in the United States Supreme Court, asking for a summary judgment ruling that the boundary was the middle of the river where the highway sign said it was. Months later, Louisiana responded with a long brief of its own, and the Court appointed a special master, U.S. District Judge Robert Van Pelt of Nebraska, to hear the case. He was to report his findings to the Supreme Court.[5]

Meanwhile, as Daniel was preparing this case, another request was about to affect his life dramatically. At this point in his career, he had already lived up to most of the lofty ambitions he had set for himself in politics. However, one big challenge remained. Since his graduation from Baylor, he was skilled in the art of courtroom persuasion. He loved the process of taking on a long-shot case and developing it into a finely tuned argument. Having served successfully in the legislative and executive arenas, in the back of his mind he had always hoped for an opportunity to participate in the judicial branch of government. This opportunity came in December 1970, when Governor Preston Smith appointed him to a seat which had been vacated on the Texas Supreme Court. Daniel was so proud of the appointment that he hailed it the biggest honor in all his years as a public servant.[6]

Chief Justice Robert W. Calvert was a stickler for precise time. Under his direction, the Court convened each day at its exact scheduled time, not a minute sooner or later. Daniel, on the other hand, well known for being perpetually late, learned quickly to adhere to Calvert's schedule. The day of his swearing-in, he was taking his time before the ceremony began, standing in a side hallway shaking some hands. As the clock struck 10:00, Calvert walked to the door of the robing room and motioned to the justices to take their seats. "But Judge!" one member exclaimed. "You can't do that. It's Price's ceremony!" Without a moment's hesitation, Calvert once again motioned for the justices to take their seats. The ceremony proceeded for a couple of minutes, still without its inductee, until eventually a back door opened and a red-faced Price Daniel tip-toed to his chair.[7]

The investiture also provided the Court with its first taste of Daniel's humor. Calvert asked him to repeat the oath of office, saying: "I, Price Daniel, will do my best to uphold this office to which I was elected." But when repeating, Daniel responded that he would uphold the office to which he was "appointed," defiantly stressing the latter word. The room immediately broke up in laughter.[8] In his acceptance remarks, thanking Governor Smith for the appointment, he quipped: "I always knew [he] was a good governor!"

Then, turning serious, Daniel underscored what he considered to be the critical roll of the judiciary. "We are living in an age," he asserted, "when a small but vocal and violent minority has no respect for that portion of the law with which it disagrees." Claiming that "they misuse their freedoms to trample upon the rules and institutions which form the greatest safeguards of their right to freedom, liberty and justice," he reminded all present that "without a system of laws and a dedicated judiciary to interpret and administer the laws, individual rights and freedoms would not be of any lasting value."

He could not resist adding how refreshing it was to take an oath without having to follow it with the presentation of a platform, promises, and issues which had been "the case on all of the 18 previous occasions when that oath was administered to me."[9]

Although now a Supreme Court justice, Daniel was still involved on the other side of the bench in the Texas-Louisiana dispute. In fact, Judge Van Pelt had set a June hearing date in New Orleans. Daniel arrived for the proceedings, saying he had paid his own way and that "I am no longer employed in the case. I am here only as an observer."[10]

When the hearing began on June 9, working with Assistant Attorney General Houghton Brownlee, he became what one Louisiana newspaper called a "very active observer." The account was correct. Daniel contended that an 1848 measure passed by Congress put the boundary at midriver and was not contested by Louisiana. He also introduced into evidence a 1938 oil lease signed by the governor of Louisiana which described the boundary "as outlined by the Act of 1848." In addition, he forced the executive secretary of the Louisiana Mineral Board to admit that since 1942 Louisiana had not leased or tried to collect royalties on leases on the western part of Sabine Lake, thereby acknowledging the midlake boundary.[11]

After listening to both states' arguments, Judge Van Pelt concluded the hearing in two days but waited eleven months to announce a decision. On May 5, 1972, he declared Texas the victor. Crawford Martin, understandably elated, hailed the decision as the second-largest land suit settlement in Texas history. Only the tidelands win was bigger. He estimated the victory to be worth at least a billion dollars to the state, the public school fund, and the cities of Port Arthur and Orange. He also reminded Texans that more than 35,000 acres of land, four producing oil wells, and $2,660,568 in legal bonuses already collected by Texas were directly involved in the litigation.[12]

As expected, Louisiana appealed. In March of the following year, however, the Supreme Court, in an eight-to-one ruling, upheld much of Van Pelt's decision. Only Justice William O. Douglas dissented. Left unsettled was ownership of some islands in the western half of the Sabine, but the Court ruled that the boundary was the middle of the river and Texas owned the oil-rich land beneath the western half. It was a resounding Texas win.[13]

One newspaper claimed that Daniel had "added another jewel to his public service crown."[14] By now he was also well into his Supreme Court duties. Actually, he was no stranger to the judiciary. As governor, he had appointed more of its judges than any other chief executive in the state's history. Rumors even surfaced of there being a "Daniel wing" on the Court. "If there was a 'Daniel wing' on the Court," one justice would later recall, "it was not participated in by Price Daniel."[15]

With so many high-profile political positions on his rèsumé, Daniel surprised many observers with the soft-spoken, back-seat role he chose to take on the Court. Instead of leading in the asking of questions, as some would expect of a former chief executive, he preferred to remain silent until the dust settled. As a former justice recalled: "A lot of judges very forthright ask a lot of questions so that the attorneys will know that they had read the briefs. Price was not sensitive to that at all. It was of no consequence to him what they thought."[16]

Daniel quickly earned the respect of his colleagues. Charles Barrow, who shared the bench with him for two years, remembered being impressed by the way Daniel was so "committed to deep research, to finding answers. He was a lawyer while so many remain politicians. You can't count votes and be a judge."[17] And Justice Sam Johnson, who would soon replace Daniel as the lowest-ranking justice in seniority on the Court, recalled: "He was the most accurate appraiser of people that I ever saw. He knew what made people think, how people were probably going to think, and how they would think tomorrow, even if they were not thinking that today."[18]

A stern advocate of the process of selecting appellate judges under a nonpartisan, appointive system, Daniel outlined his beliefs in a speech before the State Bar of Texas: "Senators, governors, and legislators must take their cases to the people because they are the representatives of the people in making or advocating changes in our laws. Not so with judges; they are not supposed to make or change the laws; they do not represent the people in such activities; it is their duty to interpret the law as they find it to be and apply it to the facts. In this way they should be free from the political necessities of partisan campaigns and the expense, pressures, abuse, conscious or sub-conscious feelings of obligations, and the time-consuming tasks which are inherent in the usual election campaigns."[19]

Daniel had several law clerks, but nevertheless always insisted on writing his own opinions. And even this late in life, he preferred working into the wee hours of the morning. Barrow, later to become dean of the Baylor Law School, fondly recalled a weekend in which he was the guest of Daniel at his Liberty ranch: "We visited in his study until I decided to retire about ten o'clock. He advised me that he wanted to work some on an opinion he was writing. About six the next morning, I arose and went looking for a cup of coffee. I found him at his desk, just finishing the opinion, which he telephoned to his secretary that morning. One week later, the opinion was unanimously approved by the Court with very few 'fly specks.'"[20]

In his eight years on the Supreme Court, from 1971 to 1978, Daniel drafted seventy-three majority opinions. Cases appealed to the state's highest Court ranged from zoning conflicts to contract disputes, divorce settlements to insurance claims, as well as actions involving land, water, and minerals.[21] His views proved to be highly influential on improvement of groundwater law, underground and surface minerals, and his self-proclaimed specialty—law dealing with land. From his early days in law school to his recent venture in settling state boundaries, he was more fascinated by determining property lines than winning a sensational murder trial. So when such a case was appealed to the Court, he was always at his best.

Chief Justice Joe Greenhill, Calvert's successor, counted among Daniel's major contributions his opinion in a controversial and complex case twice before the Court, *Reed v. Wylie,* on which Greenhill and Daniel originally disagreed.[22] The landowner claimed right to surface and subsurface minerals, in this case coal and lignite. The Court, in a majority opinion written by Justice Tom Reavley, held that the landowner, or surface owner, in order to claim a mineral, must prove that "extraction of the surface mineral would necessarily have consumed or depleted the land surface." Daniel argued in a dissenting opinion that the Court's wording required a burden more difficult and complicated than the law intended. The controlling principle in the law, he concluded, was "the [mineral's] existence so near the surface that it formed a part thereof rather than a part of the 'minerals.'" He predicted that the majority decision would tie up the courts with lawsuits and result in inequity.[23]

In his polite but firm style, Daniel wrote, "With due respect, I question the soundness of the manner in which the majority reached its result and believe that it will lead to ownership uncertainties and litigation almost on a tract-by-tract basis whenever and wherever title to lignite coal is concerned." Daniel reported that fourteen friend-of-the-court briefs had been filed "by prominent law firms from every section of the state" arguing against the majority's language regarding proof. He wrote, "Minerals have been a blessing to Texas, but the term has plagued our courts in efforts to determine what is covered by the term in various leases, reservations and conveyances. Much of this is because of the failure to enumerate specific minerals intended to be dealt with...."[24]

When the Reed case was again appealed to the Supreme Court

in 1980, after Daniel had left the bench, the majority opinion, written by Greenhill, adopted the less stringent method of determining surface minerals and overruled portions of its earlier opinion. The majority affirmed Daniel's earlier dissenting opinion defining ownership: If the surface owner establishes ownership of the substance at or near the surface, he also "owns the lignite, iron, or coal beneath such land at whatever depth it may be found." [25] The subsequent Reed case, overruling the original decision, was a landmark decision regarding ownership of minerals.

Said Greenhill later, "Judge Daniel was a realist. He did not think our Reed I and Reed II opinions would work. That's the view that ultimately prevailed. He respected the Court's previous opinions; but if he thought the Court was wrong, he felt free to suggest a change. Either we did [change], or he would dissent." [26]

Another of Daniel's major contributions in the area of change dealt with water law and the subsidence issue. Under an old Texas statute, landowners were free to produce as much water from under their land as they desired. But in a case appealed to the Supreme Court, a major oil company had pumped water in such quantity and speed that the surrounding land in the Houston and Galveston area sank as much as five to nine feet. The Court followed the prevailing law, but in the majority opinion written by Daniel said that water must be extracted in the future with regard to the rights of others. He asserted, "As to the future subsidence caused by wells hereinafter drilled or produced, this Court... will recognize and apply the law of negligence along with willful waste and malicious injury as limitations on the present rule.... The right of capture did not carry with it the right to destroy or interfere with the geology beneath another's land." [27]

Daniel's writing style, while formal and always respectful, was also forthright and at times acerbic. An example was his majority opinion on the question of whether Southwestern Bell Telephone Company could build a parking lot on adjacent residentially zoned land. Basing its case on a 1927 law, the City of Spring Valley had sought an injunction preventing the construction. Wrote Daniel, "Perhaps parking facilities were not so essential to the use of commercial and other buildings in 1927, but the statute was not limited to uses and needs of the year of its enactment. Being still in effect, it speaks for the uses and needs of 1972." With that logic, the Court upheld the decision of the lower court in denying the city an injunction.[28] In another case, Daniel wrote concerning language used in a law: "By substituting 'the work' for the longer phrases of the former statute, the Hardeman Act of 1961 simply said in 59 words the same thing which took 78 words in the previous version."[29]

While Daniel was a strict constructionist in reading the law, he was also flexible in its interpretation. Commenting on a rule from *Kennedy v. Brown* in the Court's *Sullivan v. Barnett* decision, he wrote, "Equity and justice being the ultimate aims of all rules of law, this and other courts have not been so rigid in their application of this rule. Numerous exceptions are as well established as the rule itself."[30]

Daniel's commitment to integrity and ethics also surfaced in his opinions. In an insurance claim case in which conflict of interest became an issue regarding an attorney, he wrote, "These are serious questions involving legal ethics and public policy with which this Court has not dealt under like circumstances. Counsel concedes... that guidelines from this Court would be welcomed...." Said Daniel, "Such attorney becomes the attorney of record and the legal representative of the insured, and as such he owes the insured the same type of unqualified loyalty as if he had been originally employed by the insured... the attorney owes a duty to the insured to immediately advise him of the conflict."[31]

Daniel was also particular about how cases were presented. Once, when a lawyer had purposely propped a map up on an easel with the north and south arrows pointing east and west, and the wording right side up, Daniel was bewildered. At first he laid his head sideways on the table, trying to make what little sense he could out of the map. But before long, he spoke up: "Counsel, I'm sorry. As far as one judge on this Court is concerned, I cannot understand it unless you've got an arrow running north and what you want me talking about running north." The lawyer hesitantly obliged by correcting the arrows on his map.[32]

On January 12, 1978, to the surprise of many, Daniel announced that he would not be a candidate for another six-year term. "It is an honor and a highly rewarding experience to be a member of this Court," he issued in a press release. "I shall look forward to completing my present term, which ends on December 31, 1978. At that time, I will have served eight years and will be 68. After that, God willing, I would like to have time to engage in some activities which would be less confining. Therefore, I have decided not to offer for an additional six-year term. For the opportunity of serving our state on the Supreme Court and in other capacities, I express my appreciation and shall always be grateful to the people of Texas." [33]

By this time Daniel's son, Price, Jr., was running for attorney general of Texas. Because the attorney general's opinions are often appealed to the Supreme Court, Daniel knew that a father on the Court with a son in the attorney general's office would be a political issue. While he insisted publicly that he would not allow a conflict to arise, he also did not want to hurt his son's election chances. [34] Despite having a substantial lead in early polls, Price, Jr., would ultimately be defeated. His opponent, Mark White, had greatly benefited from a late surge of expensive television commercials. White would serve four years as attorney general and then become governor.

On his last day as a member of the Court, Daniel recalled that forty years earlier, almost to the day, he was sworn in as a member of the Texas legislature, his start as a public servant. His voice broke as he told the Court good-bye: "It has been hard work, but the time passed rapidly because it was enjoyable work. And I want to make it clear that I am surrendering this chair but I am not surrendering my interest in government and our judiciary. I am not retiring and there will be no lessening of my interest in our government and our laws." [35]

Tributes to Daniel were many and came from across the state, especially in the form of newspaper editorials. "A long and distinguished career is coming to an end," claimed one. [36] Another called his "a career record of almost unbelievable breadth" that represented "voter confidence and support justified by Daniel's conduct in each office he has filled." [37]

"I was privileged to serve with Price Daniel for approximately eight years on the Texas Supreme Court," remembered Joe Greenhill. "He was a careful and studious judge. He was a champion for fairness and simplicity in the rules of civil procedure promulgated by the Court." [38]

On June 6, 1979, Daniel was honored at a huge appreciation dinner at the Hyatt Regency Hotel in Houston. Publicizing the $25-a-plate event, the *Abilene Reporter-News* called Daniel "a great Texan worthy of inclusion with the likes of Stephen F. Austin and Sam Houston. In truth, there are not many like him. The good news is that there are some.... Hope they have a really big banquet room—they'll need it." [39] Personal tributes that night were presented by Greenhill, Leon Jaworski, Governor Bill Clements, longtime friend Fred Hartman, Congressman Jake Pickle, and every living former governor—Allan Shivers, Dolph Briscoe, John Connally, and Preston Smith. Lady Bird Johnson was also in attendance. [40]

Some years later, when a state building was named for Daniel, Greenhill summarized his colleague's contribution to the Court. Recalling concern about a Daniel wing forming, Greenhill said, "In a large sense, there was a 'Daniel wing' of admirers, all of those who respected his hard work on the Court. He was an able lawyer, a great and honorable man, a person who was proud but not arrogant, always sensitive to the rights of litigants and other persons, and in my opinion, one of the ablest judges who ever sat on this Court." [41]

CHAPTER 16

The Later Years

While many people look forward to retirement, Price Daniel abhorred the thought. After forty years at the center of power, having routinely made momentous decisions that affected the lives of countless people, he found it difficult to relegate himself to an observer's role. Always active, he continued to immerse himself in an abundance of activities. He even rekindled some youthful passions, such as his love for the Trinity River and his self-built Texana collection, and he continued to engage in new business dealings, law cases, writing projects, and much more. Starting the day after he stepped down from the Court, Daniel kept a log in which he recorded his daily schedule. On January 23, 1979, he wrote: "Awoke at 3:30 A.M.—ready to go—shaved—read—back to bed at 5:30 A.M. and up again at 7:00 A.M." The following day's entry read: "Up at 3:30 A.M.—full of energy, but rested until 4 A.M.—back to bed at 5:45 A.M.—up at 7 A.M. for the day—and to bed at 11:30 P.M." [1]

Daniel soon formed a law firm with two of his sons, Houston and Price, Jr., and began to spend more time at Holly Ridge. It was a place where he was in charge and could make decisions on land sales, cattle feed, ranch hands, round-ups, and oil drilling. He would schedule morning meetings over coffee with his senior ranch hand to discuss plans for the day, a far cry from his daily briefings with George Christian in the Governor's Mansion. But Daniel relished making decisions on which fields needed mowing, which cows should be moved to a different pasture, and whether or not to plant soybeans across the lake. He often fed the cattle himself, driving his old Chevrolet Blazer into distant pastures with tall bags of Beefmaster. He would bounce along, blowing the horn and occasionally singing the first verse to "Amazing Grace," the only hymn he seemed to remember, as a hundred head of cattle anxiously surrounded his vehicle. To him, this was heaven on earth.

The ranch house had been sawn in half when moved from Sour Lake, and a careful observer could still see where it had been put back together. Though appearing rustic on the outside, it had all the modern conveniences inside. Over the years Daniel supervised gradual expansion projects on the house, eventually making the accommodations suitable for his family of six and a live-in nanny.[2] Upon completion, the home contained seven bedrooms, two kitchens, three living rooms, two working offices, a game room, and an outdoor swimming pool. The furnishings were sundry—a weathered polyester couch sat in the same room as precious original paintings and a replica of Sam Houston's bed. A six-vehicle carport stretched along the front lawn, although a majority of the spaces were filled with motorized toys for visiting grandchildren. And out the main living room windows was a great view of the lake Daniel had constructed, complete with stocked fish and alligators, the latter a gift from a former governor of Florida.

He even purchased a large, ten-seat, pontoon-style boat to take people for rides on the ranch lake. He loved to crank it up to full speed, causing the craft to tilt upward at a steep angle and, playing to the fear of his passengers, head full speed toward a small bridge, letting up on the gas just as the nose of the boat had time to drop enough to slip through. But his favorite activity was heading out in his ten-year-old, beat-up Blazer to survey his land. The vehicle's tags had expired long ago and the rear license plate, dangling from a single screw, swung back and forth at every bump in the road. There were also indentions in the bumpers where he had butted against huge trees, trying to shake pecans loose. But on many occasions, having driven off in the Blazer, he would return hours later on foot. "I think he likes to get stuck," a ranch hand once told Jean, referring to how many times he had been sent to pull the governor's vehicle out of muddy trenches.[3]

Daniel's departure from public life was a personal success. He did not suffer political withdrawal pains, as many longtime public servants do after retirement. To the contrary, he experienced a liberating autonomy that politics had seldom allowed. He traveled freely, read books for pleasure, planned trips with his grandchildren, and poked around his ranch. This was one of the best times of Daniel's life. But his absence from the public eye soon ended as a result of a family tragedy.

On January 19, 1981, Daniel's oldest son was shot to death by his wife, Vickie, in a domestic dispute. Price, Jr., thirty-nine, had served not only as Speaker of the Texas House of Representatives but also as president of the 1974 Texas Constitutional Convention. His death received prominent play from both state and national press. In fact, throughout Texas, the shooting upstaged Ronald Reagan's presidential inauguration and shared the front page of both Houston dailies with details of ex-President Carter's deal for the release of American hostages with Iran.

Perhaps at no time were Daniel's convictions better displayed than in the aftermath of this tragedy. While devastated by the untimely death of his son and by the way he felt Price, Jr.'s reputation was slandered in the courtroom and libeled by the press, he remained tight-lipped in an attempt to preserve the relationship with his two grandchildren born to Price and Vickie. He counseled family members to put aside hate and bitterness toward Vickie, to remember that God is the ultimate arbiter of human affairs, and to find ways to forgive because, as he would often say, "That is what Jesus would do." Even during the bitter custody trial in which Price's daughter Jean sought custody of her slain brother's two young sons—and despite the fact that he resented the tactics of Vickie's lawyer, the famous Texas trial attorney, Richard "Racehorse" Haynes—Daniel spoke of forgiveness and his belief that the Almighty would eventually square all things. When the court allowed Vickie to keep the children, and when, in a second trial, she was found not guilty of murder, he still refused to allow rancor or bitterness to get the best of him.

Price and Jean continued their passion for history, delving into several writing projects. In 1969 they had co-written a critically acclaimed book, *Executive Mansions and Capitols of America*, which contained illustrations and historical data on all the governors' mansions and capitols. In the preface, Lady Bird Johnson wrote: "I am delighted that Jean Houston Daniel, one of the most gracious and history-minded First Ladies to occupy an Executive Mansion, has compiled the stories of the official residences and their Capitols. No one could be more ideally equipped for such a task by heritage, association and experience. I believe this book will bring all of us closer in this delightful demonstration of the historical, architectural, political and spiritual ties which bind us together in 'a more perfect Union.'"[4]

Years later the Daniels collaborated with Dorothy Blodgett on another book, *The Texas Governor's Mansion, A History of the House and Its Occupants*. They turned down lucrative offers from at least four commercial publishers, preferring instead to make the book a nonprofit venture associated with the state. The result of twenty years of research on every detail of the mansion, the book also contained biographical sketches of all former Texas governors and first ladies. "History has been made in the mansion longer than in any other State building," wrote Jean in the preface. "Thirty-two years older than our imposing granite Capitol, it is the oldest structure in the Capitol complex. Yet, soon after I became an occupant of the Mansion, as the wife of a Texas governor in 1957, I realized that this historic house had been slighted by the writers of Texas books; that it deserved a book of its own; and that I would attempt the task."[5] The finished product became a successful book for the Texas State Library and Archives Commission.[6]

In 1973 the Daniels had donated a 110-acre segment of the Liberty ranch to the Texas State Library and Archives Commission. A building was to be constructed on the land to house regional historical resources for ten counties of southeast Texas. As a result, the Sam Houston Regional Library and Research Center was dedicated in 1977.[7] It has since grown into the largest regional historical depository in Texas. The depository was to serve the ten southeast Texas counties carved from the original Atascosito-Liberty district of the Republic of Mexico—Chambers, Hardin, Jasper, Jefferson, Liberty, Newton, Orange, Polk, San Jacinto, and Tyler. The Sam Houston Center was later expanded to provide teaching and research facilities and valuable library collections on Texas and general history, government, and religion.[8] Daniel made several substantial donations to the depository, most notably the journal of Jean Laffite. He took great pride in bringing this beautiful facility to southeast Texas and often played a hands-on role in its day-to-day operations. For instance, when an encrusted chain surfaced that was believed to be from the *Black Cloud*, a Trinity River steamboat whose wreckage was discovered in 1963, Daniel told one of his ranch hands to clean it up so that it could be placed on exhibit with other *Black Cloud* artifacts. Later, seeing the finished product in near perfect condition, Daniel thought it looked too new for the museum's exhibit. He then instructed his worker to drop the chain in the lake behind his house for a few weeks and bring it back to the library after it looked rusty and timeworn again.[9]

A trip related to the depository led Daniel into another major retirement project. In San Antonio to investigate how to frame documents for display, he and Jean stopped at a small night spot on the River Walk to listen to music and noticed that the entire building was for sale. The seven-story structure, built in the 1920s, had housed the YMCA for years but was now abandoned. It caught Daniel's attention as a good prospect for downtown apartments. Accordingly, he arranged a loan, purchased the property, which he named Riverside, gutted it, and created five floors of apartments. Over the next several years he invested time and money to improve the project and make it profitable.[10]

Another of Daniel's dreams was to build on the lot across from the Sam Houston Regional Library and Research Center a replica of the Texas Governor's Mansion, with the addition of two wings which had been in the original design but were never constructed in Austin. While recovering from a carotid artery operation in a Houston hospital room, he spread the blueprints for this project across his lap, determined the structure would be built in his lifetime. He returned from the hospital to oversee construction. When finished, the home provided additional archival space and housed Daniel's private collections. Both the home and the Sam Houston Library and Research Center have been deeded to the state of Texas. They stand side-by-side today along quiet Farm Road 1011 just outside of Liberty. Daniel had intended to live with Jean in the east wing of the newly constructed mansion and had it equipped with a separate kitchen, breakfast room, bedroom, and a private study. But despite the appeal of the lavish quarters, located just a half mile from the ranch house, he never made the move. He was too at home in the old house.

One of Daniel's more actively pursued causes in his later years was the fight against widespread vulgarity and pornography on television and the big screen, which he feared was corrupting the minds of younger generations and assaulting important religious standards. In a public address he claimed: "The most important thing in the life of our nation today could be the restoration of Judeo-Christian morality and ethics. We hear great cries against pollution of our air, streams and lands, but the greatest danger to this country is the pollution of the minds and souls of our young people by dealers in dope and pornography, and the daily depiction of violence, vulgarity, and crime on the television and movie screens of America."[11]

On April 7, 1984, Daniel broke his six-year silence on political matters to condemn House Speaker Gib Lewis' instructions to state agency heads to prepare no-growth budgets for the legislature's consideration. "It's been a long time since I took on a speaker of the House and a chairman of the appropriations committee in this building," he said at a state capitol press conference. "But I am forced to do so by their arrogant and intimidating letter recommending that all state agencies prepare a no-growth budget."[12] As a member of the State Library and Archives Commission, he was outraged that Lewis was demanding a no-growth budget during a time when the commission could not maintain vital programs under the previous budget. With a tenure of sixteen years, Daniel eventually served longer on the commission than any other member.[13]

Daniel also used this rare public opportunity to come to the defense of his deceased colleague, Lyndon Johnson. Swindler Billie Sol Estes had told a Robertson County grand jury that the former president arranged the 1961 slaying of Henry H. Marshall, an Agriculture Department official based in Bryan. "Knowing the two men, I know that Billie Sol Estes is a liar and I wouldn't believe a thing he said," Daniel remarked. "You can give Lyndon Johnson all the black points you want, but he'd not be a party to that. It's just somebody else trying to blacken the name of a dead man."[14]

Religion was still the cornerstone of his life. If he was not on the back pew of Liberty's United Methodist Church on Sundays, he could be found at home sitting in his recliner, listening to the worship service on a small transistor radio. He had read the Bible cover to cover several times and could quote numerous scriptures by heart. In 1985 Daniel published a small pamphlet entitled "The Most Important Thing on Earth: A Layman's Viewpoint," consisting of excerpts from his previous speeches that best exemplified his religious faith. "The most important thing in the world to every human being, the rich and the poor alike," one passage read, "is to have the right relationship with God and our fellow men." [15] He printed the pamphlets at his own expense and distributed them to family and friends.

By the mid-1980s, Daniel had numerous health afflictions, most notably a light stroke that damaged his vision. He also underwent an operation on his left knee to repair an injury that had been hampering him since the 1940s, when a horse he was riding slammed him into a fence. This procedure required months of extensive therapy and resulted in his having to use a walking cane. [16]

Even in poor health, the governor made a diligent effort to keep in touch with old friends and colleagues. Often chauffeured by his twenty-something granddaughter in a rugged 1968 Ford Mustang, he still attended numerous social functions in Austin. [17] And he kept in close touch with Fred Hartman, his Baylor classmate who had become highly successful in the newspaper publishing business. On one of their last meetings, Daniel and Hartman were headed to their fiftieth class reunion at Baylor. "They missed the flight," remembered Daniel's daughter, Jean, "and then asked me to go ahead and drive them from Dallas to Waco for the reunion. Those two men, both in their seventies, sat in the back seat together the whole way giggling as they flipped through an old Baylor yearbook and talked about college girlfriends." [18]

Daniel finally made amends with longtime political foe Ralph Yarborough. After taking part in one of the ugliest gubernatorial races in state history, the two men eventually joined forces in working to preserve the Big Thicket wilderness area in East Texas, as well as helping the state's two Indian tribes, the Alabama-Coushatta and Tiguas, in their disputes with the federal government. [19] In December 1985, at a joint press conference on behalf of the tribes, Daniel used the occasion to express his reconciliation with Yarborough. "Senator Yarborough's erstwhile opponents and the news media have not given him the recognition that his public service deserves," he stated, fighting back tears. "As one of those opponents I would feel remiss if I did not use this occasion to say that when objective historians of the future lay aside all the political differences of this era they will rank Ralph Yarborough along with former Governor Jim Hogg in his work for the people and in his accomplishments for the Permanent School Fund; and they will place him alongside Sam Houston in his love for the Texas Indians and in his accomplishments for Texas while in the United States Senate." [20]

Yarborough, jumping to his feet and grasping Daniel's hand, returned the praise. "I ran for governor a number of times," he said, "and every opponent I had was telling about how much he loved Texas. But none of them ever did anything about it except Price Daniel[21].... There were a lot of vicious things said in that campaign (1956), but he never said any of them. He was a nice fellow." [22] At one point, displaying their commitment to the Alabama-Coushattas and Tiguas as well as their renewed friendship, Daniel and Yarborough posed for photographers wearing colorful Indian war bonnets.[23]

In the spring of 1988, in what would be the last months of his life, Daniel was still active and busy. From San Antonio he called for the establishment of a regional archive in Bexar County, which he termed the most historic region in the state. He had been advocating it for years and was ready to resume the fight. "I can't keep up with him!" Jean once exclaimed, noting that on a recent walk he had carried a large metal cane but never let it touch the ground.[24] May of that year marked the one-hundredth anniversary of the State Capitol in Austin. Daniel had served on the Capitol Centennial Committee and, along with other former governors, he rode up Congress Avenue in an antique carriage and reviewed the parade from a special stand erected in front of the Governor's Mansion.[25]

Daniel made his final public appearance before the United Methodist congregation in Liberty. Using no prepared text, he described his personal relationship with Jesus Christ. "He spoke straight from the heart and soul," remembered Jean. "It was a real gem." [26] Just days later, on August 25, 1988, Daniel suffered a massive stroke at his ranch, shortly after having put his youngest grandchild to bed. He was pronounced dead on arrival at Yettie Kersting Hospital in Liberty.

At the time of his death, three files were found neatly stacked on his office chair, each containing details of active projects that the seventy-eight-year-old crusader was pursuing. Age had not yet taken his mind, resolve, or sense of duty.[27]

More than eight hundred mourners gathered at First United Methodist Church in Liberty to pay their last respects. "He was a giant in his service to the nation, the state and the community," said the Reverend Charles L. Allen to the entourage of the governor's family members, friends, acquaintances, and admirers. "More importantly, he was a giant in his service to his family and other relationships."[28] In attendance was Senator Lloyd Bentsen, who at the time was running with Michael Dukakis on the Democratic presidential ticket. "He was a giant among Texans, a dear friend and a great public servant who was full of integrity," Bentsen told reporters as he exited the chapel doors. "He epitomized all we strive for in public service."[29]

The following day another memorial service was held in Austin's First Baptist Church. A "who's who" entourage of Texas politicians, including then-Vice President George Bush, attended. "I'll never forget our first meeting, although I had lived in Texas four or five years prior to that," Bush told a small crowd of reporters standing outside after the service. "We admired this man, like all Texans. We just wanted to fly over and pay our respects not only from this generation of Bushes but from the previous one."[30] Governor Bill Clements released a statement from his Austin office saying, "No man has ever done more for our state than Price Daniel."[31] And across town Lieutenant Governor Bill Hobby called Daniel "one of our Texas heroes... No other Texan served with such distinction in all three branches of government. His accomplishments make us all humble."[32]

Daniel's silver coffin, draped with white roses and escorted by an honor guard of Texas troopers, was buried on a Holly Ridge hilltop in the tree-shaded family cemetery near the grave of his eldest son and namesake. Many times the governor had walked over the plot where his body now lay, extolling the beauty of the countryside. It was the place he said he never wanted to leave.

Perhaps no story better described Price Daniel than one which appeared in *The Dayton News.* Writer Jim Kyle recalled his first visit with him: "I'll have to admit that while sitting in the kitchen of the governor's ranch house, I didn't know what kind of man he was," remembered Kyle. "I was a little nervous awaiting his early morning arrival from the bedroom.... When he walked in, I noticed right off he had on a pair of old pants that had dried mud stains from the ankles to the knees on the inseams. He was ready to go to work.... I never dreamed that before my day with Governor Daniel was over that I would meet a lawyer, a judge, drop him off on a farm road to meet a man in a helicopter, and drive about 250 miles to such places as Moscow, Point Blank, Ames, Livingston, and back roads of East Texas no one ever heard of." [33]

Kyle recalled Daniel driving him north on Highway 146 to pick up a judge. "When we picked up the judge in Livingston and headed around the courthouse," he wrote, "an old three-story brick building was visible on one corner of the courthouse grounds. The governor stopped the car and had the judge tell him everything he knew about it. The judge ended the story by telling the governor the building was going to be torn down.... Four hours later when we returned to Livingston, Daniel went out of the way to stop near the old building." He gazed out the window, then reflected: "I'll never see this building again and I just want to sit here for a few minutes so I can remember what it looks like." [34]

Throughout his life's journey, Price Daniel never sold himself short. "I discovered that people will respect you if you fight for what you think is right, even if they don't agree with you," he had once remarked. "My maternal grandmother Partlow—she ruled her family until she died at ninety-two—always hated people who wouldn't take a stand. She used to say, 'Show your backbone.'

"I've tried to do that." [35]

ACKNOWLEDGMENTS

I am deeply grateful for the efforts of many individuals who have assisted me in the process of writing this biography. Special thanks are due to those friends, family members, and colleagues of Price Daniel who took the time to give interviews for this project. Also providing ample assistance were the folks at the Texas State Library and Archives, the Lyndon Baines Johnson Presidential Library and Museum, the Center for American History at the University of Texas at Austin, the Sam Rayburn Library, and the Sam Houston Regional Library and Research Center. Other important contributors were J.C. Martin, Robert L. Schaadt, John W. Storey, George Christian, Joe Greenhill, Ned Price, Sam Johnson, H.G. Dulaney, Tom Daniel, Frank Daniel, Houston Daniel, Tim Daniel, Jean Murph, Marilyn Murph, my editor, Melissa Roberts, and former President George Bush.

I am most heavily indebted, however, to my father, David Murph. He took the initiative to interview Price Daniel on numerous occasions and to document a good portion of Daniel's life in his 1975 Ph.D. dissertation, entitled "Price Daniel: The Life of a Public Man." Without the framework provided by this extensive work, along with his countless hours of editing, traveling and counseling, this project in its present form would not have been possible.

Finally, I would like to thank my grandmother, Jean Daniel, for her tireless assistance with this project. Her response to my endless requests for documents and newspaper clippings, as well as answers to a barrage of questions asked over a span of seven years, is most appreciated. Paul Healy once wrote in *The Saturday Evening Post* that "Price Daniel got his comeuppance early. In college they shaved his head to puncture his ego. The girl he chose snubbed him as a 'little country politician.' So he took his cue from the Bible, rose to become a U.S. senator and new champion of the rights of Texas. And he married the girl!" I know my grandfather would agree that, taking everything into consideration, the latter was his wisest decision.

SOURCES AND NOTES

Much of this manuscript was written at my grandfather's desk in Liberty, Texas. In his private office, I had incredible access to a variety of sources, many of which have yet to be turned over to state archival collections. Often, when searching for a letter or document, it was as simple as thumbing through a filing cabinet or looking in a drawer. For the majority of my sources, however, I relied on collections housed in many fine libraries across the state. Of these, the most helpful were the Texas State Library and Archives, the Lyndon Baines Johnson Presidential Library and Museum, the Center for American History at the University of Texas at Austin, the Sam Rayburn Library, and the Sam Houston Regional Library and Research Center.

A full bibliography for this book would include a plethora of materials concerning many of the leading players and events that shaped the history of Texas and the nation in the twentieth century. It would be a book in itself. In my eight years of research, I was influenced by hundreds of books, reports, and articles that dealt with Daniel and his contemporaries. In addition, I examined most available oral history collections, research papers, newspaper clippings, letters, pictures, and documents related to Price Daniel's life and career. Listing them all, I believe, would serve little purpose. I have therefore chosen to cite in the notes only those books and articles that are quoted or otherwise mentioned in the text.

Chapter 1: The Early Years

1. Price Daniel, interview with David Murph, December 28, 1973.

2. David Murph, "Price Daniel: The Life of a Public Man," Ph.D. diss. (Texas Christian University, 1975), 2–3.

3. Price Daniel, interview with David Murph, December 28, 1973.

4. David Murph, "Price Daniel: The Life of a Public Man."

5. M.P. Daniel letterhead inscription; copy in author's possession.

6. I.H. Devine, *Daniel Family in Texas* (Waco, 1961), Apendix I.

7. *Liberty Vindicator,* December 24, 1909.

8. David Murph, "Price Daniel: The Life of a Public Man," 7.

9. *Houston Post,* October 20, 1910.

10. Ibid.

11. Miriam Partlow, interview with David Murph, August 12, 1974.

12. Price Daniel, interview with David Murph, December 27, 1974.

13. *Teague Daily Herald,* April 1, 1912.

14. M.P. Daniel to Nannie Daniel, June 3, 1912.

15. *Teague Daily Herald,* July 1, 1912.

16. Price Daniel, interview with David Murph, December 27, 1974.

17. Miriam Partlow, interview with David Murph, August 12, 1974.

18. William P. Daniel, interview with David Murph, August 12, 1974.

19. Price Daniel, interview with David Murph, December 27, 1974.

20. Price Daniel, interview with Fred Gantt, February 25, 1967.

21. Miriam Partlow, interview with David Murph, August 12, 1974.

22. Price Daniel, interview with David Murph, December 28, 1973.

23. Ibid.

24. Ellen V. Daniel, interview with David Murph, March 12, 1974.

25. Jean Daniel, interview with author, April 11, 1993.

26. David Murph, "Price Daniel: The Life of a Public Man," 21.

27. Miriam Partlow, *Liberty, Liberty County, and the Atascosito District* (Austin: Pemberton Press, 1974).

28. Price Daniel, interview with David Murph, December 28, 1973.

29. Ibid.

30. Ibid.

31. David Murph, "Price Daniel: The Life of a Public Man," 25–26.

32. Ibid., 26.

33. Ibid., 28.

34. *Liberty Vindicator,* date unknown.

35. David Murph, "Price Daniel: The Life of a Public Man," 29.

36. Undated, untitled clipping in Price Daniel files.

37. Price Daniel to M.P. and Nannie Daniel.

38. David Murph, "Price Daniel: The Life of a Public Man," 30.

39. Ibid.

40. Ibid.

41. *Fort Worth High School Student,* date unknown.

42. David Murph, "Price Daniel: The Life of a Public Man," 31.

43. Undated, untitled clipping in Price Daniel files.
44. David Murph, "Price Daniel: The Life of a Public Man," 32.
45. Ibid.
46. Ibid., 31.
47. Author interview with Jean Daniel, August 14, 1997.
48. Dave Cheavens to Price Daniel, August 25, 1927.
49. Price Daniel to congregation of College Avenue Baptist Church, Fort Worth, August 29, 1927.
50. David Murph, "Price Daniel: The Life of a Public Man," 33.

Chapter 2: Baylor University

1. E.W. Provence, "Baylor University: An Historical Sketch," in *The Diamond Jubliee: A Record of the Seventy-fifth Anniversary of the Founding of Baylor University*, edited by Henry Trantham (Waco: Baylor University Press, 1921), 13,17.
2. *Saturday Evening Post*, January 2, 1954.
3. Ibid.
4. Ibid.
5. Price Daniel essay, "My Ideal Woman in the University," 1927.
6. Jean Daniel, interview with author, July 5, 1993.
7. Price Daniel to Dean W.S. Allen, undated.
8. Dean W.S. Allen to Price Daniel, February 17, 1928.
9. David Murph, "Price Daniel: The Life of a Public Man," Ph.D. diss. (Texas Christian University, 1975), 35.
10. *Houston Post*, June 22, 1928.
11. *Houston Press*, June 22, 1928.
12. David Murph, "Price Daniel: The Life of a Public Man," 38.
13. Price Daniel press release, undated.
14. David Murph, "Price Daniel: The Life of a Public Man," 39.
15. Price Daniel, interview with Fred Gantt, February 25, 1967.
16. David Murph, "Price Daniel: The Life of a Public Man," 39–40.
17. Ibid., 41.
18. Fred Hartman to Price Daniel, January 29, 1930.
19. Price Daniel to Fred Hartman, January 23, 1929.
20. Fred Hartman to Price Daniel, January 29, 1930.
21. Ibid.
22. David Murph, "Price Daniel: The Life of a Public Man," 37.
23. M.P. Daniel to Price Daniel, July 22, 1928.
24. *The Daily Lariat*, March 5, 1929.
25. Senator Tom Connally to Price Daniel, March 14, 1929.
26. *The Daily Lariat*, May 23, 1929.
27. "Ox" to Price Daniel, May 24, 1929.
28. *The Daily Lariat*, September 18, 1929.
29. Dorothy Stokes essay, "Personality Sketch," November 6, 1929.
30. Charles D. Johnson to Price Daniel, July 24, 1929.

31. *Waco Times-Herald,* December 4, 1929.
32. Ibid.
33. David Murph, "Price Daniel: The Life of a Public Man," 44.
34. Ibid.
35. Fred Hartman to Price Daniel, January 20, 1930.
36. Jean Daniel, interview with author, July 5, 1993.
37. Fred Hartman to Price Daniel, March 6, 1987.
38. *The Daily Lariat,* 1931 (exact date unknown).
39. Baylor *Round-Up,* 1930–31 (Jefferson City, Missouri, 1931).
40. Stokes, "Personality Sketch."
41. Price Daniel Armistice Day Speech excerpt, November 11, 1930.
42. Pat Neff to Price Daniel, May 6, 1931.
43. *Liberty Vindicator,* date unknown.
44. Price Daniel to Nannie Daniel, March 16, 1931.
45. Ibid., November 12, 1931.
46. David Murph, interview with author, June 29, 1998.
47. Undated, untitled clipping in Price Daniel files.
48. David Murph, "Price Daniel: The Life of a Public Man," 47.
49. Philip Hyatt to Price Daniel, August 1, 1929.
50. Price Daniel to Nannie Daniel, March 16, 1931.
51. Ibid., November 12, 1931.
52. Ibid., January 6, 1932.
53. Baylor *Round-Up,* 1930–31.
54. Price Daniel to Nannie Daniel, October 21, 1931.
55. "Clarence" to Price Daniel, December 29, 1929.
56. Price Daniel to Nannie Daniel, January 20, 1932.
57. M.P. Daniel to Price Daniel, February 7, 1932.
58. Price Daniel, interview with Fred Gantt, February 25, 1967.
59. Ibid.
60. *Liberty Vindicator,* June 8, 1932.
61. Dr. Herbert H. Reynolds open letter, undated.
62. M.P. Daniel to Price Daniel, June 2, 1932.
63. Bill Daniel to Price Daniel, undated.

Chapter 3: Country Lawyer
1. *Texas Almanac,* 1940, 61.
2. Jean Daniel, interview with author, August 13, 1996.
3. *Saturday Evening Post,* January 2, 1954.
4. Price Daniel to Dean Allen G. Flowers, June 16, 1932.
5. *Liberty Vindicator,* March 9, 1933.
6. David Murph, interview with Thomas J. Hightower, December 28, 1973.
7. *Houston Chronicle,* March 8, 1997.
8. *Liberty Vindicator,* March 9, 1933 .
9. David Murph, interview with Ellen Daniel, March 12, 1974.

10. *Houston Chronicle*, March 11, 1933.
11. Ibid.
12. Ibid.
13. David Murph, interview with Price Daniel, March 29, 1974.
14. David Murph, interview with Thomas J. Hightower, December 28, 1973.
15. *Liberty Vindicator*, November 24, 1933.
16. David Murph, interview with Ellen Daniel, March 12, 1974.
17. *The Daily Courier*, 1933 (exact date unknown).
18. *Liberty Vindicator*, 1933 (exact date unknown).
19. David Murph, interview with Price Daniel, February 25, 1967.
20. M.P. Daniel, Sr. to Mrs. M. Moefield, December 9, 1933.
21. M.P. Daniel, Sr. to Ed Brookins, November 16, 1933.
22. M.P. Daniel, Sr. to Hon. Martin Dies, November 11, 1933.
23. M.P Daniel, Sr. to C.R. Newton, December 8, 1933.
24. C.R. Newton telegram to M.P. Daniel, Sr., December 9, 1933.
25. Congressman Martin Dies to M.P. Daniel, Sr., December 4, 1933.
26. M.P. Daniel, Sr. to Congressman Martin Dies, December 7, 1933.
27. *Liberty Vindicator*, November 24, 1933.
28. David Murph, "Price Daniel: The Life of a Public Man," Ph.D. diss. (Texas Christian University), 61.
29. Texas election returns, State Library and Archives.
30. *The Daily Courier*, 1933 (exact date unknown).
31. M.P Daniel, Sr. to Bertis Foster, December 22, 1933.
32. Fred Gantt, interview with Price Daniel, December 25, 1967.
33. David Murph, interview with Thomas J. Hightower, December 28, 1973.
34. David Murph, interview with Ellen Daniel, March 12, 1974.
35. David Murph, interview with Thomas J. Hightower, December 28, 1973.
36. Undated and untitled newspaper article in Price Daniel files.
37. David Murph, interview with Thomas J. Hightower, December 28, 1973.
38. *Daily Courier*, 1934 (exact date unknown).
39. Ibid.
40. Price Daniel, interview with author, August 10, 1987.
41. David Murph, "Price Daniel: The Life of a Public Man," 68–69.
42. Ibid., 69–70.
43. David Murph, interview with Thomas J. Hightower, December 28, 1973.
44. *Liberty Vindicator*, November 30, 1938.
45. *Dallas Morning News*, October 28, 1938.
46. Price Daniel to W.C. Morgan, February 1, 1943.
47. Undated and untitled article in Price Daniel files.
48. Robert L. Schaadt, interview with author, 1999.

49. *Beaumont Enterprise*, January 28, 1938.
50. Undated and untitled article in Price Daniel files.
51. Fred Gantt, interview with Price Daniel, February 25, 1967.
52. David Murph, "Price Daniel: The Life of a Public Man," 73–74.
53. *Beaumont Enterprise*, November 3, 1938.

Chapter 4: Look Out, Austin!
1. Ned Price, interview with author, October 27, 1993.
2. *Austin Statesman*, January 10–12, 1939.
3. Ibid., January 17, 1939.
4. Ibid., January 18, 1939.
5. Price Daniel, interview with Fred Gantt, February 25, 1967.
6. McKay, *O'Daniel*, 176–177.
7. Ibid., 180–181.
8. *Fort Worth Star-Telegram*, March 20, 1927.
9. Price Daniel, interview with Fred Gantt, February 25, 1967.
10. David Murph, "Price Daniel: The Life of a Public Man," Ph. D. diss. (Texas Christian University), 83–84.
11. Price Daniel, interview with Fred Gantt, February 25, 1967.
12. David Murph, "Price Daniel: The Life of a Public Man," 84.
13. *Dallas Dispatch*, April 1, 1939.
14. Ibid.
15. *Cleveland Advocate*, March 29, 1939.
16. Price Daniel, interview with Fred Gantt, February 25, 1967.
17. Ned Price, interview with author, October 27, 1993.
18. Price Daniel, interview with Fred Gantt, February 25, 1967.
19. Jean Daniel, interview with author, August 7, 1993.
20. Ibid.
21. Ibid.
22. *Dallas News*, May 20, 1939.
23. *Beaumont Enterprise*, May 21, 1939.
24. Drew Pearson column, undated and untitled.
25. David Murph, "Price Daniel: The Life of a Public Man," 89–90.
26. *Liberty Vindicator*, June 26, 1940.
27. Price Daniel, interview with Fred Gantt, February 25, 1967.
28. Jean Daniel, interview with author, August 7, 1993.
29. Ibid.
30. Ibid.
31. Ibid.
32. Price Daniel, interview with Fred Gantt, February 25, 1967.
33. Ibid.
34. Ibid.
35. Ibid.
36. *Hull-Daisetta News*, July 26, 1940.
37. *Texas Almanac*, 1941, 384.

38. Price Daniel, interview with Fred Gantt, February 25, 1967.
39. Ibid.
40. Jean Daniel, interview with author, August 7, 1993.
41. *Houston Post*, January 19, 1941.
42. David Murph, "Price Daniel: The Life of a Public Man," 96–97.
43. *Austin Statesman*, May 2, 1941.
44. Price Daniel, interview with Fred Gantt, February 25, 1967.
45. Ibid.
46. David Murph, "Price Daniel: The Life of a Public Man."
47. Price Daniel, interview with Fred Gantt, February 25, 1967.
48. Ned Price, interview with author, October 27, 1993.
49. Jean Daniel, interview with author, August 7, 1993.
50. Price Daniel, interview with Fred Gantt, February 25, 1967.
51. Price Daniel to Rep. Morris Roberts, May 21, 1942.
52. Price Daniel, interview with Fred Gantt, February 25, 1967.
53. Price Daniel to Ned Price, May 20, 1942.
54. *Houston Post*, October 3, 1942.
55. Price Daniel to J.R. Lindley, August 17, 1942.
56. Price Daniel to S.B. McAlister, October 2, 1942.
57. *Houston Chronicle*, February 7, 1942.
58. *Corpus Christi Times*, June 13, 1942.
59. Price Daniel, interview with Fred Gantt, February 25, 1967.
60. Rep. Everett Hutchinson to Price Daniel, undated.
61. *Austin Statesman*, January 11, 1943.

Chapter 5: Running the House
1. Price Daniel, interview with Fred Gantt, February 25, 1967.
2. Jack C. Estrin, *American History Made Simple* (New York, 1968), 167–168.
3. Texas Legislature, *House Journal*, 48th Legislature, 6–9.
4. Price Daniel to unknown, undated letter in Price Daniel files.
5. David Murph, "Price Daniel: The Life of a Public Man," Ph.D. diss. (Texas Christian University).
6. Price Daniel to Pete Jones, February 16, 1943.
7. Price Daniel, interview with Fred Gantt, February 25, 1967.
8. David Murph, "Price Daniel: The Life of a Public Man," 109–110.
9. Ibid., 108–109.
10. *Austin Statesman*, May 9, 1943.
11. Price Daniel, interview with Fred Gantt, February 25, 1967.
12. *Abilene Reporter-News*, March 4, 1943.
13. Price Daniel, interview with Fred Gantt, February 25, 1967.
14. Ibid.
15. Price Daniel, interview with Joe B. Frantz, June 5, 1970.
16. Ibid.
17. Ibid.

18. *Austin Statesman,* May 12, 1943.

19. *Houston Press,* May 12, 1943.

20. *Houston Post,* May 13, 1943.

21. *Fort Worth Star-Telegram,* May 13, 1943.

22. Ibid., May 14, 1943.

23. *Austin Statesman,* May 9, 1943.

24. Ibid.

25. Clarence (last name unknown) to Price Daniel, undated.

26. Virgil McPhail to Price Daniel, July 2, 1943.

Chapter 6: Humble Soldier

1. Price Daniel Diary, "The Life of a Public Man," 1943.

2. Ibid.

3. Ibid.

4. Ibid.

5. Ibid.

6. *Houston Chronicle,* August 5, 1943.

7. David Murph, "Price Daniel: The Life of a Public Man," Ph.D. diss. (Texas Christian University), 118.

8. Price Daniel, interview with Fred Gantt, February 25, 1967.

9. Price Daniel to Sam Rayburn, 1944 (undated), Sam Rayburn Library.

10. Sam Rayburn to Price Daniel, February 23, 1944, Sam Rayburn Library.

11. Jean Daniel, interview with author, August 7, 1993.

12. Jack C. Estrin, *American History* (New York, 1968), 167–168.

13. Jean Daniel, interview with author, August 7, 1993.

14. V Amphibious Corps unit introductory packet, 1945.

15. David Murph, "Price Daniel: The Life of a Public Man," 119.

16. Ned Price, interview with author, October 27, 1993.

17. Pat Neff, Sr. to Price Daniel, December 12, 1945.

18. David Murph, "Price Daniel: The Life of a Public Man," 120.

19. Ibid., 122.

Chapter 7: I'm Not Afraid of Anybody

1. Price Daniel radio broadcast, KTHT radio, Houston, July 20, 1946.

2. Ibid.

3. Price Daniel radio broadcast, KWBU radio, June 22, 1946.

4. Booth Mooney press release from Price Daniel state headquarters, Austin, date unknown.

5. *Saturday Evening Post,* January 2, 1954.

6. Price Daniel speech excerpt, June 22, 1946.

7. Ibid.

8. *Dallas Morning News,* January 2, 1947.

9. Joe Greenhill, interview with author, October 25, 1993.

10. Ibid.

11. Price Daniel, interview with Fred Gantt, February 25, 1967.

12. David Murph, "Price Daniel: The Life of a Public Man," Ph.D. diss. (Texas Christian University), 132–133.

13. Michael L. Gillette, *Southwestern Historical Quarterly*, 324.

14. V.O. Key, Jr. *Southern Politics in State and Nation* (New York: Alfred A. Knopf, 1949), 254.

15. Michael L. Gillette, "Blacks Challenge the White University," *SWHQ*, Vol. 86 (October 1982): 325.

16. *Newsweek*, December 30, 1946, 74.

17. Gillette, *Southwestern Historical Quarterly*, 324.

18. Ibid., 326.

19. *Newsweek*, December 30, 1946, 74.

20. Orville Bullington to John A. Lomax, January 7, 1944.

21. Henry Allen Bullock, "Negro Higher and Professional Education in Texas," *Journal of Negro Education* 17 (Summer 1948): 379.

22. Texas Poll, January 26, 1947: Alan Scott, "Twenty-Five Years of Opinion on Integration in Texas," *Southwestern Social Science Quarterly* 48 (September 1967): 157.

23. Price Daniel, "Constitutionality of Segregated Schools in Texas," argument in the Austin Court of Civil Appeals in the case of *Heman Marion Sweatt v. T.S. Painter* (January 29, 1948): 2.

24. Senate Bill 140, General & Special Laws of the State of Texas passed during the Regular Session of the 50th Texas Legislature.

25. Gillette, *SWHQ*, 327.

26. Ibid., 328.

27. *Austin American*, May 13–17.

28. Thomas R. Cole, *No Color Is My Kind* (Austin: University of Texas Press, 1997), 62–63, 73.

29. Michael Davis and Hunter Clark, *Thurgood Marshall: Warrior at the Bar, Rebel on the Bench* (New York, 1992), 142.

30. *Mexia News*, May 16, 1947.

31. *Beaumont Journal*, January 30, 1948.

32. Ibid.

33. *Dallas News*, November 16, 1947.

34. *Mexia News*, May 16, 1947.

35. *Tyler Telegraph*, May 15, 1947.

36. *Houston Post*, May 14, 1948.

37. *Negro Labor News*, May 24, 1947.

38. *The New York Times*, May 17, 1947.

39. "Lessons in Race Relations," n.p., n.d., Price Daniel Papers, clipping file, 1947.

40. *Waco News-Tribune*, January 20, 1950.

41. *Dallas News*, July 28, 1948.

42. Jean Daniel, interview with author, April 11, 1993.

43. Joe Greenhill, interview with author, October 25, 1993.

44. David Murph, "Price Daniel: The Life of a Public Man," 134–137.

45. Stuart Long, syndicated columnist, untitled, Price Daniel files, December 1948.

46. Price Daniel press release, July 1960.

47. *Current Biography,* 1956.

48. Price Daniel excerpt from speech to American Legion, date unknown.

49. Joe Greenhill, interview with author, October 25, 1993.

50. *Dallas Times Herald,* August 16, 1949.

51. David Murph, "Price Daniel: The Life of a Public Man," 148–149.

52. *Corpus Christi Caller,* September 8, 1949.

53. *Austin Statesman,* September 9, 1949.

54. Sam Rayburn to Fagan Dickson, January 25, 1949.

55. Price Daniel radio broadcast on KWBU, June 22, 1946.

56. Sam Rayburn to Price Daniel, February 19, 1949.

57. *Beeville Bee-Picayune,* January 5, 1950.

58. *Austin Statesman,* April 5, 1950.

59. *Dallas News,* March 28, 1950.

60. Roger Goldman and David Gallen, *Thurgood Marshall: Justice For All* (New York, 1992), 89.

61. Ibid., 89–90.

62. *Austin American-Statesman,* January 25, 1993.

63. Goldman and Gallen, *Thurgood Marshall: Justice For All,* 90.

64. Price Daniel, interview with Joe B. Frantz, June 5, 1970.

65. *Austin American-Statesman,* January 25, 1993.

66. Joe Greenhill to Harry McMullan, June 14, 1950.

67. Price Daniel to Herbert B. Harlow, June 15, 1950.

68. *The New York Times,* June 6, 1950.

69. Gillette, *SWHQ,* 342.

70. Gillette, "Heman Marion Sweatt," 157–158.

71. *Texas Almanac,* 1952–1953.

72. Price Daniel, interview with Fred Gantt, February 25, 1967.

73. Seth Shepard McKay, *Texas and the Fair Deal* (San Antonio: Naylor Co., 1954), 347–348.

74. *Fort Worth Press,* April 2, 1951.

75. Price Daniel, interview with Fred Gantt, February 25, 1967.

76. David Murph, "Price Daniel: The Life of a Public Man," 153–154.

77. *Dallas Morning News,* August 7, 1951.

78. Price Daniel, *Texas Publication Laws* (Austin, 1951), passage from preface by Fred Massengill, Jr.

79. Ibid.

80. Price Daniel biographical sketch, July 1960.

Chapter 8: The Tidelands

1. Woodrow Wilson, *Constitutional Government in the United States* (New York: The Columbia University Press, 1908), 174.

2. Price and Jean Daniel and Dorothy Blodgett, *The Texas Governor's Mansion* (Austin: Texas State Library and Archives, 1984), 208.

3. D. B. Hardeman and Donald C. Bacon, *Rayburn* (Austin, 1987), 351.

4. Ernest R. Bartley, *The Tidelands Oil Controversy* (Austin: University of Texas Press, 1953), 4.

5. *New York Times,* August 2, 1946.

6. Untitled, undated article in Price Daniel files.

7. *United States v. California,* 392 U.S. 19.

8. *Texas Spectator,* July 7, 1947.

9. Daniel and Daniel, *The Texas Governor's Mansion,* 208.

10. Price Daniel telegram to Beauford Jester, July 16, 1947.

11. Price Daniel, interview with Fred Gantt, February 25, 1967.

12. Price Daniel, interview with Joe B. Frantz, June 5, 1970.

13. Price Daniel brief to U.S. Supreme Court, July 14, 1947.

14. Price Daniel to Beauford Jester, December 28, 1947, Beauford Jester Papers, Texas State Archives.

15. *Beaumont Enterprise,* September 2, 1947.

16. Ibid.

17. Price Daniel statement, undated, in possession of Texas State Library and Archives.

18. Hardeman and Bacon, *Rayburn,* 352.

19. Price Daniel to Sam Rayburn, January 19, 1948.

20. Hardeman and Bacon, *Rayburn,* 352.

21. *Houston Chronicle,* January 16, 1948.

22. Curtis Morris to Beauford Jester, January 10, 1948, Beauford Jester Papers.

23. Price Daniel to Beauford Jester, February 12, 1948, Beauford Jester Papers.

25. Jester telegrams to governors, February 14, 1948, Beauford Jester Papers.

25. David Murph, "Price Daniel: The Life of a Public Man," Ph.D. diss. (Texas Christian University).

26. Price Daniel, interview with Fred Gantt, February 25, 1967.

27. Sam Rayburn to Price Daniel, May 7, 1948.

28. *Austin American,* September 28, 1948.

29. Price Daniel, interview with Fred Gantt, February 25, 1967.

30. *Houston Chronicle,* December 22, 1948.

31. Beauford Jester to Sam Rayburn, December 23, 1948, Beauford Jester Papers.

32. Price Daniel, interview with Fred Gantt, February 25, 1967.

33. *Houston Chronicle,* January 16, 1949.

34. Curtis Morris to Price Daniel, February 3, 1949, Price Daniel Papers.

35. Curtis Morris to Beauford Jester, March 12, 1949.

36. Price Daniel to Lyndon Johnson, March 7, 1949.

37. Lyndon Johnson to Price Daniel, March 11, 1949.

38. *Fort Worth Star-Telegram*, March 27, 1949.

39. *Daily Texan*, 1949 (exact date unknown).

40. Seymour V. Connor, *Texas: A History* (Arlington Heights, IL: AHM Publishing Corp., 1971), 368.

41. Tom Pickett to Beauford Jester, May 12, 1949, Jester Papers.

42. Lyndon Johnson to Beauford Jester, May 10, 1949.

43. Price Daniel brief to U.S. Supreme Court, May 9, 1949.

44. *Houston Chronicle,* May 17, 1949.

45. Price Daniel, interview with Anthony Champagne, January 10, 1979.

46. Daniel and Daniel, *The Texas Governor's Mansion,* 208–209.

47. Price Daniel, interview with Anthony Champagne, January 10, 1979.

48. *Austin Statesman,* May 17, 1949.

49. Hardeman and Bacon, *Rayburn,* 352–354.

50. *Dallas Times Herald,* May 23, 1949.

51. David Murph, "Price Daniel: The Life of a Public Man," 171.

52. Price Daniel, interview with Anthony Champagne, January 10, 1979.

53. Sam Rayburn to Howard D. Dodgen, March 3, 1950.

54. Hardeman and Bacon, *Rayburn,* 352–354.

55. Daniel and Daniel, *The Texas Governor's Mansion,* 208–209.

56. Beauford Jester to Sam Rayburn, May 30, 1949, Jester Papers.

57. Daniel and Daniel, *The Texas Governor's Mansion,* 209.

58. Ibid.

59. Ibid., 208–209.

60. Hardeman and Bacon, *Rayburn,* 353.

61. Price Daniel, interview with Fred Gantt, February 25, 1967.

62. Untitled, undated article in Price Daniel files.

63. Allan Shivers, interview with Thomas Brewer, April 8, 1966.

64. *Houston Chronicle,* July 23, 1949.

65. Sam Kinch and Stuart Long, *Allan Shivers, The Pied Piper of Texas Politics* (Austin, 1973), 86.

66. George Norris Green, *The Establishment in Texas Politics* (Westport, Connecticut, 1979), 142.

67. *Austin Statesman,* April 25, 1950.

68. *Beaumont Enterprise,* August 30, 1949.

69. *Fort Worth Press,* March 10, 1950.

70. *Saturday Evening Post,* January 2, 1954.

71. Jean Daniel, interview with author, April 11, 1993.

72. *Houston Post*, March 25, 1950.
73. Price Daniel brief to U.S. Supreme Court, March 28, 1950.
74. *Saturday Evening Post*, January 2, 1954.
75. Jean Daniel, interview with author, April 11, 1993.
76. *Sherman Democrat*, April 9, 1950.
77. *Beaumont Journal*, April 1, 1950.
78. *Houston Chronicle*, date unknown.
79. Alfred Steinberg, *Sam Johnson's Boy* (New York: Macmillan, 1968), 357.
80. *New York Times*, June 6, 1950.
81. Ibid.
82. Ibid.
83. Ibid.
84. *Saturday Evening Post*, January 2, 1954.
85. *New York Times*, June 6, 1950.
86. Price Daniel speech excerpt, October 10, 1950.
87. Anthony Champagne, *Congressman Sam Rayburn* (New Brunswick, NJ: Rutgers University Press, 1984), 142.
88. Green, *The Establishment in Texas Politics*, 142.
89. Hardeman and Bacon, *Rayburn*, 354.
90. Ibid.
91. Price Daniel address to Texas State Bar Convention, July 5, 1951.
92. *New York Times*, August 28, 1951.
93. Ibid.
94. Green, *The Establishment in Texas Politics*, 142.
95. Allan Shivers, interview, February 28, 1973, LBJ Library.
96. Allan Shivers, interview with Joe B. Frantz, May 29, 1970; Allan Shivers interview with Tom Brewer, April 8, 1966.

Chapter 9: I Like Ike!

1. George Norris Green, *The Establishment in Texas Politics* (Westport, Connecticut, 1979), 149.
2. Tom Connally and Alfred Steinberg, *My Name is Tom Connally* (New York, 1954), 76–81, 245, 344–345.
3. Price Daniel radio broadcast, WFAA Radio, Dallas, Texas, January 21, 1952.
4. Ibid.
5. *Saturday Evening Post*, January 2, 1954.
6. *Liberty Vindicator*, January 24, 1952.
7. Alfred Steinberg, *Sam Johnson's Boy* (New York: Macmillan, 1968), 325.
8. Price Daniel, interview with Joe B. Frantz, June 5, 1970.
9. *Abilene Reporter-News*, February 24, 1952.
10. Daniel telegram to Tom Connally, March 24, 1952.
11. Green, *The Establishment in Texas Politics*, 148.

12. Allan Shivers, interview with Thomas Brewer, April 8, 1966.
13. Allan Shivers statement, April 14, 1952, Allan Shivers Papers.
14. Steinberg, *Sam Johnson's Boy*, 325.
15. Ronnie Dugger, *The Politician* (New York, 1982), 374.
16. Price Daniel, interview with Joe B. Frantz, June 5, 1970.
17. *Houston Post*, April 16, 1952.
18. *The Longview Journal*, April 16, 1952.
19. *The Sherman Democrat*, April 14, 1952.
20. Price Daniel, interview with Joe B. Frantz, June 5, 1970.
21. Price Daniel Senate candidacy speech excerpt, January 21, 1952.
22. Ibid.
23. Price Daniel, interview with Anthony Champagne, January 10, 1979. (While interviewing Daniel, Champagne says that Lindley Beckworth faced "almost certain defeat" in his decision to enter the Senate race.)
24. Green, *The Establishment in Texas Politics*, 150.
25. *Denison Herald*, June 15, 1952.
26. Jean Murph, interview with author, June 28, 1998.
27. Price Daniel speech text, May 29, 1952, Waco, Texas, Price Daniel Papers.
28. *Saturday Evening Post*, January 2, 1954.
29. Green, *The Establishment in Texas Politics*, 150.
30. *Texas Almanac*, 1954–1955, 447.
31. Files of the Republican National Committee, 1932–1965.
32. Allan Shivers, interview with Thomas Brewer, April 8, 1966.
33. Price Daniel speech excerpt, August 25, 1952.
34. Price Daniel, interview with David Murph, May 6, 1967.
35. Paul Casdorph, *The Republican Party in Texas, 1865–1965* (Austin, 1965), 195.
36. *Amarillo Daily News*, September 10, 1952.
37. *Dallas Morning News*, September 10, 1952.
38. Price Daniel, interview with David Murph, May 6, 1967.
39. Jean Daniel, interview with author, April 11, 1993.
40. *Houston Chronicle*, October 15, 1952.
41. *Saturday Evening Post*, January 2, 1954.
42. *Houston Post*, October 18, 1952.
43. Ibid., October 22, 1952.
44. Price Daniel, interview with David Murph, May 6, 1967.
45. Hardeman and Bacon, *Rayburn*, 371.
46. Price Daniel, interview with Anthony Champagne, January 10, 1979.
47. *Texas Almanac*, 1990-91, 365.
48. Casdorph, *The Republican Party in Texas*, 196.
49. Price Daniel, interview with Anthony Champagne, January 10, 1979.

Chapter 10: Washington
1. Roger Dallek, *Lone Star Rising* (New York, 1991), 428–429.
2. *Saturday Evening Post*, January 2, 1954.
3. Ibid.
4. *U.S. News & World Report*, August 22, 1952.
5. *Newsweek*, April 28, 1952.
6. *Saturday Evening Post*, January 2, 1954.
7. Price Daniel, interview with Joe B. Frantz, June 5, 1970.
8. Ibid.
9. Ibid.
10. David Murph, "Price Daniel: The Life of a Public Man," Ph.D. diss. (Texas Christian University, 1975), 222–223.
11. Price Daniel, interview with Joe B. Frantz, June 5, 1970.
12. *Saturday Evening Post*, January 2, 1954.
13. Booth Mooney, *LBJ: An Irreverent Chronicle* (New York: Crowell, 1976), 22.
14. *Congressional Record*, 83rd Congress, 1st session, 2815–2817.
15. Ibid.
16. *Fort Worth Star-Telegram*, April 9, 1953.
17. *Saturday Evening Post*, January 2, 1954.
18. *Fort Worth Star-Telegram*, April 9, 1953.
19. *Houston Post*, April 10, 1953.
20. *Washington Post*, April 28, 1953.
21. Price Daniel, interview with Joe B. Frantz, June 5, 1970.
22. Ibid.
23. *Hubbard News*, May 22, 1953.
24. Price Daniel, interview with Fred Gantt, May 6, 1967.
25. Jean Daniel, interview with author, April 11, 1993.
26. *Saturday Evening Post*, January 2, 1954.
27. Jean Daniel, interview with author, April 12, 1993.
28. Price Daniel, interview with Joe B. Frantz, June 5, 1970.
29. Ibid.
30. *Saturday Evening Post*, January 2, 1954.
31. Ibid.
32. David Murph, "Price Daniel: The Life of a Public Man," 229.
33. *Dallas Morning News*, March 17, 1956.
34. David Murph, "Price Daniel: The Life of a Public Man," 229–233.
35. *La Croix*, June 19, 1953.
36. *Common Sense*, April 1950.
37. Price Daniel, interview with Fred Gantt, May 6, 1967.
38. Price Daniel, interview with Joe B. Frantz, June 5, 1970.
39. *New York Times*, June 20, 1954.
40. Price Daniel, interview with Fred Gantt, May 6, 1967.
41. *Congressional Record*, 83rd Congress, 15845–15873.
42. Price Daniel, interview with Fred Gantt, May 6, 1967.

43. Letters regarding Joseph McCarthy are in Price Daniel files.
44. Don E. Carleton, *Red Scare! Right-Wing Hysteria, Fifties Fanaticism, and Their Legacy in Texas* (Austin: Texas Monthly Press, 1985), 100–147.
45. Price Daniel to E.M. Biggers, January 4, 1955.
46. *Austin Statesman*, December 2, 1954.
47. *Congressional Record*, 83rd Congress, 16328–16329.
48. Thomas Reeves, *The Life and Times of Joe McCarthy*, 662, 665, 671.
49. Price Daniel, remarks made during a debate on April 1, 1954.
50. *Congressional Record*, 83rd Congress, 6742.
51. Price Daniel speech text, May 1954.
52. *Houston Post*, May 19, 1954 .
53. Price Daniel, interview with David Murph, February 8, 1975.
54. Monroe Lee Billington, *The Political South in the Twentieth Century* (New York: Charles Scribner's Sons, 1975), 110.
55. J. William Fulbright, *The Price of Empire* (New York, 1989), 93–94.
56. Billington, *The Political South*, 110.
57. Excerpts from text of Southern Manifesto, Library of Congress.
58. Fulbright, *The Price of Empire*, 93–94.
59. Billington, *The Political South*, 111.
60. Price Daniel to Mildred Brockemeyer, March 23, 1956.
61. Price Daniel, interview with Fred Gantt, May 6, 1967.
62. David Murph, "Price Daniel: The Life of a Public Man," 235–236.
63. Ibid.
64. Ibid., 238–239.
65. Price Daniel to Mrs. Floy Satterfield, December 8, 1955.
66. *Washington Post*, December 20, 1955.
67. *Congressional Record*, 84th Congress, 2nd session, 268–278.
68. Ibid.
69. *Dallas Morning News*, January 11, 1956.
70. *Congressional Record*, 84th Congress, 2nd session.
71. David Murph, "Price Daniel: The Life of a Public Man," 241.
72. *Saturday Evening Post*, January 2, 1954.
73. Jake Pickle, *Jake* (Austin, 1997), 151.
74. J.C. Martin, interview with author, October 27, 1993.
75. Jean Daniel, interview with author, April 11, 1993.
76. David C. Whitney, *The American Presidents* (New York: Doubleday, 1967), 202.
77. *Austin American-Statesman*, February 6, 1956.
78. Ibid., March 11, 1956.
79. James McGregor Burns, *John Kennedy: A Political Profile* (New York, 1961), 171.
80. *Austin American-Statesman*, March 16, 1956.
81. Burns, *John Kennedy: A Political Profile*, 172.
82. Ibid., 172–173.

83. Ibid., 173–174.

84. Robert S. Parmet, *Jack: The Struggles of John F. Kennedy* (New York, 1980), 343.

85. Burns, *John Kennedy: A Political Profile,* 174.

86. *Dallas Morning News,* March 29, 1956.

87. Ibid.

88. George Norris Green, *The Establishment in Texas Politics* (Westport, Connecticut, 1979), 166 .

89. Joe B. Frantz, *Texas: A Bicentennial History* (New York, 1976), 191.

90. Jean Daniel, interview with author, April 11, 1993.

91. Douglas Cater, "The Trouble in Lyndon Johnson's Backyard," *The Reporter,* December 1, 1955, 32.

92. William G. Phillips, *Yarborough of Texas* (Washington, D.C.: Acropolis Books, 1969), 42.

93. *Beaumont Enterprise,* March 15, 1956.

94. Price Daniel, interview with Joe B. Frantz, June 5, 1970.

95. Allan Shivers, interview AC 74–42, LBJ Library.

96. George E. Reedy, *The U.S. Senate* (New York, 1986), 169.

97. Ibid.

Chapter 11: Race of '56

1. Alfred Steinberg, *Sam Johnson's Boy* (New York: Macmillan, 1968), 442.

2. George Norris Green, *The Establishment in Texas Politics* (Westport, Connecticut, 1979), 174.

3. Joe B. Frantz, *Texas: A Bicentennial History* (New York, 1976), 190.

4. Rupert N. Richardson, *Texas: The Lone Star State* (Englewood Cliffs, New Jersey, 1958), 369.

5. *San Antonio Express,* June 5, 1956.

6. *Houston Post,* June 6, 1956.

7. *Dallas Morning News,* June 5, 1956.

8. Price Daniel speech excerpt, March 12, 1956.

9. J.C. Martin, "The First Administration of Price Daniel," thesis (University of Texas at Austin, 1967), 18.

10. Price Daniel form letter to county campaign managers, August 1956.

11. *Austin Statesman,* April 13, 1956.

12. *Austin American,* April 20, 1956.

13. Sam Kinch and Stuart Long, *Allan Shivers, The Pied Piper of Texas Politics* (Austin, 1973), 88.

14. Richardson, *Texas: The Lone Star State,* 369.

15. *Austin American,* May 2, 1956.

16. Ralph Yarborough speech text, June 1, 1956, Ralph Yarborough Papers.

17. Ibid., undated.

18. *Houston Post*, June 22, 1956.

19. Green, *The Establishment in Texas Politics*, 175–176.

20. Price Daniel speech excerpt, El Paso, Texas, June 5, 1956.

21. Green, *The Establishment in Texas Politics*, 175–176.

22. Fred Gantt, Jr., *The Chief Executive in Texas* (Austin: UT Press, 1964), 278.

23. *Austin American*, June 17, 1956.

24. Green, *The Establishment in Texas Politics*, 175–176.

25. *Houston Post*, June 22, 1956.

26. *Kountze News*, January 1, 1956.

27. Ralph Yarborough speech, Corsicana, Texas, July 20, 1956.

28. Gantt, *The Chief Executive*, 294.

29. *Dallas Morning News*, June 24, 1956.

30. *Austin Statesman*, July 11, 1956.

31. Kenneth Towery column, source unknown.

32. *Houston Post*, July 7, 1956.

33. Ibid., July 17, 1956.

34. Jean Murph, interview with author, June 29, 1998.

35. *Austin American*, July 24, 1956.

36. Texas Press Association, "Campaign Advertising," Yarborough Papers.

37. *Austin Statesman*, July 8, 1956.

38. *Austin American*, July 28, 1956.

39. Green, *The Establishment in Texas Politics*, 175–176.

40. Ibid.

41. Steinberg, *Sam Johnson's Boy*, 442.

42. James Reston, Jr., *The Lone Star* (New York: Harper and Row, 1989), 142.

43. Untitled clipping in Ralph Yarborough Papers, July 9, 1956.

44. Ibid., August 13, 1956.

45. Green, *The Establishment in Texas Politics*, 175.

46. Earl Black, *Southern Governors* (Cambridge, Massachusetts: Harvard University Press, 1976), 382–383.

47. Untitled clipping in Ralph Yarborough Papers, August 8, 1956.

48. Ibid., August 7, 1956.

49. Green, *The Establishment in Texas Politics*, 176.

50. Price Daniel speech excerpt, Dallas, Texas, August 20, 1956.

51. Martin, "The First Administration of Price Daniel," 37.

52. *Texas Almanac*, election tables.

53. Green, *The Establishment in Texas Politics*, 176.

54. Untitled clipping, Lyndon Baines Johnson Library.

55. *Texas Almanac*, election tables; Reston, *The Lone Star*, 142.

56. Steinberg, *Sam Johnson's Boy*, 442.
57. *Fort Worth Star-Telegram*, August 28, 1956.
58. Ibid., August 30, 1956.
59. William G. Phillips, *Yarborough of Texas* (Washington, DC: Acropolis Books, 1969), 43.
60. Ralph Yarborough speech text, September 4, 1956, Ralph Yarborough Papers.
61. Frantz, *Texas: A Bicentennial History*, 191.
62. Sam Rayburn to Ava I. Humphreys, April 9, 1956.
63. Green, *The Establishment in Texas Politics*, 171–173.
64. Don E. Carleton, *A Breed So Rare* (Austin: Texas State Historical Association, 1998), 467.
65. Price Daniel, interview with Anthony Champagne, January 10, 1979.
66. *The New Republic*, September 24, 1956.
67. Price Daniel, interview with Anthony Champagne, January 10, 1979.
68. *The New Republic*, September 24, 1956.
69. Allan Shivers, interview with Frantz.
70. *Fort Worth Star-Telegram*, September 6–7, 1956; Jim Wright, interview with David Murph, February 10, 1999.
71. *Fort Worth Star-Telegram*, September 9, 1956.
72. Jim Wright, interview with David Murph, February 10, 1999.
73. Green, *The Establishment in Texas Politics*, 177.
74. *Fort Worth Star-Telegram*, September 9, 1956.
75. Ibid., September 8, 1956.
76. Green, *The Establishment in Texas Politics*, 177.
77. *Fort Worth Star-Telegram*, September 10, 1956; Jim Wright, interview with David Murph, February 10, 1999.
78. *Fort Worth Star-Telegram*, September 9, 1956.
79. Ibid., September 11, 1956.
80. Ibid.
81. *Fort Worth Star-Telegram*, September 11, 1956.
82. Green, *The Establishment in Texas Politics*, 177.
83. *The New Republic*, September 24, 1956; *Fort Worth Star-Telegram*, September 11–12, 1956.
84. Harry Provence, *Lyndon B. Johnson* (New York: Fleet Publishing Corporation, 1965), 73.
85. Price Daniel, interview with David Murph, June 29, 1998.
86. *Fort Worth Star-Telegram*, September 12, 1956.
87. *The New Republic*, September 24, 1956.
88. Price Daniel, interview with David Murph, May 20, 1999.
89. Martin, "The First Administration of Price Daniel," 64.
90. Gantt, *The Chief Executive in Texas*, 319–320.
91. *Texas Almanac*, 1966–67, 575.

92. Price Daniel, interview with David Murph, June 29, 1998.

93. Jean Daniel, interview with author, April 11, 1993.

94. Steinberg, *Sam Johnson's Boy*, 448.

95. Price Daniel campaign press release, August 8, 1956.

96. Richard Harwood and Haynes Johnson, *Lyndon* (New York: Praeger Publishers, 1973), 201.

97. Price Daniel to Allan Shivers, November 2, 1956.

98. Allan Shivers to Price Daniel, November 12, 1956.

99. Price Daniel press release, November 13, 1956.

100. Price Daniel to Allan Shivers, November 21, 1956.

101. Price Daniel to Sam Rayburn, November 24, 1956, Sam Rayburn Library.

102. Price Daniel, interview with Anthony Champagne, January 10, 1979.

103. Price Daniel, interview with David Murph, June 9, 1982.

104. Harwood and Johnson, *Lyndon*, 201.

105. Ibid.

106. Steinberg, *Sam Johnson's Boy*, 448.

Chapter 12: A Dream Come True

1. Ross Phares, *Texas Tradition* (New York: Henry Holt & Co., 1954), 192.

2. *San Antonio Express*, January 15, 1957.

3. Chandler Davidson, *Race and Class in Texas Politics* (Princeton University Press, 1990), 29.

4. *Austin Statesman*, January 15, 1957.

5. Ibid.

6. *Dallas News*, January 16, 1957.

7. Price Daniel inaugural speech, January 15, 1957.

8. *Houston Post*, January 16, 1957.

9. *Dallas News*, January 16, 1957.

10. *Houston Post*, January 16, 1957.

11. Ibid.

12. *Dallas News*, January 7, 1957.

13. *San Antonio News*, January 16, 1957.

14. Author interview with Price Daniel.

15. Price Daniel speech text, January 17, 1957, Price Daniel Papers.

16. *Dallas News*, January 18, 1957.

17. *Austin Statesman*, January 18, 1957.

18. *Dallas News*, January 18, 1957.

19. Price Daniel legislative address, January 17, 1957.

20. *San Antonio Express*, January 18, 1957.

21. *Federationist*, January 18, 1957.

22. Author interview with George Christian, October 25, 1993.

23. Price Daniel legislative address, February 19, 1957.

24. George Christian memorandum to Price Daniel, date unknown.

25. Price Daniel press release, February 26, 1957.

26. Price Daniel speech excerpt, March 25, 1957.

27. Price Daniel message to Texas Legislature, 1957.

28. John Crosthwait, source unknown.

29. *Liberty Vindicator*, August 28, 1988.

30. Fred Gantt, Jr., *The Chief Executive in Texas* (Austin: UT Press, 1964), 248.

31. Ibid.

32. Price Daniel legislative address, January 17, 1957.

33. Jerry Sadler to John Osorio, date unknown.

34. John Osorio to Jerry Sadler, date unknown.

35. Untitled, undated document in Price Daniel files.

36. Price Daniel address to insurance board, date unknown.

37. Joe B. Frantz, *Texas: A Bicentennial History* (New York, 1976), 192.

38. Untitled, undated document in Price Daniel files.

39. George Norris Green, *The Establishment in Texas Politics* (Westport, Connecticut, 1979), 201.

40. Richard Morehead, *Fifty Years in Texas Politics* (Burnet, Texas: Eakin Press, 1982), 137.

41. John Ben Shepperd arguments before U.S. Supreme Court, April 13, 1955.

42. Texas Poll, Report 528, April 7, 1955, in Alan Scott, "Twenty-five Years of Opinion on Integration in Texas," *Southwestern Social Science Quarterly*, 48 (September 1967): 155, 160.

43. Robyn Duff Ladino, *Desegregating Texas Schools* (Austin: UT Press, 1996), 21.

44. Texas Poll, in *Southern School News*, July 1956.

45. *Dallas Morning News*, February 4, 1956.

46. Ladino, *Desegregating Texas Schools*, 136–137.

47. Green, *The Establishment in Texas Politics*, 190.

48. Frantz, *Texas: A Bicentennial History*, 204–205.

49. *Christianity Today*, 1958.

50. Numan V. Bartley, *The New South, 1945–1980* (Baton Rouge: Louisiana State University Press, 1995), 213.

51. Billington, *The Political South*, 123.

52. Jean Daniel, interview with author, August 10, 1995.

53. *Texas House Journal*, 1957.

54. Ladino, *Desegregating Texas Schools*, 139.

55. Betty Bean Fielder, "Price Daniel, Texas and Segregation," thesis (Lamar Univ., 1997), 135.

56. Price Daniel telegram to Dwight Eisenhower, October 19, 1957.

57. Dwight Eisenhower to Price Daniel, November 7, 1957.

58. Price Daniel, interview with Joe B. Frantz, June 5, 1970.

59. Price Daniel legislative address, November 20, 1957.

60. *Texas Senate Journal*, 1957, 118.

61. *Dallas News*, November 28, 1957.

62. Ibid., November 30, 1957.

63. Price and Jean Daniel and Dorothy Blodgett, *The Texas Governor's Mansion* (Austin: Texas State Library and Archives Commission, 1984), 219.

64. *Laws*, Republic of Texas, 1:133; Gammel, *Laws of Texas*, 1:1193–1194.

65. Price Daniel, interview with Frantz.

66. Sam Kinch and Stuart Long, *Allan Shivers, The Pied Piper of Texas Politics* (Austin, 1973), 85–86.

67. Price Daniel, interview with Anthony Champagne, January 10, 1979, Sam Rayburn Library.

68. Figures released August 31, 1983 by Jack Gibson of the General Land Office.

69. Author interview with Jean Daniel, October 30, 1993.

70. Price Daniel, *Report to the Legislature*, January 9, 1963, 121.

71. Gantt, *The Chief Executive in Texas*, 255.

72. *Texas Outlook* magazine, September 1959.

73. *Texas House Journal*, 1957.

74. *Liberty Vindicator*, August 28, 1988.

75. *Austin American-Statesman*, September 4, 1988.

76. Ibid.

77. Ibid.

78. Mary Farrell and Elizabeth Silverthorne, *First Ladies of Texas* (Belton, Texas, 1976), 378.

79. Ibid., 379.

80. Author interview with Jean Daniel, October 30, 1993.

81. Ibid.

82. *Dallas Times Herald*, August 25, 1988.

83. *National Municipal Review*, May 1921.

84. George Christian, interview with author, October 25, 1993.

85. Morgan and Webb, *Making the Most of Your Life* (New York: Garden City Publishing Company, Inc., 1932), 7.

86. Llerena Friend, *Sam Houston: The Great Designer* (Austin: UT Press), 39.

87. Dale Carnegie, *How to Win Friends and Influence People* (New York: Simon and Schuster, 1936), 76.

88. Jean Daniel, interview with author, August 14, 1995.

89. George Christian, interview with author, October 25, 1993.

90. Ibid.

91. Price Daniel, *Report to the Legislature*, January 9, 1963.

92. Price Daniel televised speech, June 1957.

93. *Dallas News*, date unknown.

94. Untitled, undated document in Price Daniel files.

95. Price Daniel speech in Huntsville, Texas, September 10, 1957.

96. Clifton McCleskey, *The Government and Politics of Texas* (Boston: Little, Brown and Company), 176.

97. Price Daniel message to Texas Legislature, October 14, 1957.

98. *Liberty Vindicator*, August 28, 1988.

99. Ibid.

100. Gantt, *The Chief Executive in Texas*, 320.

101. Ibid.

102. Julie Leininger Pycior, *LBJ and Mexican Americans* (Austin: University of Texas Press, 1997), 103.

103. *Houston Chronicle*, August 26, 1988.

104. Sam Rayburn to Jesse Andrews, August 25, 1958.

105. Sam Rayburn to Price Daniel, August 25, 1958.

106. Gantt, *The Chief Executive in Texas*, 320–321.

107. *San Antonio Express*, September 10, 1958.

108. McCleskey, *The Government and Politics of Texas*, 243.

109. Author interview with David Murph, October 28, 1995.

110. *The Hondo Anvil Herald*, September 15, 1988.

111. Author interview with George Christian, October 25, 1993.

112. Jake Pickle, *Jake* (Austin, 1997), 201–202.

113. Ibid.

114. Richard Morehead, *Fifty Years in Texas Politics* (Burnet, Texas: Eakin Press, 1982), 137–139.

115. Untitled, undated document in Price Daniel files.

116. *Dallas News*, February 1, 1959.

117. Institute of Public Affairs, University of Texas, *The 56th Legislature: A Review of its Work*, 3–9.

118. Author interview with George Christian, October 25, 1993.

119. *Dallas News*, February 1, 1959.

120. *The Tipro Reporter*, August 1961.

121. Price Daniel, interview with David Murph, June 10, 1982.

Chapter 13: A Penny for Price

1. Price Daniel, interview with David Murph, November 25, 1982.

2. Ibid.

3. Ibid.

4. Ibid.

5. Ibid.

6. Alfred Steinberg, *Sam Johnson's Boy* (New York: Macmillan, 1968), 508.

7. Booth Mooney, *LBJ: An Irreverent Chronicle*, 125.

8. Price Daniel, intyerview with Anthony Champagne, January 10, 1979.

9. Author interview with Jean Daniel, April 11, 1993.

10. Fred Gantt, Jr., *The Chief Executive in Texas* (Austin: UT Press, 1964), 321.

11. Rupert N. Richardson, *Texas: The Lone Star State* (Englewood Cliffs, New Jersey, 1958), 370.

12. Texas Election Returns, Texas State Library and Archives.

13. Earl Black, *Southern Governors and Civil Rights* (Cambridge, Massachusetts: Harvard University Press, 1976), 129, 191, 198, 392; *Texas Observer*, 1962.

14. Steinberg, *Sam Johnson's Boy*, 539.

15. Ibid.

16. Gantt, *The Chief Executive in Texas*, 321.

17. Steinberg, *Sam Johnson's Boy*, 539.

18. O. Douglas Weeks, *Texas in the 1960 Presidential Election* (Austin: University of Texas Press, 1961), 49.

19. Steinberg, *Sam Johnson's Boy*, 539.

20. Gantt, *The Chief Executive in Texas*, 322.

21. James Reston, Jr., *The Lone Star* (New York: Harper and Row, 1989), 203.

22. Price Daniel to Pauline Yelderman, July 26, 1965.

23. Clinton McCleskey, *The Government and Politics of Texas* (Boston: Little, Brown and Company, 1963), 213.

24. Price Daniel, *Report to the Legislature*, January 9, 1963.

25. Report of House Committee, December 21, 1961.

26. Price Daniel, *Report to the Legislature*, January 9, 1963.

27. *The Hondo Anvil Herald*, September 15, 1988.

28. Gantt, *The Chief Executive in Texas*, 118–119.

29. Ibid., 112.

30. Price Daniel, interview with Pauline Yelderman, April 5, 1960, University of Houston Television.

31. Author interview with George Christian, October 25, 1993.

32. Price Daniel, interview with Corrinne E. Crow, November 17, 1977, ETSU Oral History.

33. Ibid.

34. Gantt, *The Chief Executive in Texas*, 115.

35. *Austin American-Statesman*, July 31, 1961.

36. Gantt, *The Chief Executive in Texas*, 245.

37. Marvin P. Baker, "The Executive Veto in Texas," unpublished M.A. thesis, University of Texas, 1933; 54.

38. *Austin American*, May 22, 24, 28, 1961.

39. Gantt, *Chief Executive*, 251–252.

40. George Norris Green, *The Establishment in Texas Politics* (Westport, Connecticut: Greenwood Press, 1979), 201.

41. Seymour V. Connor, *Texas: A History* (New York: Crowell, 1971), 373.

42. Daniel, interview with Crow, November 17, 1977.

43. Daniel, *Report to the Legislature.*
44. *Austin American,* October 17, 1960.
45. Sam Rayburn to Price Daniel, September 26, 1961, Sam Rayburn Library.
46. Gantt, *The Chief Executive in Texas,* 294.
47. Ann Fears Crawford and Jack Keever, *John B. Connally: Portrait in Power* (Austin: Jenkins, 1973), 86–87.
48. Ibid., 86.
49. Ibid.
50. Ibid.
51. Author interview with George Christian, October 25, 1993.
52. John Connally quote as recounted by Price Daniel to both Jean Daniel and George Christian. (Author interview with Jean Daniel, April 11, 1993, and author interview with George Christian, October 25, 1993.)
53. Crawford and Keever, *John B. Connally: Portrait in Power,* 87.
54. Gantt, *The Chief Executive in Texas,* 295–296.
55. Crawford and Keever, *John B. Connally: Portrait in Power,* 87.
56. McCleskey, *The Government and Politics of Texas,* 209.
57. Clyde Johnson to George Christian, March 27, 1962.
58. Ibid.
59. Undated, untitled document in Price Daniel files.
60. Author interview with George Christian, October 25, 1993.
61. Reston, *The Lone Star,* 210.
62. Author interview with George Christian, October 25, 1993.
63. *Chicago Tribune,* n.d., 1961, Price Daniel Papers.
64. Charles Ashman, *Connally: The Adventures of Big Bad John* (New York: William Morrow, 1974), 98–99.
65. Ibid., 98.
66. Steinberg, *Sam Johnson's Boy,* 591.
67. Crawford and Keever, *John B. Connally: Portrait in Power,* 89.
68. Gantt, *The Chief Executive in Texas,* 278.
69. *Washington Post,* April 17, 1962.
70. Price Daniel 1962 campaign itinerary.
71. Price Daniel press release, May 2, 1962.
72. Ibid.
73. Ibid.
74. Crawford and Keever, *John B. Connally: Portrait in Power,* 91.
75. Connor, *Texas: A History,* 373.
76. George Christian, interview with author, October 25, 1993.
77. *Texas Observer,* 1962.
78. *Houston Chronicle,* n.d., Price Daniel Papers.
79. *The Lubbock Avalanche-Journal,* n.d., Price Daniel Papers.
80. Author interview with Jean Daniel, April 11, 1993.
81. *New York Times Magazine,* 1962.
82. Daniel, *Report to the Legislature,* January 9, 1963.

83. Ibid.
84. Ibid.
85. Author interview with George Christian, October 25, 1993.
86. Untitled, undated article in Price Daniel files.

Chapter 14: Lyndon's Request
1. George Christian, interview with author, October 25, 1993.
2. Ibid.
3. Jean Daniel, interview with author, April 11, 1993.
4. Jim Keahey, LAWtoons, date unknown.
5. Ibid.
6. Ibid.
7. Jean Daniel, interview with author, April 11, 1993.
8. Lyndon Johnson to Price Daniel, May 1, 1965, LBJ Library.
9. Price Daniel to Lyndon Johnson, July 3, 1964, LBJ Library.
10. Marvin Watson to Lyndon Johnson, August 2, 1965, LBJ Library.
11. Jean Daniel, interview with author, April 11, 1993.
12. Ibid.
13. David Murph, interview with author, June 1, 1996.
14. Jean Daniel, interview with author, April 11, 1993.
15. James Reston, Jr., *The Lone Star* (New York: Harper and Row, 1989), 346.
16. Jean Daniel, interview with author, April 11, 1993.
17. Price Daniel, interview with David Murph, June 10, 1982.
18. Ibid.
19. Jean Daniel, interview with author, April 11, 1993.
20. Price Daniel, interview with David Murph, June 10, 1982.
21. Reston, *The Lone Star,* 346.
22. Jean Daniel, interview with author, April 11, 1993.
23. Price Daniel, interview with David Murph, June 10, 1982.
24. Public Papers of the Presidents, February 29, 1968, 298.
25. David C. Whitney, *The American Presidents* (Garden City, New York: Doubleday & Company, Inc., 1969), 343.
26. J.C. Martin, interview with author, October 27, 1993; this Price Daniel quote was told to Martin by a former White House photographer who witnessed the exchange.
27. Records of the National Security Council, LBJ Library, FG 11-6.
28. For an example of this, see Price Daniel to Lyndon Johnson, April 25, 1968, LBJ Library.
29. Price Daniel to Lyndon Johnson, February 14, 1968, LBJ Library.
30. Jean Daniel Murph, interview with author, May 23, 1999.
31. Lyndon Johnson, *Vantage Point* (1971), 431.
32. Ibid., 526–529.
33. Ibid.
34. Price Daniel to Lyndon Johnson, November 12, 1968, LBJ Library.

35. John Connally to Price Daniel, January 13, 1969.
36. Lyndon Johnson to Price Daniel, January 22, 1969, LBJ Library.

Chapter 15: Boundaries and Courts

1. *Houston Post*, May 28, 1971.
2. *Shreveport Times*, June 10, 1971.
3. *Houston Post*, May 6, 1972.
4. Jean Daniel, interview with Jean Murph, June 28, 1998.
5. *Wall Street Journal*, March 21, 1973.
6. Jean Daniel, interview with author, April 12, 1993.
7. Sam Johnson, interview with author, October 24, 1993.
8. Jean Daniel, interview with author, April 12, 1993.
9. Excerpt from handwritten notes in author's possession.
10. *Morning Advocate*, June 10, 1971.
11. *Dallas Times Herald*, June 10, 1971.
12. *Fort Worth Star-Telegram*, May 7, 1972.
13. *Wall Street Journal*, March 21, 1973.
14. *Beaumont Enterprise*, March 25, 1973.
15. Joe Greenhill, interview with author, October 25, 1993.
16. Sam Johnson, interview with author, October 24, 1993.
17. *Houston Chronicle*, August 26, 1988.
18. Sam Johnson, interview with author, October 24, 1993.
19. Price Daniel speech excerpt before State Bar, 1965.
20. *Baylor Law Review*, Fall 1988.
21. Texas Supreme Court Records.
22. Joe Greenhill, Texas Supreme Court's Price Daniel Memorial Service, May 22, 1989.
23. *Reed v. Wylie*, 554S.W.2d169.
24. Ibid.
25. Ibid.
26. Greenhill, Daniel Memorial Service, May 22, 1989.
27. *Friendswood Development Co. v. Smith-Southwestern Industries, Inc.*, 576S.W.2d21 (Texas, November 29, 1978).
28. *City of Spring Valley v. Southwestern Bell Tel. Co.*, 484S.W.2d579 (Texas, July 19, 1972).
29. *Hayek v. Western Steel Co.*, 478S.W.2d786 (Texas, March 15, 1972).
30. *Sullivan v. Barnett*, 471S.W.2d39 (Texas, June 23, 1971).
31. *Employers Cas. Co. v. Tilley*, 496S.W.2d552 (Texas, June 13, 1973).
32. Sam Johnson, interview with author, October 24, 1993.
33. Price Daniel press release, January 12, 1978.
34. Jean Daniel, interview with author, April 11, 1993.
35. Associated Press, January 1979.
36. *San Angelo Standard*, January 19, 1978.
37. *Corpus Christi Caller*, January 17, 1978.
38. Joe Greenhill, memorial, 1993.

39. *Abilene Reporter-News,* May 7, 1979.
40. Price Daniel Appreciation Dinner program, June 6, 1979.
41. Joe Greenhill address, Price Daniel Building dedication, date unknown.

Chapter 16: The Later Years
 1. Price Daniel personal health log.
 2. Jean Daniel, interview with author, April 11, 1993.
 3. Ibid.
 4. Price and Jean Daniel, *Executive Mansions and Capitols of America* (Wisconsin, 1969), Preface.
 5. Ibid., 9.
 6. Ron Tyler to Joe Greenhill, August 18, 1993.
 7. *Austin American-Statesman,* August 26, 1988.
 8. Sam Houston Regional Library and Research Center plaque.
 9. Price Daniel, interview with author, August 10, 1985.
10. David Murph, interview with author, June 28, 1998.
11. Price Daniel, *The Most Important Thing on Earth,* 1985.
12. *Dallas Times Herald,* April 7, 1984.
13. Robert L. Schaadt, interview with author, February 12, 1999.
14. Associated Press, April 1984.
15. Price Daniel, *The Most Important Thing on Earth,* 1985.
16. Jean Daniel, interview with author, April 11, 1993.
17. Marilyn Murph, interview with author, June 24, 1998.
18. Jean Murph, interview with author, June 28, 1998.
19. *Austin American-Statesman,* August 26, 1988.
20. Price Daniel and Ralph Yarborough joint press conference text.
21. *Austin American-Statesman,* August 26, 1988.
22. *Houston Post,* August 26, 1988.
23. AP photograph appearing in the *Houston Post,* August 26, 1988.
24. Jean Daniel, interview with Jean Murph, June 28, 1998.
25. Houston Daniel, interview with David Murph, June 28, 1998.
26. Jean Daniel, interview with author, April 11, 1993.
27. Ibid.
28. Reverend Charles L. Allen message at Price Daniel funeral, August 27, 1988.
29. *Houston Chronicle,* August 28, 1988.
30. *Fort Worth Star-Telegram,* August 29, 1988.
31. Governor Bill Clements press release.
32. *Liberty Vindicator,* August 28, 1988.
33. *Dayton News,* September 5, 1974.
34. Ibid.
35. *Saturday Evening Post,* January 2, 1954.

INDEX